First Among Equals

First Among Equals

U.S. Foreign
Policy in a
Multipolar World

Emma Ashford

Yale UNIVERSITY PRESS
New Haven & London

Published with assistance from the foundation established in memory of Philip Hamilton McMillan of the Class of 1894, Yale College.

Yale University Press books may be purchased in quantity for educational, business, or promotional use. For information, please e-mail sales.press@yale.edu (U.S. office) or sales@yaleup.co.uk (U.K. office).

Set in ITC Galliard and Gotham type by IDS Infotech, Ltd.
Printed in the United States of America.

ISBN 978-0-300-27954-2 (hardcover)
Library of Congress Control Number: 2024950826
A catalogue record for this book is available from the British Library.

Authorized Representative in the EU: Easy Access System Europe, Mustamäe tee 50, 10621 Tallinn, Estonia, gpsr.requests@easproject.com

10 9 8 7 6 5 4 3 2 1

Contents

Preface

In 1930, the Italian communist Antonio Gramsci wrote a treatise on the political malaise of the moment from his exile in a fascist prison cell. The people had become disaffected with elites, he argued, who continued to exercise power mostly due to inertia. There was little in the way of coherent opposition to those moribund elites. The crisis, he wrote, arose from the fact that the old world was dying, and the new was not yet born. Until it was, "a variety of morbid symptoms" would continue to appear.

This book was written before the election of 2024 that returned Donald Trump to the presidency, and even before Joe Biden's unceremonious removal from the Democratic presidential ticket. Since that time, U.S. foreign policy has lurched from a reactionary embrace of the status quo to a chaotic roller coaster of policy change. Trump's inaugural address promised to return America to a golden age; his overtures to Russia, brusque dismissal of European allies, and aggressive tariff wars suggest that his second term could overshadow the chaos and incoherence of his first.

Yet even as the new president's policies are less predictable, they are also more clearly a break with the status quo. Trump's first term could be viewed by allies and adversaries alike as an aberration—a blip in the normal conduct of U.S. foreign policy, with his worst impulses constrained by mainstream foreign policy advisers and overturned by Biden. Now there is little doubt: the old world is dead. It is, I think, accurate to describe Donald Trump as the first post-unipolar president.

At the same time, the new world is not born either. We are mired in crisis. This book explores the direction of travel in global affairs and in U.S. foreign policy. The presidency of Joe Biden—with its reactionary denial of change in the international system—and the second term of Donald Trump—who appears to be seeking to accelerate the process of global fragmentation—are not the drivers of this change; they are instead the morbid symptoms of an ongoing transformation.

The first half of this book—which analyzes the unipolar moment and explores today's global trend lines—seeks to explain how we got here. The foreign policy debates of 2025 and 2026 will continue to center around the forces explored in this section, from the increasingly urgent need for the United States to prioritize in defense, to the unraveling of globalized trade, and the contestation within Republican and Democratic parties to frame a new foreign policy consensus.

The back half of the book offers one vision for how the United States might build something new in this post-unipolar world: a strategy of Realist Internationalism. In some areas, this vision shares common ground with the Trump administration: it advocates for burden-shifting to capable allies in Europe and argues for rigid prioritization of U.S. resources to combat China, the only truly significant threat to American interests. In other ways, however, the vision presented here is radically different from Trump's: it seeks increased global economic engagement, for one thing. Both visions are realist and nationalist, but there is a difference between Trump's coercive vision of America unchained, and my hope for a flexible, engaged America.

Fundamentally, however, the Biden administration, the Trump administration, and this book are all trying to solve the same problem: how the United States can adapt its foreign policy from the overreach of the unipolar moment to something better suited to the emerging multipolar reality. There is no more important task for policymakers in the coming decade.

This book is dedicated to my daughters—Lily and Hazel—and the hope that they and their peers can thrive in this brave new world.

First Among Equals

Introduction: A Normal Nation

> The United States performed heroically in a time when heroism was required; altruistically during the long years when freedom was endangered. The time when Americans should bear such unusual burdens is past. With a return to "normal" times, we can again become a normal nation—and take care of pressing problems of education, family, industry, and technology. We can be an independent nation in a world of independent nations.
> —Jeane Kirkpatrick, 1990

In 2023, as they do every year, global elites descended on the tiny Swiss Alpine town of Davos, arriving en masse in their private jets and sporting luxurious cold-weather gear as they navigated the frozen streets.[1] There was one term on everyone's lips: *polycrisis,* a catch-all for our increasingly troubled and interconnected global environment. The upper crust of the global establishment hobnobbed in cafés and speculated about a new kind of interconnected global crisis, one in which economic, pandemic, and climate crises each helped destabilize the other in a kind of crude Rube Goldberg crisis machine. Conspiracy theories about Davos—or the World Economic Forum, as it is more properly known—abound, but the reality is more prosaic. Davos brings together top business executives, government officials, and global movers and shakers to discuss current events and provides a convenient forum for world leaders to convene private discussions away from the prying eyes of the media. The gathering is also a buzzword generator, as participants flit year over year to the newest fads and hot topics, from artificial intelligence to decoupling. Davos, in truth, is useful primarily as a reflection of what global leaders believe is important—an insight into groupthink.

So why did they flock to embrace the notion of a "polycrisis"? As the World Economic Forum's own report put it: "Eroding geopolitical cooperation will have ripple effects across the global risks landscape over the medium term, including contributing to a potential polycrisis of interrelated environmental, geopolitical and socioeconomic risks."[2] The concept of interlocking crises reflected a level of gloom about the future and provided a convenient shorthand to describe a decade that had contained an exceptionally high level of global upheavals: the war in Ukraine; the Covid-19 pandemic and its resultant economic fallout; democratic backsliding around the world; a global migration crisis; growing conflagration in the Middle East; the impact of sanctions and war on global food and technology supply chains; the political risk associated with American domestic politics; and the start of a dangerous new nuclear arms race between Russia, China, and the United States.

The notion that this "polycrisis" is a unique phenomenon is certainly overstated; the current moment resembles earlier periods of flux in the international system, such as the interlocking economic, political, and social crises of the 1920s and 1930s, or the interrelated financial, energy, and geopolitical shocks of the 1970s. In each of these cases, as in our present moment, shifts in power in the international system and the global economy increased uncertainty for states and raised questions about what the future of the international order would look like. Today, policymakers and business elites—from Davos to Washington—are reacting to that uncertainty by looking for answers about the future shape of the world. Some assume that the future will look like the past and that China's rise will create a new bipolar Cold War, an assertion that often comes with the unstated assumption that the United States will necessarily win such a competition. But history rarely repeats itself, and current trends suggest instead that a multipolar era may be dawning, one in which China and the United States are ahead of the pack, but military and economic power are also diffusing to a broader variety of middle powers.

For the United States—the country that has ruled the international system largely alone since 1991—this moment is particularly perilous. What will the world look like in the coming decades—and what is America's place in it? How should the United States seek to engage and interact with a world of burgeoning multipolarity? And perhaps most important, can American policymakers contend with the failures of their transformational post–Cold War foreign policy and learn to live in a world in which theirs is no longer the indispensable nation?

After the Unipolar Moment

Eras can be difficult to define, particularly without the benefit of hindsight. And even once a historical consensus has formed, the big showy events that we associate with the start or end of an era are typically less important than the trends that helped set them in motion. The storming of the Bastille, for example, was not the primary cause of the French Revolution, just as the Cold War was already largely over by the time the Soviet Union collapsed in 1991. It is thus difficult to pinpoint the exact end of the period we have been living through since about 1991, a period of pronounced U.S. global predominance that many have referred to as the "unipolar moment." Some argued as early as 2008 that the global financial crisis might spell the end of American global predominance; others have argued more recently that the Covid pandemic, the war in Ukraine, or the election of Donald Trump in 2016 marks the end of the unipolar moment.[3] Perhaps it will be some event yet to come. What we can say, however, is that we are in the process of leaving the unipolar moment and entering something new.

Rather than any single historical event, it is largely because of trend lines that we can make this diagnosis. There are lots of ways one can measure power shifts, from military capabilities to industrial strength, cultural power, technological innovation, or economic dynamism. But taken holistically, the trend lines of the past few decades show some clear patterns: American power is in relative—though not absolute—decline, particularly in the economic space; China is rising, transforming its economic heft into military might as it does so; and globalization is allowing economic and technological power to diffuse to a much wider variety of states. As William Wohlforth and Stephen Brooks put it, "There is perhaps no more widely accepted truth about the world today than the idea that it is no longer unipolar."[4] Wohlforth and Brooks themselves disagree with this thesis, but they are increasingly in the minority. When the magazine *Foreign Affairs* asked a broad cross section of foreign policy experts in 2023 to assess whether the world was still unipolar, only one in four agreed that it was.[5]

Indeed, a good case can be made that the world is shifting toward a form of unbalanced multipolarity, with the United States and China as predominant powers, joined by a variety of capable second-tier powers: Japan, India, Germany, France, Australia, Russia, and others. As Mark Leonard of the European Council on Foreign Relations has noted, it is this latter shift that is perhaps the most intriguing: "In 1950, the United States and its major allies (NATO countries, Australia, and Japan) and the communist world (the Soviet Union, China, and the Eastern bloc) together accounted for 88 percent of global GDP. But today, these groups of countries combined account for only 57 percent of global GDP. Whereas nonaligned countries' defense expenditures were negligible as late as the 1960s (about one percent of the global total), they are now at 15 percent and growing fast."[6] Many of these regional powers have already started to jockey for position within the emerging system. President Emmanuel Macron of France, for example, shocked other European leaders when he said in 2023 that Europe should "seek to be a third pole" in an emerging world order.[7] India's prime minister, Narendra Modi, has openly sought to speed up the transition to global multipolarity, and the Brazilian finance minister Fernando Haddad recently told journalists that Brazil is not going to lean toward either the United States or China and is "too big to be choosing partners."[8] The message is increasingly clear: Many countries around the world believe that American dominance is ending and are hedging their bets.

For American foreign policy elites, this shift has been compounded by a period of unprecedented soul-searching created by the foreign policy failures of the unipolar moment. U.S. foreign policy over the past three decades has been governed by what the scholar Barry Posen describes as "liberal hegemony"—a bipartisan marriage of unmatched military power with radical policy aims.[9] Indeed, "radical" understates the case: U.S. foreign policy since 1991 has been profoundly transformational, with attempts to maintain American military primacy by suppressing the military capabilities of both allies and adversaries; to enforce liberal norms through international institutions; to spread democracy by the sword; and to prevent atrocities globally by rewriting the norm of sovereignty. Though U.S. policymakers themselves often portrayed these choices in terms of the preservation or defense of an existing liberal order, they were in practice trying to reshape the world. As the scholars William Wohlforth and Jennifer Lind have written, "For the past 25 years, the international order crafted by and for liberal states has itself been profoundly revisionist, aggressively exporting democracy and expanding in both depth and breadth."[10]

America's foreign policy crusades mostly failed. The war on terror yielded blowback and the rise of new terror groups, and the United States failed to transform either Iraq or Afghanistan into a stable or vibrant democracy. NATO expansion contributed to Russia's newfound territorial aggression, and trade liberalization with China—initially one of the high points of policy during this period—has come to be perceived in Washington as a mistake, empowering China while damaging U.S. domestic industries. The election of Donald Trump also acted as a shock to the system for many foreign policy elites, who had assumed that Trump—with his idiosyncratic views on foreign policy and his unwillingness to bear America's "indispensable nation" mantle—simply could not get elected. It came as a significant surprise that voters *liked* Trump's positions on foreign policy.[11] Even the Biden administration, which came into office promising to reset U.S. foreign policy to the pre-Trump norm, found it impossible to do so. For all the praise heaped on Biden's ability to build a coalition to resist the Russian war in Ukraine, for example, the administration was far more successful in corralling European allies than in persuading India, China, or states in the Global South. And although Biden himself continued to tell all who would listen that the United States was still "the most powerful nation in the history of the world," his views were increasingly out of step with those of the American public, only 20 percent of whom want the United States to play the leading role in world affairs.[12] The public, it seems, is ahead of the policy community in accepting that the unipolar moment is over.

Debating Our Place in the World

The most important question for American policymakers today is how the United States can adapt its foreign policy to better fit the twenty-first century, and in doing so, whether it can avoid the pitfalls and excesses of the past three decades. The global geopolitical shifts of recent years—combined with the unorthodox presidency of Donald Trump—have indeed prompted a long-overdue period of reflection among these policymakers about the future of foreign policy, creating a messy debate among those who seek retrenchment from the war on terror, those who seek to pivot the United States to face China, and those who want to build a new liberal order around democracy.[13] "The Blob"—a term coined by Ben Rhodes, Barack Obama's former speechwriter, to describe Washington's ossified foreign policy community—is beginning to ooze apart.[14] Russia's invasion of Ukraine in 2022 only confused matters further, bringing together unlikely bedfellows—including progressive Democrats and neoconservative Republicans—in support of Ukraine while heightening existing partisan divisions on foreign policy. Almost everyone engaged in this discussion believes that the United States made mistakes during the unipolar moment, but they differ wildly both in their diagnosis of the problem and in the solutions they offer.

Today, four tribes, split along partisan and non-partisan lines, are contending for the future of U.S. foreign policy. Each differs in how they understand and prioritize U.S. interests and in their assessment of the primary risk of conflict around the world. None of these tribes are isolationist in the conventional sense; even the most nationalistic argues that the United States should use military force when needed, and even the most dovish aims to stay connected with the world through non-military means. But although they may agree with the necessity of U.S. global engagement, these groups differ widely in how expansive they think that engagement should be. Does the United States need to transform the world? Or just achieve a narrow set of security-based interests? Is America a champion for democracy everywhere? Which tools should the United States prioritize: military force, diplomatic ties, or economic engagement? Is the United States stronger with allies, or simply tied down by them? Though these questions seem simple, the answers suggest that Washington is clustering around four highly distinctive visions for how and why the United States should engage globally.

The first of these groups is the "America-first hawks," a continuation of the Jacksonian tradition in foreign policy, albeit one with Trumpian characteristics. Though inward-looking, members of this group are more than willing to use military force or economic coercion when necessary. The core of this worldview is its strong emphasis on American sovereignty and unilateralism. Its proponents are profoundly hostile to international institutions—this hostility is characterized by a rejection of nation-building and democracy promotion—and are increasingly narrowly focused on the challenge of a rising China.[15]

The second group is made up of proponents of "liberal primacy," who fundamentally accept the notion, as Bob Kagan has put it, that "the only hope for preserving liberalism at home and abroad is the maintenance of a world order conducive to liberalism, and the only power capable of upholding such an order is the United States."[16] Strong continuity exists with Washington's long-running consensus, but today's liberal internationalists tend to eschew the worst nation-building excesses of the war on terror. It is perhaps too sober to say that those in this group are committed to U.S. alliances around the world; they often regard alliances as "sacred commitments" and view them as an end, rather than a means, in U.S. foreign policy.[17]

A third group, centered mostly among the far-left progressive wing of the Democratic Party, might be described as "progressive worldbuilders." Although the roots of their anti-war, socialist-derived philosophy clearly go back further than the past few decades, the rapid growth of this group owes much to the anti-war activism surrounding the war of 2003 in Iraq. They are highly intellectually diverse but typically believe in building a better world through non-military tools, while benefiting domestic constituencies, with a redistributionist bent.[18] Although this view is still fundamentally transformative, progressives are far more skeptical of the utility of military force.[19]

Finally, a combined group of "realists" and "restrainers" adds a fourth approach to the world that emphasizes American security and the costs and risks of an overly adventurous foreign policy. They tend to favor some level of U.S. military retrenchment, along with prioritization among regions, and a narrowing of U.S. interests to form a more modest approach to foreign policy.

The stakes of this debate are high. In an emerging multipolar era, the United States risks becoming overstretched if it pursues too ambitious a foreign policy—something the past few years of crises from Europe to the

Middle East make only too clear—and risks stumbling into a conflict if it is too assertive. At the same time, if it is too passive or uninvolved, the United States risks ceding ground to rising powers like China. Yet given the course of U.S. foreign policy over the past few decades and the mindset of much of Washington's professional foreign policy class, the risk of the former is far higher than the risk of the latter.[20] Of the approaches suggested above, only a more realist or restrained foreign policy represents a true shift from the ambitious overtones of our post–Cold War foreign policy and toward a more modest, realistic approach to the world. It is to this approach that this book is dedicated.

Realist Internationalism

Americans are used to the notion of the imperial presidency, to one man wielding executive power. For thirty years, the United States has taken an analogous role in the world, proposing ambitious policies from on high. But the global future may well look more like a parliamentary system: the United States as first among equals, but with many other factions, interests, and veto-wielding actors that must be accommodated. In that multipolar context, America's post–Cold War approach to the world, with its hegemonic, transformative overtones, will not suffice. That approach will produce overstretch and alienate potential partners around the world. The United States also does not need a *new* strategic vision; there have been far too many innovative, revolutionary grand strategies in recent years, from Bill Clinton's strategy of "engagement and enlargement" to George W. Bush's "freedom agenda" or Hillary Clinton's "smart power." Instead, it needs to return to a more pragmatic, realist set of strategic principles, principles that have guided us well in past decades.

Ken Waltz, the godfather of structural realism, once noted that realism is not a theory of foreign policy but rather a theory of international relations. He meant that the structural form of realism he advocated did not necessarily tell policymakers how to behave in any specific situation; instead, it simply predicted that states that deviated too far from the realist prescription would eventually be punished for it. But there are a variety of realist theories, from classical to structural, and many realist thinkers who make clear policy prescriptions.[21] Realism has also featured as a central tendency in U.S. foreign policy throughout American history; cautious pragmatism and national interest have often formed one of the two poles around which foreign policy debates have clustered, acting as a foil against unfettered idealism.

U.S. policymakers have most often returned to their realist roots in times of significant international turmoil. Dwight Eisenhower's realism—which manifested as "studied under-reaction and . . . easygoing unsentimentality"—enabled the United States to navigate the difficult and dangerous days of the early Cold War, when the risk of nuclear use remained high and the risk of a direct confrontation with the Soviet Union could not be discounted.[22] Richard Nixon may have been the most hated president in American history, but he embraced the realism of hard choices in the 1970s, when global financial upheavals, energy crises, wars, and anti-colonial movements threatened to undermine the foundations of U.S. power. Even during the most recent moment of significant geopolitical upheaval, the end of the Cold War, George H. W. Bush was guided by a strongly realist worldview. Not only did Bush—who formed a realist troika with his advisers Brent Scowcroft and James Baker—resist regime change in Baghdad at the close of the Gulf War in 1991, thus making it one of the few wars in the past half century from which the United States has managed a short, victorious withdrawal. He also managed the decline and collapse of the Soviet Union with more pragmatism and magnanimity than one might have expected after five decades of struggle.[23]

In each case, these policymakers' decisions were guided by practicality and a view of the world as it is, rather than by grand proclamations of the world as we wish it to be. Their approach to the world differs strongly from the way policymakers since 1991 have thought about the world; most of them have wholeheartedly embraced the tenets of liberal hegemony and its transformational ethos. This may sound counterintuitive. After all, some today would argue that Eisenhower, for example, was among the architects of America's global alliance network, a core tenet of liberal internationalism. He supported alliances, however, not because they were a "sacred obligation" but because those partnerships served U.S. interests in that time and place. America needs to reclaim that realism, engaging with the world on its own terms. Policymakers must navigate this period of shifting geopolitical winds while prioritizing the security and interests of the American people.

Realism is also not necessarily the same thing as a "restrained" foreign policy. Realists have in recent years become associated with the movement for restraint in U.S. foreign policy. In large part, this is because their policy prescriptions mostly ran in the same direction during a period of U.S. overextension. Although the grand strategy of restraint is built on realist principles, it is not the only possible way to interpret those principles. Indeed, realism is not a monolith.[24] Realism instead comprises a variety of models for thinking about the world, each characterized by pragmatism and the art of the possible. Realists can be hawks or doves, as "realism is not rigidly anti-interventionist or passive; by definition, it is not rigidly anything."[25] Instead, realists are guided by a sense that global order can be managed but not transformed. Today, realists and restrainers broadly agree on the need for U.S. retrenchment from Europe and the Middle East but vary widely on their willingness to counterbalance a rising China. This book advocates a balanced middle road: retrenchment where necessary to rebalance America's strategic commitments, and engagement where it is not; avoiding war whenever possible, but not at *any* cost.

Many will recoil at the idea of U.S. retrenchment, which is often regarded as a dirty word in Washington. Even limited retrenchment from the Middle East under the Obama administration—effectively the drawdown of U.S. troops following the surges in Iraq and Afghanistan—was painted by opponents as "excessive and ill-managed," a self-inflicted blow to U.S. power and prestige.[26] But occasional retrenchment is an inevitable part of coherent strategy, realigning means and ends as circumstances change. And it is also a vital part of adjusting to headwinds in the international system. The research on this is clear: Great powers that retrench when necessary often regain prominence over time, but those that fail to retrench do not typically recover.[27] It is precisely this kind of recalibration that allowed the United States to weather the chaos of the 1970s, for example. By abandoning some elements of the Bretton Woods system, ending the war in Vietnam, and opening to communist China, the United States rebalanced its global commitments and refocused in areas where it had the most potential to push back on the Soviet Union.

This book explores what a pragmatic realist reorganization of U.S. foreign policy would look like over the coming decades. In doing so, it emphasizes several general principles that should guide U.S. policymakers.

Narrow Interests Make Better Policy

Questions of interests are always fraught. Whose interests are served by foreign policy? Which interests should be prioritized over others? Simply talking about the "national interest" does little to answer these complicated questions.[28] But there is no denying that in recent years, American interests have become so broad as to be almost meaningless. U.S. interests are routinely conflated with those of our allies, and with global security or regional peace more broadly. The list of "interests" claimed by U.S. policymakers grew exponentially during the unipolar moment: military primacy, humanitarian intervention, democracy promotion, counterterrorism, the building of international institutions, nuclear nonproliferation, and so on. Most of these are not core American interests. Certainly, Americans would prosper in a more peaceful and democratic world—or one with fewer nuclear weapons. But the cost of getting to these ambitious goals also needs to be considered; policymakers should prioritize core interests over these expansive theories of transformation. In short, the most important step policymakers could take to bring a sense of realism back into the policy process is to define U.S. goals and interests more narrowly as we head into the 2030s. This book argues for a narrow definition of U.S. interests, confined primarily to territorial security, nuclear deterrence, American democracy and prosperity at home, and the avoidance of the rise of a peer hegemon elsewhere in the world that could threaten the nation over the long term.

Big Questions Aren't Irrelevant

Realists often get a bad rap from their critics for being excessively focused on the theoretical rather than on how things work in the "real world." But everyone has a theoretical model of the world in their heads, or at least an intuitive understanding of how the international system works. It is simply that most policymakers do not make these beliefs explicit and rely instead on implicit assumptions in making their policy decisions. Yet many of the toughest policy choices facing policymakers—Taiwan, for example, or what to do about Russia—have their roots in big theoretical debates about polarity, hegemony, alliances, or spheres of influence. How we conceptualize hegemony, for example, is critical to how we think about U.S. policy toward China in Asia. Do we care only about territorial revisionism (that is, the Chinese conquest of the region by force), or do we care more broadly about Chinese coercion? Even the question of why we care about Chinese hegemony is relevant. Is it because regional hegemons tend to "roam" outside their home region, much as the United States has done for decades? Or is it simply because a hegemon can deny the United States access to its region? Though these questions are highly theoretical, answering them is a core part of formulating U.S. policy responses, and it is far better to do so explicitly and allow our assumptions to be tested and examined.

Great Power Competition in the Nuclear Age

Many of our models of great power competition come from an era before nuclear weapons, when great powers could in practice fight each other with a lower risk of disastrous outcomes. This is not to say that catastrophic outcomes did not happen—consider the burning of Moscow during the Napoleonic Wars, or a generation of young men sent to the trenches of World War I—but nuclear weapons greatly increase the risk of catastrophic outcomes at a planetary level. At the same time, there are voices that argue that avoiding conflict with other great powers is in effect appeasement, a form of nuclear blackmail allowing these countries to dominate their neighbors because of an unjustified U.S. fear of nuclear escalation.[29] Critics often argue that this is a new phenomenon, but it was the de facto state of being during the Cold War, as both the United States and the Soviet Union largely avoided direct conflict out of such fears. Indeed, as Richard Betts pointed out, often "Washington had a more frequent interest in nuclear blackmail than Moscow did."[30] Today, policymakers must again learn to avoid unnecessary conflict with other nuclear powers. This cannot mean avoiding conflict at all costs, a proposition that would allow adversaries to coerce the United States with the threat of escalation. But what policymakers can do is draw clear lines for themselves about where confrontation may be worth the risk of escalation—something policymakers during the Cold War did in Berlin, for example—and where it is not. When no vital U.S. interests are threatened, policymakers must be mindful of the risk of nuclear escalation.

Reconceptualizing Alliances for Multipolarity

Alliances have become a flash point in U.S. foreign policy debates. Many would correctly argue that during the Cold War, U.S. alliances were an asset, particularly in Europe. But alliances have also changed substantially. Today, they are more typically a U.S. security guarantee to weaker powers, and to many policymakers they are as much an end as a means of U.S. policy. Indeed, policymakers often worry that specific policy choices will undermine U.S. alliances—even when the interests at stake may be more important than the alliance itself. There's also a long-running assumption in Washington that simply entering into a security agreement with the United States creates effective deterrence against adversaries. This fiction will be increasingly difficult to sustain as multipolarity emerges. None of this is to say that alliances are unimportant or unhelpful; if the United States is to effectively counter China, for example, it will need reliable and capable partners in the Indo-Pacific, countries that are not purely dependent on American strength. But policymakers need to reconceptualize alliances for the modern era. This will mean more flexible partnerships and fewer rigid and unchanging security structures that lock in participants with no regard for changing circumstances. It means paying more attention to American interests and to avoiding policy capture by allies. And finally, it means a strong focus on burden-sharing within alliances, bolstering the capabilities of like-minded states and building more equal defense partnerships wherever possible.

Expanding the Boundaries of Grand Strategy

Realists have often been guilty of ignoring non-military aspects of international affairs. As Jonathan Kirshner describes it, "realist analysis throughout history has had a tendency to be tone deaf to questions of political economy."[31] This blind spot is politically and theoretically problematic for realists. The use of economic statecraft has become increasingly central to U.S. strategy over the past few years: The post-9/11 use of sanctions has led to innovations in financial tools and export controls, and growing concerns about the impacts of globalization at home have undermined elite support for free-trade policies. The peculiar period of Cold War bipolarity—when economies largely operated in self-contained blocs and thus could be more easily disaggregated from security choices—is long gone. The result is the return of geo-economics, in which the building of an effective military force is contingent on domestic economic capacity, countries are dependent on international markets for their energy security and supply chain needs, and any successful strategy must incorporate the intrinsic links between economics and geopolitics. Other tools of statecraft—diplomacy, technological cooperation, and espionage and covert action—can also be useful in achieving a state's goals. And though these tools have often been associated more with liberal visions of international affairs, realists cannot and should not cede the non-military tools of power to liberal internationalists. To complement a realist turn in military and security affairs, policymakers must incorporate economic insights into strategy, sharply limiting the American use of coercive or negative economic statecraft and working to build a positive economic agenda focused on resilience and diversity of markets and supply chains.

What Is Grand Strategy?

Scholars often think about grand strategy in "meta" terms. It's not just a road map for policymakers; it's also a process for formulating strategy, a variable of historical study, or even the grandiose-sounding "intellectual architecture that lends structure to foreign policy," in the words of the historian Hal Brands.[32] Scholars differ, meanwhile, over whether grand strategy is primarily about military means, or whether it incorporates other tools of power.[33] They disagree about whether it can be formulated and implemented purposefully, or whether it becomes clear only in hindsight.[34] Some scholars argue that grand strategy cannot really exist in practice, whereas others argue that its utility is declining as the world becomes more complex.[35]

Hal Brands argues that "the fact that there are so many competing conceptions of grand strategy should probably tell us that the concept is subjective and ambiguous enough that it defies any singular definition. The best an analyst can do is offer a definition that is, in the strategic theorist Colin Gray's phrasing, 'right enough.'"[36] And in general terms, there is a surprising amount of consistency in how scholars define grand strategy. It is widely understood to be broader than mere military strategy or foreign policy. And it includes at least some attempt to bring a state's means and ends into alignment on the international stage. The historian John Lewis Gaddis, for example, describes grand strategy as "the alignment of potentially unlimited aspirations with necessarily limited capabilities."[37]

Put differently, grand strategy flows from how policymakers understand the world. For each state, no matter how big or small, leaders must plan how to achieve their ends in a chaotic global environment. They must have some idea of what those ends are, the means at their disposal, and both the scope and limitations of what can be achieved within those means. This mental model of the world offers the foundation for a grand strategy: the plan for how to bring means and ends into alignment.

Some policymakers may formulate grand strategy explicitly—or even have significant bureaucratic processes to produce it. Others may do so implicitly or subconsciously. Each step of the strategy-making process can be contested: Which worldview is correct? Which constraints matter? Which ends are to be achieved? But whether this process occurs formally or informally, it is in practice the same: Policymakers use a mental model of the world—their assessment of the nation's primary interests, combined with the means available to them and existing constraints—to plot a course for how that nation seeks to achieve its ends. That calculus then informs the narrower decisions taken in military strategy, diplomacy, and economic statecraft.

This book seeks to add to the grand strategic debate in several ways. The first section explores the history, trendlines, and debates that have led to the current moment of uncertainty for policymakers. Chapter 1 presents a highly condensed overview of the unipolar moment and the foreign policy choices that characterized it, before exploring why the bipartisan foreign policy consensus that had characterized U.S. foreign policy since 1991 began to splinter. Chapter 2 addresses the question of worldviews and mental models by looking at the current schisms in the U.S. foreign policy debate. There are several different worldviews held by those trying to influence U.S. foreign policy, each of which might suggest a different grand strategic approach. Though many works on grand strategy work backward from published strategic arguments, it is potentially far more revealing to consider strategy debates more broadly, as they can suggest not only existing grand strategic models but also where others might emerge in the future. Chapter 3 explores the global balance of power in the emerging multipolar world, giving us a clearer vision of the international system in which the United States must operate in coming decades, along with some of the potential constraints on U.S. power. We consider debates about polarity and how to measure power, and lay out the risks and promise of multipolarity. That chapter argues that we are entering a period of "unbalanced multipolarity" with two top powers—the United States and China—and a much wider set of second-rank or regional powers taking places alongside them. The influence and partnerships of these second-rank powers will shape the competition and interaction between the United States and China.

The second half of the book advances a new—or at least updated—grand strategy, realist internationalism, one theory for how the United States can better bring means and ends into alignment in coming decades. Chapter 4 lays the foundations for this more pragmatic, realist program of engagement with the world. We explore some of the big, seemingly abstract issues that rarely feature in day-to-day foreign policy discussions but nonetheless form the building blocks of how we make difficult and consequential foreign policy choices in practice: spheres of interest, hegemony, the scope of U.S. interests, the causes of conflict, and the ways we conceptualize alliances. In chapters 5 and 6, we get further into the practicalities of implementing this strategy over the next fifteen years. Chapter 5 addresses two regions ripe for U.S. retrenchment, Europe and the Middle East. In Europe, the question is whether European states can fill the void left by the United States and the process through which such a transition might take place. I propose a phased program of transition away from a U.S. military role on the Continent alongside a strong push to facilitate sub-NATO groupings of capable states to fill these gaps. In the Middle East, I argue that the United States must face facts and accept that there is little to be gained from retaining a significant military presence in the region. This has been clear to policymakers since at least the Obama administration; it is time to act on it and return the United States to a limited, maritime-only posture in the region.

Chapter 6 shifts from retrenchment to engagement and looks at two places where increased American engagement is needed. In the Indo-Pacific, the United States needs a more engaged, yet flexible, approach to the states of the region. This would include maintaining defensive capabilities outside the first island chain, promoting a porcupine strategy for the states closest to China, and building up defensive weaponry and capabilities that aim to deter China by making conquest far more challenging. That chapter also delves into the issue of economic statecraft. Though the United States has certainly not been absent from this arena in recent years, its approach has been almost purely coercive in nature. I argue that the United States needs to re-engage economically with the world in trade and investment terms if it is to provide a more attractive alternative to China. Finally, the conclusion discusses practical problems of implementation: how to address the temptation problem and policymakers' incentives to overreach, as well as the domestic political barriers to implementing a more realist or restrained strategy for the United States.

PART

I

A World, Transformed

1

The Decline and Fall of the Unipolar Moment

The end of the Cold War came slowly, and then all at once. Economic and societal malaise had been undermining the Soviet Union for decades. Though not always visible from the outside, sclerotic government and endemic corruption had sapped the strength of the Soviet economy; an aging parade of Soviet apparatchiks inherited leadership only to preside over stagnation and discontent, while abroad, the Cold War continued apace. With the rise of Gorbachev and a sudden, unexpected series of arms-control agreements, however, the emotional and political valence of the Cold War changed almost overnight. An era of détente emerged, and a series of popular revolutions in Eastern Europe—symbolized most dramatically by the fall of the Berlin Wall—severed the USSR from its Eastern bloc dependencies. By the time the Soviet flag was lowered on the Kremlin walls on Christmas Day 1991, the Cold War had been over for some time. The death of the Soviet Union merely put a bookend on the era in which great powers would attempt to split the world between them.

Or so it was assumed. Even before the Soviet collapse, the détente had raised hopes among policymakers that a better world might be possible. When Saddam Hussein invaded Kuwait in August 1990, both Western and Soviet leaders rallied to push back against this violation of sovereignty. As President George H. W. Bush told Congress, the dawning of something better was visible:

> No longer can a dictator count on East-West confrontation to stymie concerted United Nations action against aggression. A new

partnership of nations has begun. We stand today at a unique and extraordinary moment. The crisis in the Persian Gulf, as grave as it is, also offers a rare opportunity to move toward an historic period of cooperation. Out of these troubled times, our fifth objective—a new world order—can emerge: a new era—freer from the threat of terror, stronger in the pursuit of justice, and more secure in the quest for peace. An era in which the nations of the world, East and West, North and South, can prosper and live in harmony. A hundred generations have searched for this elusive path to peace, while a thousand wars raged across the span of human endeavor. Today that new world is struggling to be born, a world quite different from the one we've known.[1]

The collapse of the Soviet Union into its constituent states a year later merely solidified this sense among policymakers. Yes, there was the messy fallout of the collapse to manage, from loose nukes to post-Soviet border disputes. But these were not that significant when placed against the widespread euphoria and triumphalism at the peaceful dissolution of America's greatest rival. The grand international upheavals of the late 1980s would prompt fierce debates among historians as to their causes, but to the layperson it was intuitive and obvious: the United States had won the Cold War.

The implications for American foreign policy could hardly have been more profound—or more unusual. The departure of the Soviet Union from the world stage was peaceful and left only one global power standing. At the end of World War II, U.S. ambitions had been constrained by Soviet power. The hopes of policymakers in the 1940s to build global institutions shaped by liberal ideals quickly gave way to more practical partnerships that could be effective against the Soviet threat. The early 1990s offered the promise of a second chance, and policymakers began to ask themselves the question implied in Bush's speech: How should America use this power to build a better world?

Logics of Transformation

U.S. foreign policy has always been most stable and consistent when governed by a rough bipartisan consensus. Bounded bipartisanship has also been the norm on foreign policy since 1945, even in periods of significant domestic polarization.[2] This does not mean that both parties always held the exact same foreign policy views, merely that they were generally pointing the same way in strategic terms. During the Cold War, for example, there was widespread acceptance in both political parties that containing the Soviet Union should be the primary goal of U.S. foreign policy, even though different presidents might construe that goal in different ways.[3] And although it's true that bipartisan consensus has its flaws—for example, lending itself to groupthink—it also makes U.S. commitments abroad more credible, enables the negotiation of treaties, and facilitates a reliable budgetary process for the Pentagon, the Department of State, and other agencies.

As a result, the end of the Cold War was marked not only with a sense of righteous victory but also with a feeling in Washington that a new bipartisan consensus on foreign policy would need to be forged for a new world. The early 1990s played host to the "Kennan Sweepstakes" (as it would come to be derisively called), in which a variety of thinkers proposed new missions and new rationales for U.S. foreign policy. In practice, the United States faced few genuine threats, and the American electorate was preoccupied with domestic affairs.[4] But as Stacie Goddard and Ronald Krebs point out, these debates were highly important to policymakers, who sought to use liberal language to legitimate their ambitious goals, with "the Clinton administration . . . reportedly desperate to craft a successor to 'containment.'"[5] This wrangling would ultimately produce a consensus that married Republican primacists and neoconservatives to Democratic liberal internationalists: liberal hegemony.

What united both of these groups was a conviction that the United States—the "indispensable nation"—could transform the world into something better. Primacists and neoconservatives sought to use U.S. power to topple prospective enemies of the United States and further entrench primacy, whereas liberal internationalists sought to use it for humanitarian purposes. Though they started from different assumptions, these groups aligned in practice. A campaign to overthrow Saddam Hussein or Muammar Qadhafi could serve both as a human rights victory and an abject lesson to America's adversaries. NATO expansion could both grow the community of liberal democracies and buttress U.S. power against a potential Russian revival. And where tensions arose—over human rights abuses in the invasion of Iraq, for example, or on questions of sovereignty and international institutions—they were typically smoothed over in face-saving ways by Washington's foreign policy community, making foreign policy remarkably consistent even between administrations as ideologically distinct as the Clinton, George W. Bush, and Obama presidencies. Clinton and Obama may have had more recognizably "liberal internationalist" approaches, and Bush a more "neoconservative" one, but in practice all three coalesced around a broad strategy that emphasized the maintenance of American military predominance, the expansion of U.S.-led institutions and alliances, the protection and spread of democracy and human rights norms, and the expansion of free markets.[6] As John Mearsheimer points out, each of these tasks was "directly tied to the principal liberal theories of peace: liberal institutionalism, economic interdependence theory, and democratic peace theory."[7] Each administration held it as an article of faith that if America could make the world more interconnected and more liberal, it could also make the world more peaceful. This consensus would steer U.S. foreign policy from 1991 to at least 2016.

The most visible of these policies was undoubtedly the Bush administration's embrace of the "freedom agenda" after the 9/11 attacks. The administration sought to use the wars in Iraq and Afghanistan as a proving ground for the idea that one successful democratization campaign might act as a catalyst for democratic change across the whole of the Middle East.[8] U.S. military power was central to this process. "The great strength of this nation," the 2002 national security strategy document argued, "must be used to promote a balance of power that favors freedom."[9] Yet even the emergence of a messy proto-democracy in Iraq cannot justify the deaths of a quarter-million Iraqi civilians in the post-invasion insurgency and civil war. Over the following three decades, the Middle East became less the proving ground for U.S.-led democracy and human rights promotion, and more a graveyard for the notion that freedom can be built at the point of a gun. As the political scientist Dick Betts would note, America's leaders learned from the Middle East that "the overweening power that they had taken for granted . . . is not the same as omnipotence."[10] But the nation's Middle East follies are simply the best known and most visible of the arcs of transformation that characterized the post–Cold War pursuit of liberal hegemony. Each had a theory of transformation: expanding alliances, reinforcing the liberal order, protecting human rights, and spreading democracy. Each ultimately failed in a manner reminiscent of a Greek tragedy: hubris and overreach ending in predictably disastrous outcomes.

Primacy and the Quest for an Enduring Liberal Order

America ended the Cold War in an enviable position. As Michael Mandelbaum aptly put it in 2002: "In the league standings of global power, the United States occupies first place—and by a margin so large that it recalls the preponderance of the Roman Empire of antiquity. So vast is American superiority that the distinction bestowed upon it and its great rival, the Soviet Union, during the Cold War no longer applies. The United States is no longer a mere superpower; it has ascended to the status of hyperpower."[11] One of the earliest principles uniting policymakers in the post–Cold War period was the idea that the United States should try to prolong this period of American predominance. Even before George H. W. Bush had left office, the controversial defense planning guidance document produced by his Pentagon stated it bluntly: "Our first objective is to prevent the re-emergence of a new rival . . . that poses a threat on the order of that formerly posed by the Soviet Union."[12] This assessment would drive U.S. policy toward both allies and adversaries. It suggested, for example, that the United States should not withdraw from European security, keeping European allies purposefully weak. And there would be no peace dividend from the collapse of the Soviet Union; the pursuit of perpetual primacy would not permit significant spending cuts.

The idea of primacy also became increasingly conflated with notions of a liberal order and worldbuilding. The liberal internationalist consensus that animated the Clinton administration began to link America's power predominance to the network of alliances and institutions that had been constructed during the Cold War. "If the American order persists in the post–Cold War period," John Ikenberry argued in *After Victory,* "it will be due . . . to the way power and institutions operate together to make stable and legitimate relations among the industrial democracies."[13] The conclusion was logical and intuitively appealing: extend the institutions, sustain American preeminence. It was a strategy that spoke to Americans' deep-seated idealism about their own role in the world; continued American primacy could promote the common good and thereby become self-sustaining.

Expansion of U.S. alliance networks and security guarantees—most notably the expansion of NATO—was paired with efforts to bring Russia and China into international economic institutions, from the Group of Seven (G7) to the World Trade Organization (WTO). Policymakers began to think about how U.S. power could be used to align an often illiberal world with the long-running liberal aspirations of existing international institutions.

The globalization and liberalization of existing institutions are perhaps the most effective counter to those who argue that American strategy remained consistent between the Cold War and post–Cold War periods. The liberal institutions of the Cold War period were a "bounded order that was limited mainly to the West and was realist in all its key dimensions."[14] No matter what the aspirations for the protection of human rights or self-determination outlined in the United Nations Charter, for example, it was understood that the power dynamics of the Cold War trumped such concerns. But in the post–Cold War period, no similar constraints existed. If the United States wished to see the norms embodied in the U.N. Charter enforced, it could. Bill Clinton in particular came to embrace "a growing willingness to use force to vindicate the American concept of how that post–Cold War system should work."[15] The remaining constraints—the veto powers of the U.N. Security Council, for example—were no barrier; the failure to obtain U.N. approval for campaigns in Kosovo and Iraq was no obstacle to the exercise of U.S. power when policymakers were willing to work within the confines of "coalitions of the willing."

For a time, this approach seemed remarkably effective. NATO expansion helped stabilize the former communist states of Central and Eastern Europe, locking them into a Western-leaning path of economic and democratic development. Balkan and Middle Eastern interventions were generally popular among U.S. allies, and even where significant disagreements emerged—as they did in the case of the Iraq War—the pushback was limited. The German foreign minister Joschka Fischer might have infamously exclaimed about the Iraq War that "our most important partner is making decisions that we consider extremely dangerous," but what was Germany going to do?[16] Build its own military? Even the so-called soft balancing of American allies or adversaries—the use of non-military tools to "delay, frustrate, and undermine" U.S. policies—was relatively circumscribed throughout the two decades following the end of the Cold War.[17]

The effects of America's excesses of power were building, however. The American liberal vision for the international system, which one scholar described as "illiberal ordering behavior," was increasingly generating pushback.[18] U.S. policymakers, as the political scientist Nuno Monteiro points out, would repeatedly "underplay the threats to other major powers' ways of life that resulted from the consistent enlargement of the U.S. sphere of influence."[19] Even Jake Sullivan, later Biden's national security adviser, noted in 2018 that U.S. foreign policy increasingly creates an "uneasy balance between sovereignty and noninterference on the one hand, and universal values and multilateral cooperation on the other."[20] Pushback was increasingly visible after 2008. Russia's invasions of Georgia and Ukraine, for example, sought to create territorial disputes that would complicate those countries' accession to NATO, and Chinese attempts at island building—augmenting reefs to form man-made islands—in the South China Sea sought to push U.S. military power in the region further offshore.

If strategy is the balancing of means to achieve ends, then the means of U.S. strategy—enmeshing U.S. power in a web of international institutions and alliances—has remained relatively consistent from 1945 to today. But the ends to which those means were put in the post–Cold War period shifted dramatically. U.S. policymakers after 1991 sought to build an enduring liberal order, undergirded by and sustaining U.S. power over the long term. It was a fundamentally transformative strategy.

NATO Expansion and the Transformation of Europe

The fall of the Iron Curtain brought newly independent Eastern European states into political, economic, and social interaction with the West, kicking off three decades in which they would become increasingly integrated into the institutional structures of Western Europe. With this peace dividend, one might have expected that the U.S. security role in Europe would diminish. After all, despite contentious intra-alliance debates about burden-sharing and strategy, it was widely accepted in Washington's policymaking circles that American involvement in Europe was necessary primarily to deter the Soviet Union. The end of the Cold War thus raised the possibility that NATO's own success might make the alliance obsolete. But the debate over U.S. presence began even before the collapse of the

Soviet Union. Indeed, some of the most contentious of the late–Cold War debates—both inside the Bush administration and with its Soviet interlocuters—were concerned with whether East Germany would be allowed to join NATO as part of a unified Germany. The "two plus four" peace process that followed brought together the two Germanies with the four postwar occupying powers to negotiate this question; it prioritized the fraught politics of German reunification, rather than security. In demanding that a unified Germany remain inside NATO rather than becoming neutral, policymakers also inherently implied that NATO had a future role to play in European security. Discussions about whether the end of the Cold War would require some new, broader European security architecture were ultimately settled by expediency: the desire to see Germany reunified quickly and with Soviet assent. Yet as a result, they helped sow the seeds of future discord.[21]

NATO pivoted quickly after 1991 to create new forums for interaction with the countries of the former Warsaw Pact. The most notable was the Partnership for Peace, which aimed to build civilian and military ties between NATO members and former communist states, including Russia. The question of long-term alliance membership for the states of the former Warsaw Pact remained a fraught one, complete with internecine bureaucratic battles inside the Clinton administration and pushback from the Russian government under Boris Yeltsin.[22] As Yeltsin put it to Clinton in 1993, NATO expansion would be akin to "a sort of neo-isolation of our country in diametric opposition to its natural admission into Euro-Atlantic space."[23] The Partnership for Peace offered a middle road, with individualized plans for Euro-Atlantic integration, and a path for Russian involvement. But as the George H. W. Bush administration turned to the Clinton administration, trends shifted in the opposite direction. U.S. policymakers came to see enlargement as linked to the fate of NATO itself, which still had a powerful lobby in Washington. And there were domestic benefits: NATO expansion would endear Clinton to Midwestern voters of Eastern European origin and would give him a plausible-sounding foreign policy victory.[24]

This is not to say that there was no debate on expansion in Washington. A number of eminent U.S. foreign policy voices—including Sam Nunn, Marshall Shulman, Paul Nitze, and Robert McNamara—challenged the

Clinton administration's decision to expand NATO on strategic grounds. George Kennan, one of the Cold War's clearest thinkers, likewise argued that expanding NATO would be a "strategic blunder of potentially epic proportions."[25] But the normative and domestic political arguments largely carried the day. Going forward, the United States would seek to perpetuate NATO, and it was assisted in doing so by the alliance's easily adaptable bureaucratic structure. As John Kornblum, deputy to the undersecretary of state for European affairs succinctly described, "the Alliance provides a vehicle for the application of American power and vision to the security order in Europe."[26] Another U.S. diplomat was less circumspect, noting that by engaging with Europe through the framework of NATO, the United States is able to "tell the Europeans what we want on a whole lot of issues—trade, agriculture, the Gulf, you name it."[27] NATO expansion was also seen as a way to lock in stability, democracy, and economic reform in Eastern Europe, consolidate stable democratic governments in the region, and cement civilian control of the military.[28]

NATO expansion was successful beyond the wildest dreams of its advocates; through three rounds of expansion between 1999 and 2009, a dozen states joined NATO. These expansions, plus a few scattered additions since, have brought alliance membership to an unprecedented thirty-two states and added territory in the Baltics, the Balkans, the Nordics, and Eastern Europe, far beyond the geographical scope of the original alliance.

NATO's mission also shifted significantly. After all, NATO was now an organization without a clear objective. The Clinton administration thus embraced the notion of NATO as a potential humanitarian enforcer, able to act in cases in which the United Nations could not. More than sixty thousand NATO-associated troops participated in the Bosnian implementation and stabilization forces that followed the Dayton peace accords of 1995. Just four years later, NATO forces again engaged in the former Yugoslavia, this time to drive Serb forces out of the ethnically Albanian enclave of Kosovo, and then to conduct a sizable peacekeeping operation. The terror attacks of 9/11 only added to the impetus for NATO to focus on expeditionary and "out of area" capabilities. NATO, for the first time in its history, invoked Article V of its charter, and the alliance played a critical role in the International Security Assistance Force process in Afghanistan for the following decade. The Iraq War in 2003 was more controversial, surfacing differences between Eastern and Western European members on the war on terror—or as Donald Rumsfeld memorably characterized it, divisions between "new Europe" and "old Europe." By then, NATO expansion and expeditionary missions had become practically symbiotic: For newer members, providing token military forces in Iraq and Afghanistan was viewed as a quid pro quo for membership.[29]

The bubble burst in 2008 at the Bucharest summit. New Europe backed the George W. Bush administration's push to offer Georgia and Ukraine— both former Soviet states that had once been integral parts of the Russian empire—a direct path to NATO membership. Old Europe, led by Chancellor Angela Merkel of Germany, argued that these states were not ready for membership; to offer them a membership action plan might be to "poke the bear" and provoke conflict with Russia. A speech given by President Vladimir Putin of Russia just a year earlier at the Munich Security Conference had shocked the crowd, as he argued that "it is obvious that NATO expansion does not have any relation . . . with ensuring security in Europe. On the contrary, it represents a serious provocation. . . . And we have the right to ask: against whom is this expansion intended?"[30] In the end, the summit issued a milquetoast communiqué promising Georgia and Ukraine a path to NATO membership at some unspecified future date. Shortly thereafter, Russian forces invaded Georgia, advancing to within fifty miles of the capital. The war lasted less than two weeks but made clear that Russia—thanks to its role as a peacekeeper in its immediate neighborhood—had the ability to sustain territorial disputes that could prevent its neighbors from shifting westward. The Maidan revolution in Ukraine in 2014 provided an even bigger wake-up call for European and American policymakers; the Russian annexation of Crimea and support for separatist factions in eastern Ukraine that followed served to create a territorial dispute that would inhibit NATO membership.

The upsides of NATO expansion had long been clear to policymakers: (1) stabilization in Eastern Europe and the Balkans, (2) an easy way to bring states that did not yet meet European Union fiscal requirements into the Western liberal community, and (3) a way to maintain U.S. influence and drum up support for U.S. policies within Europe.[31] The downsides of NATO expansion now also became apparent. Over the previous twenty years, the United States had committed to defend thousands more square

miles of European territory. NATO allies Lithuania and Poland now sur-
rounded the Russian enclave of Kaliningrad, placing Russian troops behind
NATO's front lines in any potential conflict and allowing Russian air defenses and missiles to expand their range of targets inside NATO's territory.
The Baltic states posed the biggest concern. A Rand Corporation wargame
in 2014 suggested that Russia could likely seize Tallinn and Riga within
three days of launching an attack, which would present NATO with the
unpalatable choice of retaking territory by force, escalating to the nuclear
level, or conceding.[32] The unstated assumption during expansion had always
been that NATO's defensive commitments to the Eastern European states
would never be called into question. The Pentagon had not even bothered
with formal defense planning during the accession process for many of
these states. Now the United States, as the primary security provider within
NATO, suddenly faced a credibility problem: Forces in Eastern Europe
were insufficiently credible to deter Russia.

Alliance expansion also worsened the nuclear extended deterrence problem. Policymakers during the Cold War wondered whether Americans
would truly be willing to trade Chicago for Berlin; by 2014, they had to
wonder whether Americans would exchange New York for Tallinn, an even
less likely proposition. Continued reliance on U.S. forces inhibited the
development of any homegrown European defense-industrial base throughout the post–Cold War period; Washington even purposefully undermined
discussions on joint European defense within the framework of the European Union for fear that it would undermine NATO in the long term.
The Obama administration's European Reassurance Initiative, which tem-
porarily rotated U.S. divisions and armor into Eastern member states,
was a Band-Aid applied to the problem.[33] It was never intended to fully
resolve the problem of deterrence in Eastern Europe—and did not. Poland
and the Baltic states increased military spending after 2014, but states
farther west in Europe still saw no real reason to strengthen their military
capabilities.[34]

Debates about NATO expansion have been fraught and contentious,
particularly in the past few years.[35] But the top-line picture is fairly clear:
NATO expansion improved the security prospects of the newly independent
nations of Eastern Europe but contributed to rising tensions between
Russia and the West. As the historian Mary Sarotte put it, "Expansion

itself was a justifiable response to the geopolitics of the 1990s. . . . What was unwise was expanding the alliance in a way that took little account of the geopolitical reality."[36]

The Balkans and the Rise of R2P

The U.N. Charter, signed in the aftermath of World War II, makes clear that genocide and crimes against humanity should not be tolerated by the international community. Its lofty ideals, however, were rarely enforced during the Cold War, and prosecution of perpetrators was typically stymied by the realities of power politics. Governments with poor human rights records would seek to pit the United States and the Soviet Union against each other, and in many cases—such as the Bangladeshi genocide or Cambodia's killing fields—perpetrators of crimes against humanity were viewed as too strategically important to condemn. For many, the post–Cold War period seemed to be a golden opportunity to rectify this flaw. But the early 1990s were characterized mostly by the failure of the international community to respond effectively to genocide and human rights abuses, first during the violent breakup of the former Yugoslavia, and then in the Rwandan genocide. As the journalist and human rights advocate Samantha Power pointed out, "despite the consensus that genocide should 'never again' be allowed, and a good deal of triumphalism about the ascent of liberal democratic values, the last decade of the twentieth century was one of the most deadly in the grimmest century on record."[37] Many of these abuses were broadcast worldwide to a horrified public by the emerging cable news phenomenon, a so-called "CNN effect" that increased the salience of public pressure on humanitarian issues.

These tensions came to a head in the former Yugoslavia, an area right on Western Europe's doorstep that during the mid-1990s was rapidly descending into civil war and ethnic cleansing. The United Nations acted quickly, passing various Security Council resolutions and creating an international peacekeeping force to protect safe areas for civilians within the conflict zone. Member states, however, were generally unwilling to provide the level of force necessary to carry out these ambitious missions. In perhaps the most infamous case, Dutch peacekeepers were unable to defend the town of Srebrenica—a U.N.-designated civilian safe zone—from an advancing Serb army. Some of the peacekeepers fled in the face of overwhelming odds; others were used as human shields to deter Western air strikes. Serbian forces then committed genocide, killing more than eight thousand men and boys. The disaster was a clear-cut case of a mismatch between resources and commitments. According to the U.N. report on Srebrenica, "The safe areas were established by the Security Council without the consent of the parties and without the provision of any credible military deterrent. . . . The International Community as a whole must accept its share of responsibility for allowing this tragic course of events by its prolonged refusal to use force in the early stages of the war."[38] An assumption was born among foreign-policy makers: If the international community wanted to prevent atrocities in future, members would have to commit appropriate force.

The concept of the "responsibility to protect" (R2P) emerged from this period. It was an astounding philosophical break from the principle of sovereign inviolability. A book published in 1996 by the Brookings Institute, titled *Sovereignty as Responsibility,* made the argument plain: If a state did not or could not protect its own citizens, norms of sovereignty should no longer apply to that state. The international community, it argued, was obligated to intervene to protect civilians, although in practice it would be the United States and Western Europe that would have to provide the necessary resources.[39] Humanitarian concerns soon surfaced again in the Balkans, as conflict broke out between Serbian forces and Kosovar separatists. With Russia and China both unwilling to authorize U.N. intervention, however, NATO forces—primarily American—instead engaged in an air campaign designed to force Serbia to accept a peace deal. It was, as legal experts put it, simultaneously illegal and "legitimate" in its attempts to protect civilians, and further bolstered the idea in the West that something akin to R2P was necessary to overcome the veto at the U.N. Security Council.[40] By 1999, Kofi Annan, the U.N. secretary-general, confidently told the *Economist* that "state sovereignty, in its most basic sense, is being redefined." He continued: "States are now widely understood to be instruments at the service of their peoples, and not vice versa."[41]

For all the general acquiescence around the idea of R2P, it remained fuzzily defined, with the areas of greatest agreement in preventive and non-military responses. The language of R2P proponents tactfully emphasized these elements, "the 'responsibility to protect' being much less inherently abrasive than the 'right to intervene,' " as the human rights advocate Gareth Evans put it.[42] The newly elected Obama administration in Washington was increasingly on board. That included notable human rights advocates in the president's inner circle of advisers, such as Hillary Clinton and Samantha Power, along with Susan Rice, Obama's chief of staff. By 2011, when the Arab Spring began to spread across the Middle East, policymakers were primed to see military intervention as the obvious solution. Mass protests in Libya were among the first to spill over into open civil war; as violence spread across much of the country, Western policymakers began to toy with the idea of a no-fly zone designed to protect civilians from the regime's air forces. The debate was given added urgency by Qadhafi's inflammatory comments promising "no mercy" to those in rebel-held towns, and representatives of the newly established transitional government in Libya directly used the language of R2P in their appeals.[43] On March 17, the U.N. Security Council authorized a no-fly zone in Libya, with Russia and China abstaining. NATO-led airstrikes on Libyan government forces began the next day. The mission shifted rapidly from civilian protection to regime change. NATO provided air support for rebel forces and engaged in attempted decapitation strikes on Qadhafi.[44]

The killing, however, didn't end, and Libya spiraled into a bloody multi-sided civil war. The political scientist Alan Kuperman describes the fallout thus: "NATO's intervention backfired: it increased the duration of Libya's civil war by about six times and its death toll by at least seven times, while also exacerbating human rights abuses, humanitarian suffering, Islamic radicalism, and weapons proliferation in Libya and its neighbors."[45] Since Srebrenica, the assumption—particularly in Washington—had been that preventing atrocities was largely a question of willpower and domestic politics. But as Libya proved, the dilemmas seen at Srebrenica were common to complex, multi-sided wars, in which it was difficult to separate victims from perpetrators. Most states were unwilling to countenance the costs of post-conflict reconstruction in Libya, and policymakers began to sour on the notion of R2P. By 2013, the question of intervention in Syria, which also experienced an Arab Spring civil war, had become a proxy in Washington debates for whether the United States should regularly engage in humanitarian intervention.[46] Proponents argued that America had a moral obligation to intervene, whereas opponents pointed to the vanishingly low odds of success. Though Bashar al-Assad was undoubtedly responsible for crimes against humanity, Obama's reticence to intervene in Syria was a clear sign of how Washington's political winds were shifting. It was a bitter pill for R2P proponents to swallow. As Leon Wieselter wrote in the *Atlantic*, "This is what the world looks like when the United States has abandoned its faith in its power and its duty to do good."[47]

But for President Obama—and for many others in Washington—the desire to do good in the world had run up against harsh reality. "A president," Obama told the *Atlantic*'s Jeffrey Goldberg, "does not make decisions in a vacuum. He does not have a blank slate. . . . Any thoughtful president would hesitate about making a renewed commitment in the exact same region of the world with some of the exact same dynamics and the same probability of an un-satisfactory outcome."[48] The fortunes of R2P rose and fell in just two decades, as policymakers shifted from a post–Cold War sense that anything was possible to the realization that too much of the American human rights agenda was, as the 2022 national security strategy put it, "underpinned by an unrealistic faith in force and regime change to deliver sustainable outcomes."[49]

Entr'acte: Consensus Splinters

In December 2015, under the bright lights of a Las Vegas auditorium, more than a dozen Republican presidential hopefuls took to the stage to brandish their hawkish foreign policy credentials and make the case why they should be the one to face off against the Democratic candidate, Hillary Clinton, in the 2016 general election. But then a funny thing happened. Donald Trump attacked his primary opponents, criticizing their willingness to intervene in Iraq and elsewhere:

> In my opinion, we've spent $4 trillion trying to topple various people that frankly, if they were there and if we could've spent that $4 trillion in the United States to fix our roads, our bridges, and all of the other problems; our airports and all of the other problems we've had, we would've been a lot better off. I can tell you that right now. We have done a tremendous disservice, not only to Middle East, we've done a tremendous disservice to humanity. The people that have been killed, the people that have wiped away, and for what? It's not like we had victory."[50]

Trump was immediately criticized for this departure from Republican orthodoxy. But it did little to dent his popular support. It didn't even seem to matter that Trump himself was lying about his own prior support for the war. By 2015, more than half of all Americans had come to believe that the invasion of Iraq was a mistake.[51] For the media, Trump's comments on Iraq in 2015 might have been gauche enough to be outside "the bounds of normal political discourse."[52] For voters, it was past time someone said it.

Today, two-thirds of Americans believe that the invasion of Iraq was a mistake.[53] And that once unthinkable position has so thoroughly entrenched itself in elite discourse that a recent report from the patrician Council on Foreign Relations described the war as "a major strategic blunder that destabilized the Middle East, consumed significant American resources, and sapped the power of the United States."[54] During the presidential campaign of 2020, the Democratic candidates vying to face by then President Trump in the general election all argued some variant of this position. Many went further, committing to remove U.S. troops from Afghanistan, revive the Iran nuclear deal, and adopt a less militarist foreign policy.[55] These sudden shifts in U.S. foreign policy debate resulted from several factors: the rise of China, the failures of the war on terror, the decade-long fallout of the 2008 financial crisis, and even the shock election of Donald Trump. The result has been a half decade of ideological ferment in U.S. foreign policy, as divides have emerged both between the political parties and within them.

The Political Fallout of the War on Terror

By the start of Obama's first term in office, cracks in the consensus were starting to show. The war-on-terror campaigns in Iraq and Afghanistan were not going well—and Washington's foreign policy ecosystem spun itself in circles debating the causes and the solutions. There was a growing network of groups affiliated with al Qaeda stretching across the Middle East and North Africa, and a rapidly expanding set of U.S. troop deployments and drone strikes in countries from Djibouti to Yemen. Obama himself had run on a campaign that opposed the war in Iraq, arguing that the war on terror should be narrower and involve fewer troops. America, he argued, had "spent nearly a trillion dollars, alienated allies and neglected emerging threats—all in the cause of fighting a war for well over five years in a country that had absolutely nothing to do with the 9/11 attacks."[56] His policies, however, contradicted those arguments: He "surged" tens of thousands of troops to Afghanistan and relied heavily on targeted killings, drone strikes, and security assistance to partner forces overseas.[57]

Tough congressional hearings—with representatives and senators keen to show the public that they were taking the issue seriously—grilled generals on the slow progress in Iraq and Afghanistan and pressed them on whether the surge would be successful. Behind the scenes, however, policymakers were largely mollified by the early successes of the surge in Iraq and by reassurances from General David Petraeus—the mastermind behind the surge strategy—that Afghanistan had finally turned a corner. He emphasized "important but hard-fought progress" in the country, but that phrasing quickly became infamous, a bumper sticker for a strategy that over the next few years proved itself to be little more than a military Ponzi scheme.[58] The temporary troop increases of the surge did indeed dampen levels of violence, first in Iraq and then in Afghanistan, but did nothing to resolve the underlying governance, corruption, or political problems of each country. When troops were withdrawn, violence and instability returned. By 2011, when negotiations with the government of Iraq over a residual U.S. force presence collapsed, more than 75 percent of Americans supported the withdrawal of troops from the country.[59]

By 2014, there was also a general sense that the global security situation was headed in the wrong direction; the Russian invasion of Crimea shocked the world, and the Arab Spring uprisings had created an explosive mixture of weapons, extremist ideologies, and frustrated populations in the Middle East. The Obama administration's intervention in Libya was initially viewed in Washington as a grand triumph of "light touch" intervention. But the chaos, civil war, and refugee crisis that followed all took their toll on public opinion. At home, the Benghazi embassy siege became a centerpiece of Republican attack ads against Obama during the 2014 midterms. Next came rapid territorial gains by the newly formed group ISIS in Iraq and a series of high-profile terror attacks in Europe. Public opinion swung toward redeploying troops to Iraq, and Republicans had a field day, criticizing Obama as soft on terror. Similar dynamics characterized the negotiations and implementation of the Iran nuclear deal. Obama was determined to achieve a deal with Iran, but the deal became a touchpoint for opposition to his foreign policy. Hostility ran particularly strong in Congress, where both Republicans and conservative Democrats painted the deal as a capitulation to Tehran and an attack on Israel. Progressive groups rallied around the Obama White House, but the result was a bruising fight that drained much of the administration's political capital.

By the end of Obama's second term, foreign policy was a notable drag on his approval ratings; his foreign policy approval rating lagged his overall popularity by more than ten points.[60] He had failed to follow through on his promises to extract the United States from open-ended wars in the Middle East—he started new wars and continued old ones—and had failed to convince Washington that a new approach to foreign policy was needed. Obama had drawn bipartisan praise for managing the global financial crisis early in his first term in office and had even green-lighted the Special Forces raid that finally killed Osama bin Laden in 2011. But in many ways, this merely highlighted the problem: Bin Laden was dead, but if anything, the terrorism problem had worsened. It was no surprise that voters were frustrated with Obama's record, and with foreign policy elites more generally. By 2014, polling showed that a sizable majority of Americans wanted the United States to focus less on problems overseas and more on domestic policy.[61] By 2019, when the leak of the "Afghanistan Papers" revealed that military and civilian leaders had been misleading the public on foreign policy for almost two decades, Craig Whitlock, a journalist at the *Washington Post,* noted that the reaction was clear: "Many readers had suspected all along that the government had lied to them about the war, and they were angry."[62]

Dismantling the Washington Consensus

The end of the Cold War didn't just vindicate democracy. It was also widely perceived to have vindicated liberalism and free-market capitalism. The West had outpaced the Soviet Union though superior economic performance, which delivered tangible benefits to populations in Western Europe and the Americas. As Fritz Bartel highlights in his history of the end of the Cold War, "democratic capitalism prevailed because it proved capable of imposing economic discipline on its own citizens. Communism collapsed because it could not."[63] Governments from Prague to Beijing took note; capitalism—or neoliberalism, as some described it—was on the march. The end of the Cold War thus supercharged a process of globalization that had begun two decades earlier. An intensive process of economic restructuring—or "shock therapy"—got under way in former communist countries. Meanwhile, countries in Africa and the Middle East that had previously been able to extort aid from the superpowers during the Cold War suddenly found themselves dependent on lending from international institutions such as the International Monetary Fund (IMF) and the World Bank, which required tough fiscal reforms and the liberalization of economic governance. Regional trade integration reached new heights, from the signing in 1992 of the Maastricht treaty—which transformed the European Community into a political union—to the signing of the North American Free Trade Agreement (NAFTA) by the Clinton administration.

This veritable orgy of trade liberalization peaked in 2000 with the U.S. decision to allow China to enter the World Trade Organization (WTO) for the first time. President Clinton's speech hailed it as a historic moment: "Today the House of Representatives has taken an historic step toward continued prosperity in America, reform in China, and peace in the world. . . . It will open new doors of trade for America and new hope for change in China."[64] His remarks reflected several increasingly accepted truisms in Washington. The first was the idea that economic globalization—the integration of other countries into the Western economic system through trade and financial ties—could promote peace and the maintenance of U.S. primacy. At its most facile, this argument was propounded by the *New York Times* columnist Thomas Friedman as the "Golden Arches" theory of peace: the idea that no two countries with a McDonald's had ever gone to war.[65] But more complex and academically rigorous versions of this argument also sprang up; they focused on the ways in which capitalism and interdependence might lower global hostility levels and even prevent wars.[66] Others argued that an open economic order could defuse the need for other states to challenge U.S. leadership. As Madeleine Albright, then the secretary of state, described it, the United States could try to bring China "into the fold as a responsible participant in the international system."[67] This idea became deeply entrenched in Washington's foreign policy circles.[68]

So did the idea that as countries grew rich, they would democratize. This was hardly a new idea, but in the post–Cold War period, it became a core pillar of U.S. strategy. If America could just create an "expanded community of market democracies," the thinking went, it would undoubtedly reap security and economic benefits.[69] Globalization exploded in the following years, particularly in rapidly industrializing low- and middle-income countries, where more than a billion people were lifted out of extreme poverty.[70] But there were also negative externalities associated with this rapid globalization of trade, from job losses to unequal domestic development. As the historian Adam Tooze points out, "Opinion polls, especially those commissioned by the right wing, had for a long time been recording the profound resentment among the American population at the way that both the economy and the political system seemed to be engineered to their disadvantage."[71]

It took the financial crisis in 2008 to bring dissatisfaction with globalization into the mainstream, catalyzing domestic discontent around the idea that the rich were benefiting from a system of international trade and migration that didn't benefit ordinary citizens; American reporters began to explicitly link globalization, economic malaise, and political dissatisfaction at home. This was not an entirely fair criticism. The central cause of the financial crisis was not trade globalization but the internationalization of complex financial markets. Domestic economic dislocation owed as much to technological advances in automation as it did to offshoring. But globalization was increasingly seen as a bête noire on both the left and the right of the political spectrum, from Senator Bernie Sanders to Donald Trump.[72] Similar trends played out in Europe, augmented in the European case by refugee crises that permitted right-wing Euroskeptic and populist parties to take a larger share of the vote in elections.

It did not help in any of this that China's economy continued to visibly boom—and that its political system remained firmly authoritarian. The country's economic success was astounding. As one commentator observed: "700 million people [were] . . . lifted from poverty over the past four decades. In 1986, China's per capita GDP was $282. In 2016, it climbed above $8,100. The country's middle class represented 4 percent of the population in 2002 and 31 percent in 2013."[73] Yet these very successes solidified the Communist Party's hold on power and legitimized its rule.

In light of that and the discontent surrounding trade globalization, many in Washington began to revisit the cost-benefit calculus of U.S.-China trade.

The election of 2016 brought the problem to a head. Donald Trump, true to his word, repudiated the Trans-Pacific Partnership, and Democrats—worried that globalization might have contributed to Hillary Clinton's loss in key swing states—began to tilt toward protectionism. "The foreign policy consensus that guided previous Republican and Democratic administrations," a Carnegie Endowment task force on the topic wrote, "left too many American communities vulnerable to economic dislocation and overreached in trying to effect broad societal change within other countries."[74] The inability of the United States to resolve trade disputes through long-standing methods merely added to the general distrust of international trade institutions such as the WTO. The consensus on globalization broke down quickly, particularly as it became politically advantageous to blame America's economic woes on trade openness. And foreign policy elites were quick to add their own grievances to the pile.

The Return of Revisionism

Dissatisfaction with the U.S.-China relationship was not confined to the economic sphere. Indeed, a central feature of international politics shaping Washington discourse during this period was a slow but steady trend toward challenges to the status quo by China and Russia. Revisionism—as international relations scholars would describe it—is primarily about intention. A revisionist state seeks to overturn the existing order to some extent.[75] In the case of China and Russia, their turn to revisionism was not, as the 2017 national security strategy document described it, the return of a "phenomenon of an earlier century."[76] Instead, it was the simple and expected revival of balancing behavior in the international system after a period of unusual U.S. dominance. Observers had been predicting this development since the early 1990s: Once the United States was the only superpower standing, some other country or group of states would inevitably move to balance against the United States. U.S. hegemony, however, had proved surprisingly resilient throughout the two decades following 1991. Some states engaged instead in "soft balancing," in which they used non-military tools to influence or undermine U.S. policy at the margins, but in general, states chose to prioritize growth and security under a U.S. umbrella. Those who predicted a return to balancing were lambasted.[77]

These thinkers, however, were not wrong about the return of competition among the great powers, merely about the time frame in which it would re-emerge. The most visible case of explicit balancing was Russia's seizure of Crimea from Ukraine in 2014; perhaps the most consequential has been Russia's full-scale invasion in 2022. Faced with the prospect of Ukraine slipping westward and unable to achieve any concessions from Kyiv or from Western states, Russian leaders opted to gamble on a risky and costly military intervention instead. Ukraine is hardly the only place where Russia has evinced balancing behavior. The Kremlin has been active in the Middle East, bolstering the regime of Bashar al-Assad in Syria against the wishes of Western governments. It fought Georgia in 2008 to preserve pro-Russian separatist districts in Abkhazia and South Ossetia. And it has used military force to prop up friendly authoritarian regimes in Belarus, Kazakhstan, and elsewhere. This revisionism is not intrinsic to Russia; before about 2007, there was substantially more cooperation between the United States and Russia. But relations worsened substantially thereafter, with disagreements over the Arab Spring, arms control, and the question of the extent to which NATO would expand into the post-Soviet space. Today, Russia is widely perceived in Washington to be challenging almost every aspect of the U.S.-led international order, from dollar dominance to alliance networks.

China has been more subtle and less aggressive than Russia in its shift toward balancing the power and influence of the United States. But over the past fifteen years, there has likewise been a pronounced shift toward a more assertive Chinese foreign policy. This is hardly unexpected. Although scholars disagree on the causes—revisionism may be driven by domestic political coalitions or simply by an attempt to gain more influence and status in the international system—rising powers tend to flex their muscles as they rise.[78] The earliest example was China's attempt to engage in "island building" in the South China Sea; China used dredging and modern building techniques to occupy and claim previously uninhabited rocks at places like Scarborough Shoal and thereby bolster its territorial claims to a broad sweep of Asia's maritime features. China has sought influence in other ways too. Finding itself constrained within the Bretton Woods financial system, the Chinese government opted to create parallel institutions such as the Asian Infrastructure Investment Bank. The bank's focus on development finance tied into China's Belt and Road Initiative, which sought to build ties with states across Eurasia through investment in infrastructure and trade.[79] China has intensified its ties with Russia, Iran, Brazil, and other states and has aggressively sought to place its own citizens in key roles within the U.N. system, where they can guide the development of international standards and rules.[80] In short, Chinese ambition has grown substantially in recent years.

Even Washington, often caught up in its own internal debates, has noticed these shifts. By the early 2010s, a growing chorus of voices in Washington began to call for the United States to focus less on the Middle East and more on Asia. The creation of the Trans-Pacific Partnership under Obama was designed to anchor a U.S. response to Chinese revisionism. The result has been a notable shift in the Washington consensus on China. Indeed, in just five years, we shifted from the language of China as "responsible stakeholder" to the language of "great power competition," with its open references to "ambitious, aggressive countries seeking regional dominance" and "revisionist authoritarian forces."[81] As these sentiments crystalized in Washington, they were reflected in both Trump's and Biden's national security strategy documents. For Trump—or for the team that wrote his document, at least—the revisionist threat was growing: "It is increasingly clear that China and Russia want to shape a world consistent with their authoritarian model—gaining veto authority over other nations' economic, diplomatic, and security decisions."[82]

The Trump Shock

By 2015, the message being received in Washington was clear, but corresponding policy debates continued to be remarkably slow to shift. The war on terror was on life support, yet many continued to insist that the United States should persevere in its attempts to reshape Afghanistan and Iraq. China was an increasingly visible actor on the world stage, but much of Washington was in denial about the failure of decades of Asia policy. Indeed, as late as 2016, a bipartisan study group of mainstream foreign policy experts—many of them advisers to that year's Clinton presidential campaign—argued in a report that "there is no reason for a fundamental adjustment in the approach the last eight administrations—Republican and Democratic—have taken to China. Promoting the peaceful rise of China . . . remains a sound strategy for the United States."[83] It would take one more thing—a shock to the system—to shatter the bipartisan foreign policy consensus for good. In November 2016, the election of Donald Trump provided that shock. Trump himself was certainly no foreign policy expert. Indeed, he had little real policy experience of any kind, and he furthered that deficiency by failing to incorporate D.C.'s existing policy community into his campaign. Not that they would have had him anyway: As more than a hundred Republican foreign policy hands wrote in an open letter during the 2016 primary, Trump "would use the authority of his office to act in ways that make America less safe, and which would diminish our standing in the world." It is perhaps no wonder that Washington's foreign policy elites didn't take him seriously. There was the over-the-top persona, the racist tirades against Mexican immigrants, the ridiculous ride down a golden escalator to his presidential announcement. And he didn't seem willing to learn—or even to stick to one point of view. As the open letter put it, quite accurately, Trump's "vision . . . is wildly inconsistent and unmoored in principle. He swings from isolationism to military adventurism within the space of one sentence."[84]

Media profiles nonetheless attempted to tease out Trump's views to draw a contrast with his Democratic challenger, Hillary Clinton. Perhaps the most superficial was Maureen Dowd's "Donald the Dove, Hillary the Hawk" column, which drew on Trump's criticisms of the war in Iraq and his affinity for Vladimir Putin to argue that he was less war-prone than his counterpart.[85] Such profiles were far too simplistic: As often as Trump called for an end to the war on terror, he also repeatedly used violent language and racist imagery. Indeed, what Trump's campaign mostly highlighted was a media over-reliant on simple and erroneous foreign policy binaries: If Trump was outside the status quo, then he must be anti-war. If Trump chose to use the phrase "America First" in a *New York Times* interview, then it must mean that he was hearkening back to the pro-Nazi tendencies of interwar figures like Charles Lindbergh or

Henry Ford.[86] Trump's real views were far less coherent—and far less dovish—than such profiles suggested. He certainly was no fan of the foreign policy status quo. Asked about that Republican open letter, he retorted that "the names on this letter are the ones the American people should look to for answers on why the world is a mess."[87] But Trump was not an isolationist so much as an unreconstructed Jacksonian: strongly nationalist, skeptical of alliances, and perfectly willing to use military force if needed. Washington simply didn't know what to make of him; most foreign policy hands pinned their hopes on Hillary Clinton's inevitable election victory.[88]

Trump's election in November 2016 thus came as a profound shock to the foreign policy community, as well as allies around the world. The shock was palpable; one member of a D.C. think tank took to Twitter to compare the coming struggle with Trump to the Korean War, and another compared the election to Kristallnacht.[89] But shock quickly gave way to a concerted effort to understand what Trump's foreign policy would mean for the world; the website of *Foreign Affairs*, for example, featured pieces such as "Deciphering Trump's Asia Policy" and "Reading Trump's Middle East Policy."[90] The shock also contributed to various D.C. think-tank projects over the following years that attempted to understand how the forces of globalization might have undermined popular support for liberal internationalism and sought to "educate" the public about America's vital role in the world.[91] In any normal administration, debate on foreign policy would have been shaped by the new administration and its preferred approach. But the Trump White House floundered, unable to find staff to fill vacant foreign policy positions and implement the president's foreign policy vision. Indeed, having alienated or rejected much of the Republican foreign policy elite, the administration was forced to scrape the barrel for remaining candidates who were either inexperienced or of questionable judgment; Michael Flynn, Trump's first choice for national security adviser, lasted less than a month in the job. Hiring problems were compounded by Trump's own irrational impulses and by scandals like "Russiagate." The search for qualified personnel became one of the defining characteristics of the next four years and a central reason why the Trump administration was never able to coalesce around a coherent new strategy for U.S. foreign policy.

World, Transformed

The collapse of Afghanistan was not gradual. Certainly, the mission had been faltering for years. And the Trump administration's choice to negotiate with the Taliban clearly signaled that the U.S. mission would eventually end. But no one expected an overnight collapse of the Afghan government as President Ashraf Ghani fled to Dubai in August 2021. Even the Taliban were surprised by their own catastrophic success; after twenty years of war against the United States, they nonetheless offered to give U.S. forces responsibility to secure the capital during the evacuation in an attempt to stave off chaos.[92] The Kabul airport was swarmed by thousands of terrified refugees seeking evacuation from bloody Taliban retribution. In videos reminiscent of the fall of Saigon, families clogged the airport entrances and parents threw their children into the arms of waiting marines. Desperate young men climbed onto the wheels of departing airplanes, only to fall back to earth when altitude claimed them.

So great was the chaos that the visa-processing apparatus of the U.S. government failed under the load, leaving ad hoc networks of former military and civilian specialists in Washington to work frantically to ensure the rescue of Afghans they had once worked with. The U.S. military successfully evacuated 122,000 people in just eleven days, a truly heroic feat. But it was not enough. The humanitarian horror was augmented by the many images on social media of Taliban fighters seizing the U.S. equipment supplied to the Afghan government over the previous two decades. Withdrawal—as in Vietnam—was unquestionably the correct strategic decision for Washington. But it laid bare the failures of U.S. policy and the ways in which those failures hurt the lives of ordinary Afghans and Americans.

The withdrawal from Afghanistan also had broader resonance. For all of America's power during the unipolar moment, it had not managed to transform the world—or even the domestic politics of one impoverished central Asian nation. Great strides had been made in women's literacy and economic development, but the U.S. military had been unable to resolve the deep cleavages in Afghan society. This conclusion held more broadly too. At a global level, much had been achieved in three decades of U.S. primacy; millions around the world were pulled out of poverty, for example. But the fundamental nature of the international system had not changed. The United States had sought revolutionary change after the end of the Cold War. It was no surprise that others would be threatened, and the natural global dynamics of shifting economic and military power were soon augmented by pushback from the states most concerned about America's revisionist goals. By the end of Biden's presidency, these changes had produced widespread dissatisfaction with U.S. foreign policy. Washington's bipartisan foreign policy consensus was irreparably shattered, although nothing coherent had emerged to replace it.

2

New World, New Debates

Despite all the warnings from Russia-watchers, military analysts, and even leaked U.S. intelligence sources, it is hard to describe the level of shock that hung over Western capitals in the last week of February 2022, as a seemingly never-ending stream of Russian tanks, personnel carriers, and weaponry rolled across the Ukrainian border. Major war of this kind had not been seen in Europe for a half century, and the early days of the invasion were characterized by large-scale airstrikes on infrastructure, attempted decapitation strikes on Ukraine's leadership, and aggressive Russian efforts to seize the capital of Kyiv. Western audiences watched with horror the news footage of untrained Ukrainian civilians building barricades and taking up arms while their children sheltered in subway stations. It took almost six weeks before it finally became clear that Russia had failed to achieve its most ambitious goals and that Ukraine would survive as an independent state.

During the early months of the war, the world's advanced industrialized democracies came together in a stunning show of military and economic support for Kyiv. Before the war, few would have expected European states like Germany to willingly cut their energy and trade ties with Russia, but the shock of the invasion precipitated unprecedented levels of European unity on sanctions, arms supplies, and funding to Ukraine. After years of growing concerns about American commitments to Europe, the Biden administration unquestioningly positioned additional U.S. troops in Eastern European NATO countries to deter Russia. And although the invasion of Ukraine was in many ways a worrying return to a world of state-on-state violence, it also brought a comfortable sense of purpose and clarity back to many Western capitals. The war had an unambiguous villain and hero. It suggested a future European relationship with Russia more akin to that during the decades of containment than during the messy, politically ambiguous period since 1991. President Biden's remarks on the one-year anniversary of the invasion could have been lifted straight from the Cold War: "A dictator bent on rebuilding an empire will never be able to erase the people's love of liberty. Brutality will never grind down the will of the free. And Ukraine—Ukraine will never be a victory for Russia."[1] The war in Ukraine offered a new, clear purpose to U.S. policymakers: a contest between democracy and autocracy "for the soul of mankind."[2]

But that clarity of purpose was short-lived, as all the existing problems of the post–Cold War period began to leak back in. More subtle impacts of the invasion of Ukraine took longer to be felt but created more division than unity. Food shortages and high energy prices—fueled partly by the war and partly by sanctions—were felt most strongly in the countries of the Global South, which created ill will and resentment among those who believed they should not pay the price for a faraway European conflict. Unity on sanctions has held in Europe, but public opinion is increasingly dividing; citizens of Western European states such as France, the Netherlands, and Italy are expressing a willingness to explore a negotiated peace, whereas Eastern European citizens continue to favor a long war to the bitter end.[3] And unity has begun to fracture in Washington as well. China hawks, who had expected to play a large role in the Biden administration, felt slighted by the administration's focus on Europe. Republicans have soured on the war in Ukraine, with some balking at the significant amount of money and arms being sent to a non-ally, and others worrying that the focus on Ukraine will fatally distract the United States from the growing threat of China. By August 2023, eighteen months into the war, most Americans opposed sending more aid to Ukraine.[4]

Indeed, for all the centrality and shock of the war in Ukraine over the past few years, it has done remarkably little to settle the ongoing divides in U.S. foreign policy. The Biden administration—in a hastily rewritten and reformulated national security strategy—propounded a new, post-Ukraine variant of liberal internationalism. The emerging struggle between democracy and "revisionist autocracies" (as the document describes it) is in some ways a continuation of the U.S. post–Cold War primacy-based strategy. But the administration also faced internal contention from the progressive wing of the Democratic Party, which, though content to support a fellow democracy in Ukraine, was not necessarily on board with a new global crusade against China. And across the aisle, the Republican Party's foreign policy inclinations are likewise in flux, with open contestation between those who support traditional U.S. alliances and those who want to take a harder, Asia-first line. This chapter lays out the landscape of these foreign policy debates, exploring the major camps or positions in these discussions and the ways in which their approaches to U.S. foreign policy sustain or diverge from those of the past three decades.

Four Road Maps for U.S. Foreign Policy

Many studies of grand strategy start from published academic frameworks, but the rapidity with which the U.S. foreign policy debate has shifted—and the fact that no consensus has yet emerged to replace its post–Cold War foreign policy—suggests that this may not be the best approach to understand emergent debates. Here, instead, we consider the landscape of foreign policy debates in terms of broad worldviews (that is, mental models of the world), which feed directly into the formulation of grand strategy. What has emerged over the past few years are four rough worldviews, none of which has yet coalesced into a bipartisan or partisan foreign policy consensus.

Each of these worldviews repudiates some core part of the post–Cold War consensus: nation-building, democracy promotion, globalization, trade, or even military primacy. All have differing conceptions of the scope of U.S. interests: Some remain decidedly ideological in orientation, whereas others hew toward more traditional realpolitik approaches to the world. Individuals within these groups generally differ in what they believe causes conflict—and how likely it is—and therefore differ in their preferred strategies to prevent it. They do not map neatly onto partisan political lines, although some viewpoints are more common among Democrats, and others among Republicans. And there is limited consensus even within these groupings on how to approach challenging security-adjacent problems

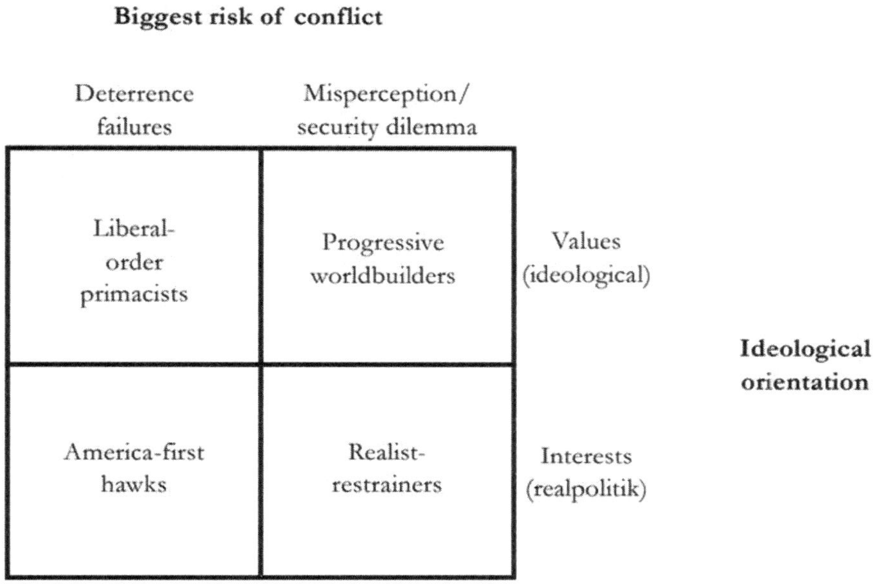

Biggest risk of conflict

Deterrence failures	Misperception/ security dilemma	
Liberal-order primacists	Progressive worldbuilders	Values (ideological)
America-first hawks	Realist-restrainers	Interests (realpolitik)

Ideological orientation

Figure 1. Cleavage lines in U.S. foreign policy debates

like trade policy or immigration. But by considering these clusters of opinion as ideal types in the Weberian sense—that is, by stressing the commonalities typically found within each group—we can better understand the logical underpinnings of these approaches and better understand how they may shape U.S. foreign policy going forward.

Existing typologies use a variety of factors to classify foreign policy or strategic thinking: How far out should the United States project its military? Is the nation's purpose found in ideology or realpolitik? How involved should the United States be in the world? Should the United States act through multilateral or unilateral means?[5] In this chapter, we focus on two deceptively simple cleavage lines around which foreign policy opinion in Washington is increasingly sorting itself (figure 1). The first concerns the role of ideology in U.S. foreign policy: Why does the United States engage with the world? Is it to reshape the international order and the domestic politics of other states into something more akin to that of the United States? Or is that engagement restricted to achieving moderate

U.S. interests within the realities of global power politics? This, in short, is a disagreement about whether U.S. foreign policy should be transformative or conservative (in the Burkean sense) in its goals.

The second concerns the causes of conflict in the international system: How should American engagement with the world be pursued? Does the United States need to provide overwhelming force to deter revisionist states around the world? Or are more cautious, diplomacy-friendly approaches less likely to provoke conflict? Though it may be tempting to frame this as a simple "hawk vs. dove" dichotomy, that is not entirely accurate. Instead, this division is driven by a fundamental difference of opinion over the causes of conflict and whether it arises mostly from deterrence failures against determined, revisionist actors or from misperceptions that drive security spiral dynamics. There is clear historical evidence that both the deterrence model and the spiral model of conflict exist, and scholars have long argued over which predominates in international affairs.[6] Yet this is no esoteric academic distinction. Indeed, the policy ramifications of this split could not be more profound: If the deterrence model predominates, then a highly militarized U.S. forward presence is required to avoid conflict. If the spiral model instead predominates, then a highly militarized approach is more likely to cause conflict.

In contrast to some traditional mappings of U.S. foreign policy, there is no clear "internationalist vs. isolationist" division in Washington today.[7] Even the most nationalistic of these groups believes in the assertive use of U.S. power when needed, and the most dovish aims to stay connected with the world through trade and diplomacy. They differ not on whether the United States should engage with the world, but instead on how and why. Though simple, the two distinctions produce four often highly distinctive visions for *how* and *why* the United States should engage globally (table 1). Let us explore each in turn.

Liberal-Order Primacists

WHO ARE THEY? This camp—a variant of liberal internationalism—is probably the one that has shifted the least in recent years, both in viewpoint and in membership. Most of this camp remains composed of mainstream Democratic foreign policy hands. They are strong believers both in American military *primacy* and in the importance of sustaining a U.S.-led *liberal order.*

Table 1. U.S. foreign policy debates: Four worldviews

	Liberal-order primacists	America-first hawks	Progressive worldbuilders	Realist-restrainers
Uniting principle	Maintain U.S. leadership; protect "liberal international order"	Prioritize American security and commercial interests above all	Foster global peace and prosperity; build a better world	Maintain American security without unnecessary wars
Core national interests	Maintain U.S. military edge and global access	Deter U.S. adversaries and ensure security of homeland	Security and prosperity, particularly for the working class	Defend U.S. homeland
	Protect U.S.-led alliance networks and postwar institutions	Maintain U.S. military edge over other states	Solidarity with oppressed peoples	Maintain U.S. economic prosperity
	Advance U.S. values and norms	Protect U.S. citizens and commercial interests abroad	Undermine the military-industrial complex	Prevent rise of peer hegemons that could threaten the United States
			Bolster global governance	
Theory of security	U.S.-led institutions and security commitments tamp down conflict and deter revisionists	U.S. military supremacy deters revisionists and ensures American security (i.e., "we fight them over there")	Resolving the underlying problems of the human condition (poverty, kleptocracy, authoritarianism) will produce greater peace and security for all	A minimally sufficient U.S. defense is most likely to create security for Americans without triggering the security dilemma
Extent of forward military presence	Expansive, multiregional	Substantial in priority regions	Minimal	Low, concentrated in priority regions
Priority regions	Asia, Europe, Middle East	Asia	All regions	Asia

Continues...

Table 1. Continued

	Liberal-order primacists	America-first hawks	Progressive worldbuilders	Realist-restrainer
View of allies and partners	Allies are the sine qua non of American security, essential to the maintenance of the liberal order; allies should be subordinate to U.S. power	Allies are helpful, often necessary, but should be challenged when they undermine U.S. interests; some concerns about free-riding	Democracies can be important partners and allies; autocratic allies should be treated with extreme caution as the United States may enable domestic repression	Allies can be useful partners on occasion but alliances should be more transactional; free-riding and extended deterrence pose significant problems for U.S. alliance commitment
Which part of previous consensus abandoned?	Regime change; forcible democracy promotion; R2P Neoliberal global trade order	Nation-building and democracy promotion International institutions	Use of force for democracy promotion	N/A
View of international anarchy	Solvable (via U.S. power, international institutions, and democratic peace)	Manageable (through superior U.S. force)	Solvable (via peacebuilding, collective security, or democratic peace)	Manageable (via diplomacy and deterrence)
Role of transnational issues	Extensive focus on climate, terrorism, etc.	Largely unimportant	Critical, particularly climate issues	Limited role for arms control, climate, or other critical issues
Approach to trade policy	Mix of free traders and pro-industrial policy advocates	Mix of free traders and pro-industrial policy advocates	Generally anti-trade	Mix of free traders and pro-industrial policy advocates
Use of force?	When the United States or allies are threatened, or when liberal principles are at stake	When U.S. security or concrete interests are threatened	In defense of U.S. or of democratic allies	When U.S. security or concrete interests are threatened
Principal flaw	Risks overextending, creating security spirals, and promoting balancing behavior in other states	Risks alienating even friendly states and isolating the United States, and risks creating security spirals	Risks neglecting or undermining concrete U.S. interests in favor of universal values	Risks balancing against revisionist states too late and failing to adequately deter conflict

And indeed, the bipartisan consensus of the post–Cold War period was always a partnership between those who supported spreading American values around the world (Samantha Power–style liberal internationalists) and those who believed that U.S. military primacy could be used to build a better world (neoconservatives such as Max Boot). If anything, these two groups have become more closely aligned over time, particularly since Trump's first presidency, which caused many neoconservatives to migrate from their *National Review*–style centrist conservatism to an ideological no-man's-land. Some took positions as columnists or television pundits at mainstream outlets (Jennifer Rubin and Max Boot at the *Washington Post,* for example, or David Frum and Anne Applebaum at the *Atlantic*); others maintain academic or think-tank sinecures (for example, Eliot Cohen at Johns Hopkins SAIS or Robert Kagan at the Brookings Institution). Most are now irrelevant in Republican politics. This means that the group is more coherent in a partisan sense than it used to be, as these former neo*conservative* thinkers are now increasingly aligned on both foreign and domestic policy with liberal internationalist thinkers in the Biden administration.

WHAT DO THEY BELIEVE? This group's views have also changed little. The group embodies the bipartisan consensus of the post–Cold War period with minimal alterations that mostly aim to blunt its worst excesses. In the security space, liberal-order primacists have (at least ostensibly) sworn off the use of force for regime change, nation-building, or democracy promotion. As the Biden administration's national security strategy put it, "We will not use our military to change regimes or remake societies, but instead limit the use of force to circumstances where it is necessary to protect our national security interests."[8] And although the notion of the responsibility to protect—the idea that the United States has a responsibility to disregard norms of sovereignty in order to protect civilians—is not dead, it is no longer widely invoked in political discussions.[9] Liberal internationalists remain committed to protecting human rights or spreading U.S. values through other means—for example, the widespread use of financial sanctions—but the failures of military intervention have taken the use of force out of the mainstream of foreign policy options for now.

In the economic space, views have changed more substantially. After Hillary Clinton's electoral loss in 2016, and fraught with concerns that the impacts of globalization and free trade at home might be undermining support for American global leadership or military spending, liberal-order primacists began to question the role of trade in U.S. foreign policy.[10] Spearheaded by Democratic foreign policy leaders including Jake Sullivan (later the national security adviser) and Salman Ahmed (later the director of policy planning at the State Department), the Carnegie Endowment launched a project centered on the creation of a so-called foreign policy for the middle class, which attempted to bring foreign policy and domestic economic policy together in a repudiation of the idea that free trade was a broadly popular, bipartisan policy.[11] This shift was exacerbated by the clear failure of "convergence," the now defunct idea that China would converge with the West both economically and in governance terms. Today's liberal internationalists have begun to reject globalization writ large. In practical terms—whether it is decoupling or the growing marriage between foreign policy and domestic industrial policy—the Biden administration largely abandoned the trade pillar of American engagement with the world.[12]

Despite these changes, liberal internationalism remains the same in most other respects: an assertive and forward-leaning strategy that seeks to leverage U.S. military and financial power for liberal ends. But I rename it here because the goal of this approach has changed: Its focus is increasingly on the protection of what proponents describe as the "liberal international order" or the "rules-based international order." The term *liberal order* is itself anachronistic; as scholars have noted, there has never been any global consensus around international liberal institutions. The Cold War order was made up of two interrelated, coexisting systems of institutions: a broad, yet largely powerless set of institutions, such as the United Nations, that included both the United States and the Soviet Union, along with a parallel club of U.S.-led alliance institutions in Europe and Asia.[13] Even the broadest norms and rules of the international system—the sovereignty norm, for example—have at times been honored, and at times been disregarded, even by the United States. But the belief in such an order is strong; its proponents argue that since the Second World War, a network of U.S.-led alliance commitments and international institutions have helped shape the rules of the road in international politics, creating a freer and more open space for international interaction than would otherwise have been the case. "For admirers," as Patrick Porter describes it, the liberal order "was a profound project that rewired the world."[14]

This renewed focus on order is a shift back to the theoretical roots of liberal internationalism as propounded by such scholars as John Ikenberry or Stephen Brooks during the 1990s. At the heart of Ikenberry's theory is the notion that an American-led order of liberal international institutions can stabilize the international system, overcome rivalries, and bring peace to the world. Today's liberal-order primacists—like Ikenberry himself—view the wars in Iraq and Afghanistan as aberrations, not as the logical extensions of liberal internationalism's attempt to rewrite the world in its own image.[15] They argue that with the liberal order under threat globally, a conservative or defensive approach to preserving this order is necessary to ensure U.S. security. A siege mentality pervades much of the writing by scholars like Robert Kagan, who notes: "The liberal world order is fragile and impermanent. Like a garden, it is ever under siege from the natural forces of history, the jungle whose vines and weeds constantly threaten to overwhelm it."[16]

Those in this camp vary on whether they think U.S. power is in decline; some believe that the unipolar moment is ending, whereas others believe that it has plenty of life left. But all agree that liberalism—or, if one is cynical, American hegemony—is under threat globally from revisionist states such as China and Russia. Others frame it more broadly: The Biden administration argued not only that "the liberal world order . . . is genuinely, seriously under assault" but also that democracy itself is being challenged.[17] Their strategies thus focus less on concrete interests and more on the preservation of the liberal order. Tom Wright, Biden's director of strategic planning at the National Security Council, argues that "responsible competition offers the best way of preserving America's status as a liberal superpower and the U.S.-led international order."[18] Mira Rapp-Hooper and Rebecca Lissner argue that the end goal of U.S. strategy should be "the pursuit of an open international system," whereas Michael O'Hanlon argues that any "new grand strategy must sustain U.S. global leadership," as "the nation's role is unique."[19]

In military terms, this means their strategy today looks similar to strategy during the post–Cold War period. Liberal-order primacists are not merely committed to U.S. alliances around the world; President Joe Biden referred to alliances as "sacred commitments."[20] Liberal-order primacists advocate maintaining a strong U.S. forward presence in all major regions, with a particular focus on containing China and Russia, along with smaller states like Iran and North Korea, all while maintaining or even growing America's alliance commitments as needed. In diplomatic terms, the new liberal internationalism is making the world an implicit—and sometimes explicit—offer: Join with America, unless you wish to live in a world dominated by China. Yet in practice, the most notable shift among liberal-order primacists is in the economic space, where the opposite is largely true. Under both Trump and Biden, the United States has adopted a significantly more protectionist approach to trade, one in which—despite the invocation of phrases like "friend-shoring"—it is increasingly difficult to advance trade liberalization.

PROBLEMS WITH THIS APPROACH A full repudiation of liberal internationalism—or its new variant—would take too much space. But many of the problems in today's liberal-order primacy approach are similar to the problems of earlier iterations of liberal internationalism. It encourages free riding by allies, who come to depend on the United States for protection and fail to build their own military capabilities. It creates significant risks of entanglement in distant conflicts, as alliances, socialization, and broad goals encourage the United States to get involved in conflicts that are at best peripheral to national interests. And it discourages the prioritization of threats, thereby increasing the likelihood of overstretch. Particularly in an era of relative U.S. decline, it is likely to become increasingly difficult to sustain the defense spending and domestic political support for this strategy.

This approach is also unpopular outside the U.S. and European policy community, and its Manichaean worldview can often be seen as overblown and tone-deaf. Take Michael O'Hanlon's description of the liberal order: "The United States led an effort after World War II that created the most stable, prosperous, and democratic period in human history. The effort achieved a bloodless final chapter of the Cold War, . . . so overwhelming was the verdict of history about which system and set of ideas should prevail."[21] That narrative is almost laughably naive about the bloodshed and risk that pervaded much of the Cold War across the developing world.

Telling citizens of Vietnam or Angola that we should return to the peaceful liberal order of the Cold War period is not likely to achieve much. Meanwhile, the growing focus on framing everything in terms of democracy versus autocracy is likely to encourage pushback and balancing behavior by threatened autocracies, just as liberal internationalism's prior focus on democratization did.

Indeed, perhaps the biggest problem with a strategy of liberal-order primacy is that it is essentially old wine in new bottles in an era of greater constraints. Despite having forsworn regime change, this approach to the world and its expansive goals are still hugely ambitious. Even at the peak of its power during the 1990s, the United States was unsuccessful at building a truly self-sustaining liberal order and in folding China and Russia into a peaceful order as "responsible stakeholders." Liberal internationalists may have rebranded and refocused their efforts, but they cannot explain how similar goals can be accomplished under the increased constraints of the post-unipolar period.

America-First Hawks

WHO ARE THEY? There has always been a hard-line, hawkish faction of the Republican Party, one that emphasizes the importance of maintaining American security and sustaining American power above all other goals. During the unipolar moment, these thinkers tended to align with the bipartisan consensus; their policy priorities were similar to those of their more Wilsonian-minded liberal internationalist or neoconservative counterparts. Just consider the differing rationales for the Iraq War: Did the United States topple Saddam Hussein out of genuine fear of weapons of mass destruction, because it wished to spread democracy, or simply to demonstrate its power and deter other states? You can find all these rationales in the historical record; hawks like Vice President Dick Cheney argued the more naked power-based case alongside more idealistic ones. The same could be said for an issue like NATO expansion, where more idealistic arguments about democratization in Eastern Europe were aligned with the arguments of those who believed that expansion would keep Russia in its place.

This brand of hawkish nationalism is often described as "Jacksonianism," a term coined by the historian Walter Russell Mead in allusion to the hawkish, populist nineteenth-century presidency of Andrew Jackson. It is thus not a new phenomenon, but one that has become visibly distinct from liberal internationalism since 2016, many of its proponents now embracing the "America first" branding that Donald Trump brought back into the mainstream. Proponents of this viewpoint include former and current Trump officials such as H. R. McMaster, Nadia Schadlow, Stephen Miller, JD Vance, and Elbridge Colby. This viewpoint is increasingly the norm at right-wing think tanks such as the Foundation for Defense of Democracies and the Heritage Foundation. It is bolstered by congressional Republicans such as Josh Hawley and Ted Cruz and is highly partisan in nature; it essentially does not exist outside the Republican Party.

WHAT DO THEY BELIEVE? "America-first hawks" believe first in the superiority of the United States and the primacy of American security and interests. Walter Russell Mead describes the Jacksonian worldview thus:

> "Don't Tread on Me!" warned the rattlesnake on the Revolutionary battle flag; Jacksonians believe that the United States should not seek out foreign quarrels, but when other nations start wars with the United States, Jacksonian opinion agrees with Gen. Douglas MacArthur that "There is no substitute for victory."[22]

In short, they are not crusaders but are more than willing to use military force—or economic coercion—when they believe it is necessary. They believe in a strong, well-funded military and the importance of military deterrence in ensuring continued peace. This is, in effect, Reagan's formula of "peace through strength," though there are some clear tensions in the modern era between the desire of the America-firsters to maintain a substantial forward military presence and their desire to minimize allies' free riding on the United States, something highlighted repeatedly during Trump's first presidency by his willingness to castigate allies for insufficient contributions and to muse about ways to "charge them" for U.S. protection.[23]

There are other clear differences from the post–Cold War consensus. America-first hawks—like their liberal internationalist cousins—have mostly repudiated nation-building and democracy promotion as a poor use of American resources. But they are more willing to leave residual force pres-

ence in various Middle Eastern countries and to engage in punitive campaigns against terrorist or rebel forces. The Trump administration's
campaign against ISIS—though it began as a continuation of the Obama
administration's policies—was a prime example of this: Most U.S. forces
were withdrawn after the military defeat of ISIS, against the wishes of local
allies. America-first hawks are generally comfortable with the use of drone
strikes and military targeting in the name of U.S. interests, regardless of
international law, as demonstrated forcefully by the assassination of the
Iranian general Qassem Soleimani. They are also open to coercion of U.S.
allies, even with sanctions. A notable example is the Nord Stream 2 pipeline;
the United States imposed sanctions to bring German energy policy more
in line with the preferred policies of the Trump administration.[24] Recent
tariffs offer another. On a broad level, although many America-firsters appreciate American alliances and partnerships, there is little question that
such alliances are a means to an end rather than an end in themselves.

Indeed, perhaps the core of this worldview is its strong emphasis on
American sovereignty as a fundamental organizing principle. Its proponents
are profoundly hostile to international institutions, drawing on a deep well
of conservative suspicion about the United Nations, as well as the World
Bank and IMF, that goes back as far as the John Birch Society in the 1960s.
This sense has been enhanced by a general sentiment that globalization,
as the former Trump official Nadia Schadlow puts it, allowed China "to
take advantage of economic interdependence to grow its economy and
enhance its military" and "subvert the liberal convergence."[25] Liberal
structures have, in other words, allowed other countries to take advantage
of American generosity. This sentiment bleeds into all kinds of foreign
policy areas. America-firsters tend to be Euroskeptic, feting the architects
of Brexit and favoring bilateral ties with individual European states rather
than stronger ties with Brussels. They are skeptical of arms-control agreements, from the Iran nuclear deal to the Intermediate-Range Nuclear Forces
Treaty, from which the United States withdrew in 2019. They prefer nuclear
supremacy and ballistic missile defense to deterrence and mutual arms
control as means of ensuring American security. In short, for the America-
first hawks, it is not important to preserve the "liberal order." Most would
deny that such a thing even exists. America succeeds not through cooperation but through the strength of its ability to coerce and deter.[26]

Again, these are not *new* views per se. John Bolton succeeded in persuading George W. Bush to withdraw from the Anti-Ballistic Missile Treaty in 2002, the event acting as a precursor to the death throes of arms control seen over the past decade. Vice President Dick Cheney was a vociferous critic of international institutions like the International Criminal Court. But their administration was at least broadly open to international cooperation when it suited them; Bush tried to get U.N. approval for his invasion of Iraq before resorting to a "coalition of the willing." Bolton was relatively isolated in his views during the Bush administration, and a later succession of failed Republican presidential candidates from John McCain to Mitt Romney would go on to endorse a liberal—if hawkish—view of the world. Today, however, Bolton's views are closer to the mainstream of the Republican Party, where traditional foreign policy thinkers are increasingly attempting to fold their own views into the new consensus. Colin Dueck, for example, argues that conservative internationalism, long the mainstay of the GOP, should be rebranded as conservative *nationalism:* the use of international means to achieve national, sovereignty-promoting ends.[27]

There is an increasing sense of urgency among many America-firsters about the threat posed by China (in both military and economic realms), along with a growing sense that European security—and the unwillingness of European states to provide for their own security—is a distraction from the potential for a hot war with China in the next decade. This stance has led some to describe America-firsters such as Elbridge Colby, the author of the first Trump administration's national defense strategy, as "Asia firsters" instead. That is not entirely accurate, but America-first hawks are certainly determined to preserve a favorable balance of power in Asia, which they view as the most important region in the world.[28] They view China not only as a territorial threat but also as a potential ideological and economic threat to the United States that must be stopped sooner rather than later. As Matt Pottinger, a former deputy national security adviser, told the House of Representatives Select Committee on China in May 2023, "It would be better to constrain and temper Xi [Jinping]'s ambitions now—through robust, coordinated military deterrence . . . and through strict limits on China's access to technology, capital, and data. . . . That's better than waiting until he has taken fateful and irrevocable steps, such as attacking Taiwan."[29]

This hawkishness bleeds into the economic realm. Though there are also domestic political imperatives pushing conservatives toward protectionism—as with liberal-order primacists, the America-first camp has soured on the domestic benefits of trade liberalization—the driving force behind much of this camp's rhetoric on trade protectionism is China. Indeed, the notion that Chinese power has been inextricably linked to American support for globalization during the post–Cold War period has enhanced the willingness of the GOP to shift away from its traditional free-trade roots. The Trump administration's aggressive use of tariffs against Chinese imports may have been self-sabotaging in an economic sense but remains popular among Republican voters.[30] This is an area of agreement with liberal-order primacists. The result has been a stronger role for economic statecraft (sanctions, tariffs, export controls, and the like) in foreign policy and an ongoing focus on decoupling from China and protecting vulnerable supply chains, particularly the Taiwanese semiconductor industry.

A final point is worth emphasizing. In addition to the growing impingement of economic and trade issues on the political space, immigration has become a prominent issue for the America-firsters over the past five years. Immigration has often been used in foreign policy debates as a foil—for example, arguments for more spending on the southern border and less in the Middle East. But discussions of migration and the border by America-firsters have themselves become increasingly securitized. The new Trump administration has sent the military to the border to reinforce the Border Patrol; and several Republican governors have already dispatched National Guard troops there as well. Others make the increasingly popular argument that unrest, increased migration, and the growth of drug-related violence in Mexico pose a national security threat, some going so far as to argue that the United States should simply send troops to enforce order. Senator Lindsey Graham, for example, argued that "if there were an ISIS or Al Qaeda cell in Mexico that lobbed a rocket into Texas, we would wipe them off the planet."[31] Overall, then, the America-first approach looks very different from the liberal-order approach in practical terms.

PROBLEMS WITH THIS APPROACH Too much of the criticism of the America-first foreign policy approach has focused on the semantic connotations of the name and its association with pro-German interwar activists like Charles Lindbergh. However, the modern doctrine bears little resemblance to the policy debates of the interwar period; it is connected to those debates mostly by a fluke of Donald Trump's memory. But that is not to say that it is without flaws. Indeed, although it is far more realistic in its approach to the world than liberal internationalism, an America-first approach carries three significant risks: It is likely to alienate countries around the world; it has diminishing utility and may be unsustainable in a post-unipolar era; and perhaps most problematically, it is likely to raise the risks of potential conflict with other states.

The most obvious of these is the distaste that many other countries—even allies—feel for this approach. This is a unilateral, militaristic, and relatively illiberal approach to the world, one in which the United States carries much of the burden for security but also expects to get its own way. In comments to the *Atlantic*, one anonymous Trump official crudely summed up this doctrine as "we're America, bitch," before adding, "The president believes that we're America, and people can take it or leave it."[32] But no one likes a bully. The crude exercise of power and coercion is widely unpopular around the world and makes cooperation with other states more difficult. An America-first strategy, as Barry Posen and Michael Beckley both describe it, is a kind of "illiberal hegemony": the exercise of power shorn of the liberal ideals that have long sought to justify American global hegemony as something more benign than traditional forms of empire.[33] America's approach to China—just as during the Cold War—will need cooperative partners; this is not a way to win them over.

A second problem is that this coercion-heavy approach may well have diminishing returns. The repeated use of extraterritorial sanctions and tariffs against allies as well as adversaries is more likely to produce pushback that could undermine sanctions capabilities and dollar dominance in the long run.[34] At the same time, the use of cyber capabilities and military strikes is likely to create incentives for states to develop their own similar capabilities. Today, China, Russia, and others are increasingly developing coercive economic tools for political ends. It remains unclear whether the United States can maintain the level of military and economic primacy required to make this strategy work; arms races are expensive, and China is not the Soviet Union. This problem will only be worsened by negative economic impacts likely to result from the relatively protectionist bent of America-firsters toward trade and immigration.

The final—and most problematic—aspect of the America-first approach to foreign policy is that it leaves the United States highly vulnerable to potential security spiral dynamics. Whether through a nuclear arms race or a flash-point conflict like Taiwan, this group's focus on militarized deterrence could wind up creating the very conflicts that we wish to avoid. The use of punitive strikes is likely to create retaliatory pressures and precedents, such as the personal targeting of U.S. officials by Iran after the killing of Qassem Soleimani. And engaging in significant saber-rattling in places like Taiwan or the South China Sea may lead China to increase its own military and coercive capabilities. In short, America-first hawks may have recognized the excesses of liberalism in foreign policy, but their approach also supercharges the excesses of militarized primacy, creating significant risk in the process.

Progressive Worldbuilders

WHO ARE THEY? As their name suggests, progressive worldbuilders are located almost entirely among the left wing of the Democratic Party. Their heritage is the anti-war, socialist left, and—although the roots of that philosophy clearly go back further than the past few decades—this viewpoint has found a rebirth in the anti-war activism surrounding the war in Iraq in 2003. Indeed, this tends to be a grassroots approach to foreign policy, albeit one with supporters in academia, left-leaning think tanks such as the Center for International Progress or the Quincy Institute, and activist organizations such as Win Without War or the Friends Committee on National Legislation. These organizations—along with a small number of high-profile columnists—provide intellectual ballast for the movement. In policy terms, this viewpoint is championed by a small but growing segment of lawmakers and staff on Capitol Hill, particularly in the Congressional Progressive Caucus.

The progressive view of foreign policy has also been elevated by the outsider presidential runs of Bernie Sanders. But it is worth noting that although progressive lawmakers are fairly coherent on international economic policy, they are far less so on questions of foreign policy. Only a few are outspoken on this topic, among them Representatives Ro Khanna,

Barbara Lee, and Sara Jacobs. The uncharitable explanation—and the criticism most often heard in Washington—is that progressives are long on criticism but short on actual ideas. But a more charitable explanation is that—apart from a few already well defined areas such as the Israeli-Palestinian conflict—progressives are simply in the process of *building* a detailed, cohesive foreign policy identity where none existed before. If so, the big question will be whether any of the obvious progressive successors to Sanders continue to make foreign policy a focus area. Perhaps unsurprisingly, few proponents of this view were found inside the Biden administration; the lack of a trained, ideologically aligned expert class of progressives who can influence foreign policy from inside the system is a key weakness for this group.[35]

WHAT DO THEY BELIEVE? Progressive worldbuilding is a strand of left thinking that has never been particularly significant in U.S. foreign policy; it was first subordinated under the anti-communism of the Cold War period, and then absorbed within the liberal internationalist consensus of the post–Cold War period. Earlier generations of progressives were dovish by inclination but typically did not challenge the liberal emphasis on human rights and democracy. When they did so, their views manifested primarily as anti-war activism—Martin Luther King's activism against the Vietnam War, for example—and as opposition to defense spending. It simply wasn't a priority topic. As Robert Farley put it in 2011, the nascent progressive movement agreed on only two broad points: "The first is that the United States should refrain from fighting stupid, random wars, while the second is that the U.S. defense budget is far, far too high."[36] Today, however, as progressives gain influence in the Democratic Party, there has been an active effort to build a more nuanced, and distinctly "progressive," foreign and defense policy framework.

In general, progressives are clearest on the broad principles that should guide U.S. foreign policy. They believe in building a better world through non-military tools and in using U.S. foreign policy to foster outcomes that are beneficial for both U.S. citizens and people around the world. For this reason, Van Jackson suggests that progressive foreign policy is best described as a form of "worldmaking," a process of trying to overcome the security imperatives of the international system and build something better.[37] It should also benefit domestic constituencies, preferably with a re-distributionist bent. As Heather Hurlburt, a well-known Democratic foreign policy hand, puts it, "Progressive foreign policy should be aimed at achieving core progressive goals for society: improving economic justice and social cohesion, defending democratic institutions and norms, and fostering a patriotism in which diverse identities belong and flourish."[38] This is not exactly a modest agenda. Indeed, one reason why it has always been difficult to differentiate this viewpoint from liberal internationalism is that both are fundamentally transformative: They seek to shape the international system, not just live within its confines.

At the same time, though, progressives are also generally skeptical of the utility of military force—and were so long before the debacles in Iraq and Afghanistan. They are wary of high levels of defense spending and worry that military force creates injustice.[39] In practical terms, this places them closer to many of their realist counterparts than to liberal internationalists and has led a number of progressive thinkers to advocate for a hybrid form of "realist pragmatism" or "progressive realism."[40] Progressives are particularly concerned about defense spending, the growth of the military-industrial complex, and the way that military spending crowds out domestic spending on health, education, and other priorities. If there is a core principle shared by most progressives, it is Eisenhower's dictum that "every gun that is made, every warship launched, every rocket fired signifies, in the final sense, a theft from those who hunger and are not fed, those who are cold and are not clothed."[41]

Progressives also typically place high levels of importance on international law and institutions but do so in a way subtly different from their liberal internationalist counterparts. Rather than emphasizing the importance of American leadership and alliance networks, progressives tend to emphasize genuinely international institutions like the United Nations and to propound the importance of international law as a stepping stone to a more just world. The blogger Robert Wright, who first coined the term *progressive realism* in 2006, suggests three key principles for U.S. foreign policy: "First, do no harm; second, respect international law; and third, nurture global governance."[42] The first of these principles also bears directly on how progressives think about alliances; it strongly prioritizes *democratic* allies and acknowledges that U.S. military support too often enables autocratic states to continue to brutalize their own citizens. This has proved a particular point of tension in the Middle East, where human rights abuses by U.S. allies such as Saudi Arabia, the United Arab Emirates, and Israel have led to contentious debates within the Democratic Party.

Progressives' fire is not trained solely on other countries. Central to this worldview is the controversial idea that "might does not make right," even when that might belongs to the United States. Progressives, particularly those in the anti-war movement, are acutely aware of the harms the United States can bring to the world and argue that Americans need to be more cognizant of, as Michael Walzer puts it, "what our own state is doing in other people's countries."[43] It is this awareness of the risks of American hegemony (or even American imperialism) that pushes some progressives toward the embrace of international law. As Robert Wright puts it succinctly: "Respecting and strengthening international law serves American interests. One benefit of respecting international law is the valuable self-restraint it can bring."[44] In short, international law should be seen as useful in constraining American power, not merely the power of its adversaries. As Kate Kizer puts it, without justice and international law, the United States cannot succeed. It "must change its relationship with accountability and instead seek to hold itself accountable to the very norms and laws it has sought to uphold."[45] This notion places progressives in opposition not just to conservative sovereignty-loving America-first hawks but also to realists and liberal internationalists.

American power itself is perhaps the most divisive topic in the progressive camp, which disagrees internally about whether the United States is the problem or the solution to the world's problems. Some progressives—described by Van Jackson as "anti-hegemonists"—argue that U.S. retrenchment could improve security globally, tamping down the security concerns that can create conflict and extremism. In contrast, other progressives—"progressive pragmatists," per Jackson—recognize that U.S. foreign policy has its flaws but argue that it is still better than the alternatives.[46] As Dan Nexon, a professor at Georgetown and an early adviser to Bernie Sanders, puts it, "The retreat of the United States will in no way create a more progressive world."[47] Most progressives fall somewhere in the middle, seeing both the risks and the prospective benefits of using U.S. power. As one might expect, this split also leads to differences in policy prescription;

progressives are more likely to align with their realist counterparts if they worry about the excesses of U.S. power, and more likely to support generally liberal internationalists otherwise.

This dichotomy also adds to the core internal contradiction in the progressive worldbuilding approach: Progressives often have a strong incentive to support interventionist military policies, even as this support undermines their broader anti-imperialist, anti-hegemonic projects. They are highly susceptible to the siren song of human-rights-related interventions and the language of "responsibility to protect," even as they understand that interventions grow the military-industrial complex, a tension that defined debate in the Democratic Party throughout the Obama administration. As Van Jackson puts it, the risk is that progressives "end up building 'national security' tools that threaten democracy," as an activist foreign policy "exploits rather than restrains U.S. power and influence, requiring a large national security state."[48] A similar tension can be seen in recent debate over Ukraine: Progressives were largely supportive of the effort to arm and fund Ukraine in its fight against Russia but were somewhat uncomfortable with the risk and levels of military spending involved.

Even aside from method, divisions exist within the progressive camp over which problems should be prioritized. Is nationalist, semi-authoritarian populism—as embodied by Donald Trump in the United States, but also by Hungary's Orbán and Turkey's Erdoğan—the biggest threat to democracy globally? Or should progressives focus more on traditional left-wing questions of capitalism, kleptocracy, and class? In practice, progressive foreign policy thought has manifested itself in two distinct areas. The first of these is arms control, which is particularly well suited to the progressive principles of cooperative threat reduction and preventive solutions to security problems. The nascent progressive wing of the Democratic Party played a pivotal role in the negotiation and—perhaps more important—in the political maneuverings surrounding the creation of the Joint Comprehensive Plan of Action (the nuclear deal) with Iran in 2014. Infamously referred to by the presidential adviser Ben Rhodes as an "echo chamber" of friendly voices, progressive organizations were pivotal in getting the deal informally approved in Congress and in sustaining it during the early years of the Trump presidency.[49] Progressives have been similarly supportive of initiatives such as expanding the New START Treaty with Russia and have pushed for opening a dialogue on arms control with North Korea and Iran. They have been highly supportive of endeavors to better integrate the Global South into U.S. diplomacy, a stance that fits well ideologically with progressive views but is often at odds both with the realities of varying interests across this bloc of states and with progressive opposition to trade policy generally.

The second area of practical impact has been at the intersection of economic and foreign policy, where progressive thinkers such as Ganesh Sitaraman—a former adviser to the presidential candidate Elizabeth Warren—have long opined about the necessity of "breaking down the silos between economics and foreign and national security policy." This was an active area of discussion for the Democratic foreign policy establishment after the 2016 election, and is perhaps the area where progressives were most effective in shaping the foreign policy of the Biden administration, which showed itself receptive to considering "how U.S. trade deals might be reimagined to solve for inequality and stagnant middle-class wages."[50] This has manifested itself in a refusal to engage in a meaningful way on trade with Asian states (the Indo-Pacific Economic Framework for Prosperity focused more on technology cooperation and it was acknowledged by the Biden administration itself as being "different" from a traditional free-trade agreement). Progressive views on political economy were also rolled into the administration's broader, sharp-edged approach to economic statecraft, including the embrace of industrial policy, "buy American" provisions for semiconductors and green technology, and even the administration's efforts to fight global kleptocracy through multilateral tax agreements.

PROBLEMS WITH THIS APPROACH With progressive foreign policy a relatively new approach, it would be easy to criticize it in any number of areas for being insufficiently detailed or coherent. Perhaps, then, it is best simply to focus on the big picture and the question whether progressive foreign policy is—in its current form—a viable replacement foreign policy for the United States. The answer, unfortunately, is no. Progressives have a series of excellent, general critiques of the way that U.S. foreign policy has been run for the past few decades; these are typically sprinkled with a healthy recognition of the limitations of U.S. power.

But when offered the chance to build their own policies, progressives too often run back to the expansive, transformational goals that have characterized U.S. foreign policy since the end of the Cold War. They have a clear picture of the world as they want it to be; they have almost no agreement on how to get there. As Tarak Barkawi describes it, progressive foreign policy is "less strategy and more progressive political imagination."[51] This is compounded by their distaste for military and economic coercion and a preference for diplomacy. Progressive foreign policy is in many ways as ambitious a strategy as liberal internationalism, yet it largely eschews the bases of U.S. power (military primacy, and financial and economic centrality) that might enable such a strategy. It thus runs the risk of simultaneously threatening autocratic states while engaging in retrenchment that weakens America's ability to handle revisionist states.

Progressive worldbuilding is a fundamentally ideological, Wilsonian view of the world, even if it is one that de-emphasizes the military tool. It is unsurprising that progressives have found themselves co-opted and ultimately disappointed by both the Biden and the Obama administrations. Until progressives can build a coherent notion of the limits of solidarity with oppressed peoples—or a better shared understanding of the extent to which the United States should be active in promoting values around the world—the movement will remain easy for liberal internationalist and neoconservative voices to co-opt. Indeed, it is increasingly clear that although progressives see their economic policies as a response to domestic inequality and the uneven distribution of the benefits from trade, these policies have been absorbed and instrumentalized by the Biden and Trump administrations for the purposes of waging a more effective geo-economic war with China.

Realist-Restrainers

WHO ARE THEY? Unlike our other three groups, which have been formed at least to some extent by the splintering of the post–Cold War bipartisan consensus, restrainers and realists have stood outside that consensus since the period preceding the Iraq War. Today, "restraint" is increasingly a Washington shorthand for any advocacy for a less militarized foreign policy—a politer version of the more polemical "isolationist." In Washington-speak, restrainers encompass academic realists, progressive

Democrats, and conservative Republicans in Congress, as well as various anti-war groups (such as Code Pink or the veterans' group Common Defense).[52] But although such groupings can be useful in the political context, they are less useful in an analytical sense; any categorization that groups John Mearsheimer together with Code Pink activists is painting with too broad a brush to be useful in understanding granular foreign policy debates. And indeed, though a broad "restraint" coalition of left and right came together during the 2010s in a relatively successful campaign to end the war on terror, that coalition has since lost some of its cohesion as disagreements over new foreign policy issues—from China to Ukraine—have taken center stage. Some of those who might have been described as "restrained" have now shifted more decisively toward hawkish America-first-style nationalism, and others toward incipient progressive worldbuilding approaches.

There remains, however, a sizable group composed of strategically inclined realists, along with a variety of fellow travelers: libertarians and anti-imperialists for whom restraint is a moral issue, and conservative deficit hawks concerned about the burgeoning national debt. Interestingly, the war on terror has yielded active veterans' groups on both sides of the aisle whose experiences over the past few decades have left them broadly predisposed to a more restrained foreign policy. There is also a small, but growing, network of restrained voices in the think-tank space. Notably, many of these programs receive funding from restraint-inclined foundations such as the Koch network, the Carnegie Corporation, and the Open Society Foundation. Though strange bedfellows on questions of domestic policy, these foundations are surprisingly aligned in terms of foreign policy. Yet the core of this worldview remains in the academy, where such academics as Barry Posen, Stephen Walt, Eugene Gholz, and others continue their long record of advocacy for a more restrained U.S. foreign policy.[53]

WHAT DO THEY BELIEVE? The remainder of this book outlines a strategy of "realist internationalism," an approach that belongs in this camp. I will thus outline the foreign policy approach of "realist-restrainers" only in broad strokes here. In general, however, members of this group agree on several core principles. They share a conviction that the United States is a remarkably secure nation. Thanks both to favorable geography (large oceans and control of the continent) and to its nuclear arsenal, the United States faces no real threat of invasion. Indeed, even in the darkest hours of the Second World War, fears of American military planners revolved much more around market access and prosperity than around the fear of direct conquest. Realist-restrainers believe that U.S. foreign policy has been characterized in recent years by unnecessary overreach and hubris, with predictably abysmal results.[54] They are also—as the name suggests—relatively restrained when it comes to the use of force. They tend to think that U.S. foreign policy is overmilitarized, believing that policymakers spend too much on defense and too quickly resort to force. Indeed, it might be simplest to say that realist-restrainers are united primarily by their opposition to primacy (or "deep engagement") and its tendency to overreach. They worry about security spirals and the potential for escalation, particularly in the context of other nuclear powers. This is the core factor that divides them from their fellow realists among America-first hawks.

Concerns about excess militarism unite progressive worldbuilders and realist-restrainers; what divides them is their goals. Whereas progressive worldbuilders hope to lessen economic inequality, improve human rights, end kleptocracy, support democracy, or achieve any number of other ambitious goals, their realist counterparts aim largely to preserve U.S. security in an uncertain world. Realist-restrainers are first and foremost pragmatic and do not believe the United States—or indeed any nation—can fundamentally alter the nature of the international system. This does not mean that they are indifferent to values; many realist-restrainers care deeply about the health of American democracy and values and worry that an overwhelming security state will undermine civil rights at home and burden the nation with debt. As Christopher Layne points out, realists are also wary of American power itself, understanding that "notions of American exceptionalism can warp U.S. grand strategy" and lead to overextension.[55] Instead, realist-restrainers argue that the United States should mostly lead by example. As Stephen Walt puts it, "If the United States wants to promote its values it ought to devote much more effort to creating an exemplary democracy here in the United States."[56]

Realists are also more conscious of the scope of American foreign policy interests and more nationalist in comparison with their progressive worldbuilding counterparts, who take a relatively universalist view. Should U.S.

foreign policy aim primarily to protect Americans? Or should it aim to benefit people around the world? The realist-restrainers argue the former: In a complex and dangerous world of states, the first priority of foreign policy must always be U.S. interests. Despite this, there is significant overlap in opinion between these groups. Some progressives explicitly adopt realist logic—attempting to place guardrails around progressive foreign policy to prevent it from sliding into interventionism. Other progressives argue, as Van Jackson puts it, that "leftists want to build a world better than the one that realists believe we're all trapped in, . . . and ideological differences stand in the way of them building a better world together."[57]

Realist-restrainers are drawing on a rich intellectual tradition and on at least two already well-identified grand strategic models of the world. The first of these is a grand strategy of "restraint" that was formulated by political scientists such as Barry Posen and Eugene Gholz, Posen's version of restraint envisaging a much smaller military based primarily within the United States.[58] Others back a strategy of "offshore balancing," a distinct but related approach—popularized by international relations theorists such as John Mearsheimer, Stephen Walt, and Christopher Layne—that also calls for downsizing the United States' global military role, but with a focus on three key global regions.[59] The distinction between the two strategies is one of degree: Posen backs an entirely offshore military presence, whereas Mearsheimer and Walt admit that the United States may occasionally need to intervene to keep a hostile state from dominating a key region. But all realist-restrainers generally agree with the proposition that, as Christopher Preble and William Ruger put it, today's foreign policy is "unnecessarily costly and unnecessarily risky" and "America's leaders should restrain their impulse to use the U.S. military when our vital interests are not directly threatened while avoiding being drawn into distant conflicts."[60]

We will have much more to say about realism, its particulars, and how it might be implemented in U.S. foreign policy in the following chapters.

PROBLEMS WITH THIS APPROACH   It would not be fair to let the realist-restrainers get away without criticism. This approach shares problems with the other approaches outlined here—and adds its own. Like progressive worldbuilders, realists argue for a smaller military, concentrated closer to home, to reduce the risks of unintentional conflict and security spiral dynamics. But a more minimal military posture runs the risk of failing to deter an aggressive revisionist state. In theoretical terms, realists are extremely wary of recreating the alliance-entrapment dynamics of the pre–World War I period; their proposed policy solutions necessarily increase the risk of a World War II–style deterrence failure. Put in more polemical language, critics of restraint would argue that appeasement feeds the appetite of dangerous states and that concessions to prevent conflict will only result in further conflicts down the road.[61] There is some truth to this concern. At a broad level, although it is rare—and can be ameliorated in various ways—restraint risks under-balancing against a determinedly aggressive state if the United States fails to react when needed.

At the same time, realism runs an entirely different set of risks—created by realists' overwhelming focus on U.S. national interest—that are more akin to those faced by America-first hawks. Wilsonian language is popular among America's democratic allies; portraying issues in pure national-interest terms is substantially less popular. In pursuing a more nationalist foreign policy, American policymakers are likely to find it more difficult to achieve coordination and cooperation on important international issues. A related problem is the future of U.S. leverage and influence. It may be that the United States enjoys more influence over some states when its foreign policy is no longer antagonizing them, but there are other states—notably close U.S. allies—with whom the United States may see a reduction in its leverage and influence as its dials down troop presence in Europe and Asia. Restraint in military affairs is no guarantee of improved diplomatic or economic relations with other states.

Finally, a more restrained U.S. foreign policy raises a series of questions about the fate of the international order: Is the postwar system of institutions that the United States created self-sustaining and independent, or does it require active American support to exist? Many liberal internationalists would argue that the benefits of decades of economic interdependence may be lost if the United States pulls back militarily from the world. They would likewise argue that in the absence of a U.S. security presence nearby, even friendly states may make poor choices, creating security spirals and incipient conflicts.[62] Restrainers may focus on the costs of U.S. global military primacy, but they tend to bracket the unknown potential costs of failing to maintain primacy. Again, this is a fair criticism. Although U.S. military presence does not necessarily increase stability, it is possible that U.S. alliances help constrain smaller regional conflicts.

Ultimately, no approach to foreign policy is without its risks and flaws, which are sometimes outweighed by the risks of other strategies. The following chapters further explore how a realist-aligned strategy could be implemented, the risks of adopting such a strategy, and—perhaps most important—how those risks can be ameliorated through smart strategy.

A New Bipartisan Consensus?

In 1988, Henry Kissinger and Cyrus Vance, both former secretaries of state, wrote a joint article in *Foreign Affairs:* "We have decided to write this article together because of our deep belief that the security of free peoples and the growth of freedom both demand a restoration of bipartisan consensus in American foreign policy. We disagree on some policy choices. But we are convinced that the American national purpose must at some point be fixed. If it is redefined—or even subject to redefinition—with every change of administration in Washington, the United States risks becoming a factor of inconstancy in the world."[63] Though focused on the specific issues of the moment—the prospects for a post-Reagan foreign policy—their arguments resonate more broadly. Foreign policy bipartisanship was most prevalent during the Cold War, but it has generally been more common than assumed, whether in Congress or between successive administrations.[64] Partisanship in foreign policy, however, has become more common in recent years and has resulted in inconsistent policy, particularly on hot-button issues like Iran, which suggests that Vance and Kissinger's concerns are to some extent warranted.

At the same time, bipartisan consensus is not an unalloyed good. Even a brief survey of some strongly bipartisan foreign policy choices over the decades—from Vietnam to Iraq—suggests that groupthink and a push for conformity in foreign policy may undermine much-needed critical thinking. "Partisan criticism," as one scholar argues, "often provides an important check on ambition, and when that check is absent, oversteering becomes harder to resist."[65] Loren DeJonge Schulman goes further: "Declaring that politics 'stops at the water's edge' of national security . . .

stifles debate about the national interest and the proper application of national resources."[66] Bipartisan foreign policy can become a straitjacket for conformity, stifling criticisms and reducing debate to personal attacks and accusations of disloyalty.

There is, then, both a positive and a negative side to bipartisanship in foreign policy. The challenge moving forward will be to build a relative bipartisan synthesis on foreign policy that becomes neither an ideological straitjacket nor a tool for partisan attacks. That is undoubtedly easier said than done. But it is worth considering where the most likely alliances between our ideal-type foreign policy groupings could arise, particularly given that these groups do not map perfectly along partisan lines (figure 2). A partnership between liberal-order primacists and America-first hawks is perhaps most logical, as it recreates in some ways the liberal-hawk synthesis of the post–Cold War period. But there are significant tensions between the two groups that might impede such a partnership—namely, on the role of the United States in Europe, prioritization, and the role of ideology in U.S. foreign policy. Progressive worldbuilders, meanwhile, are always somewhat susceptible to capture by their liberal internationalist peers in the Democratic Party (just as Republican realists are susceptible to capture by America-firsters), but both groups are likely to be less willing to go along with more hawkish foreign policy choices during a period of great power competition than they were during the unipolar moment. This book's proposed strategy of realist internationalism, though most likely to appeal to realist-restrainers, may also have appeal to some America-first hawks and some progressive worldbuilders. In short, though this is ultimately a question of political alignments and coalition building—rather than one of strategy—it is helpful to understand where the commonalities that could produce a new bipartisan synthesis for the post-post–Cold War era might arise.

A Summit for Democracy

The post–Cold War moment could be said to have ended at any of several key points: the 2008 financial crisis, the election of Donald Trump, or the U.S. withdrawal from Afghanistan. But this misses the point; what ended the post–Cold War moment was not a single event but rather

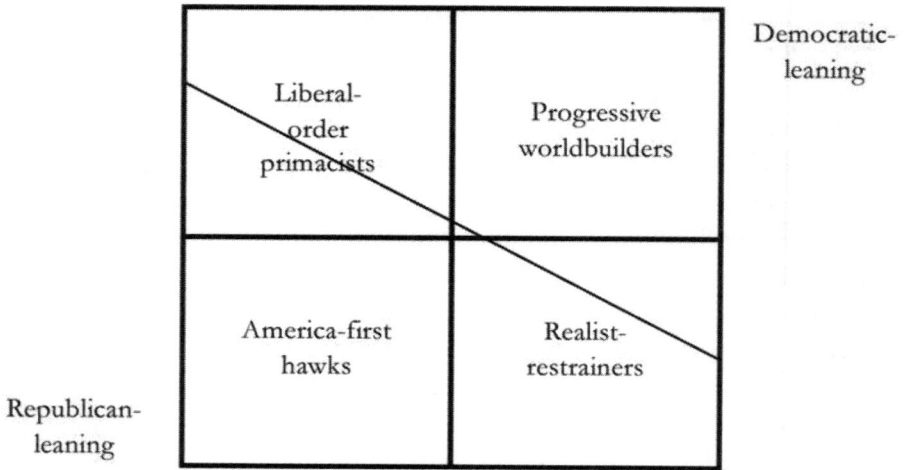

Figure 2. Foreign policy cleavages and partisan divisions

the shifting patterns of power and alignment over a decade that brought us to the precipice of a newly multipolar world. Russia's invasion of Ukraine—perhaps the most visible sign that the unipolar moment is over—was mere punctuation of a reality that already existed. This explains some of the messiness of foreign policy debates in recent years. Participants disagree not only on the best course of action but also on the very nature of the problems faced by the United States. The resultant splintering of consensus has made foreign policy less predictable and more contested.

There are few better illustrations of this than the Biden administration's attempt to build an ideological framework for foreign policy based on the superiority of democracies over autocracies—and certainly no more concise example than the utter derision with which the administration's flagship "Summit for Democracy" was met. The summit was initially promised on the campaign trail but was postponed because of Covid; the administration ended up holding a virtual summit via Zoom in late 2021. But as observers had predicted, the guest list proved challenging to manage, and both the inclusion and exclusion of certain states were met with accusations of hypocrisy and favoritism. The summit did nothing to help the administration's standing with countries in the Global South and offered little in the way of deliverables for Indo-Pacific policy.

What was notable, however, was the wide-ranging criticism leveled at the administration from all corners. Hawks attacked Biden for undermining anti-China coalition-building efforts by excluding Asian autocracies. Progressives noted that U.S. allies and partners were being given a free pass for human rights abuses. Realists pointed out the inherent contradiction in working only with democracies while claiming to represent the world. The only fans of the Summit for Democracy appeared to be a tiny slice of the NGO community dedicated to democracy-promotion efforts. The Summit for Democracy is thus a perfect example of the growing fragmentation of foreign policy opinion and how difficult it will be for *any* administration to manage foreign policy without some attempt to build a broader coalition.

3

Naval Gazing

In 2018, the Washington-based Heritage Foundation—well known for its hawkish takes on defense issues—released a report arguing that the Chinese People's Liberation Army Navy would soon comprise almost 340 ships, leaving the U.S. Navy's 280 ships in the dust. If Congress didn't authorize an increase to at least 400 ships, the author argued, "our nation's ability to deter aggression and win in conflict when necessary [would] be at risk."[1] By the release of the 2022 national defense strategy, the chief of naval operations had increased earlier estimates and was calling for an increase in the size of the U.S. fleet to over 500 ships if it was to "speak to the vulnerabilities we hear called out by the Joint Staff."[2] The media response to news that China might overtake the United States in naval strength has been hyperbolic, to say the least. As CNN put it, "China has built the world's largest navy. Now what's Beijing going to do with it?" Reuters, meanwhile, chose to publish this news under the headline "China's Vast Fleet Is Tipping the Balance in the Pacific."[3] You might be forgiven for thinking that a Chinese invasion force would soon heave into view somewhere off California's Santa Monica Pier.

A very different reaction greeted the news, early in 2023, that China's population had declined for the first time since the 1960s. As a result of the Communist Party's decades-long one-child policy, the country now faces a sharp demographic cliff. China's working-age population is destined to drop by at least a quarter before the middle of the twenty-first century, which will lead to a labor force far smaller than the elderly population it will need to support. "The Great People Shortage Hits China," announced *Business Insider,* adding that "the impact will be felt around the world."[4] The *New York Times* columnist Bret Stephens devoted an entire column to the notion that China is headed in a bad direction; as he gloated, "China's Decline Became Undeniable This Week. . . . The road downhill will not be smooth."[5] China, these reports implied, is a vast, swiftly depopulating wasteland rapidly being left behind by the Western world.

Is the United States facing a Chinese military behemoth poised to overtake it? Or will Chinese growth almost inevitably stall as demographic forces take their toll, leaving us with little to fear? Though the shifting power dynamics of the U.S.-China relationship are often understood intuitively through such attention-grabbing statistics, these sorts of headlines mostly serve to create gut reactions for policymakers that can be profoundly misleading about the future balance of power. Such headlines also tend to reinforce the assumption that we are headed into a bipolar world dominated by the United States and China, with far less attention paid to the many other states that could play a significant role in the coming decades.[6] Indeed, though China's rise is important, India's rise may be no less consequential; the country has more than a billion people, no impending demographic cliff, nuclear weapons, and no guarantee—despite its status as a democracy—that its rise will be peaceful. Russia, meanwhile, is stagnant economically, socially, and politically, but in 2022 clearly showed that it retains the capacity to act as an intentional spoiler in international affairs. America's major allies in Europe and East Asia (Germany, Japan, France, Italy, the United Kingdom, South Korea, and others) remain largely dependent on U.S. military might. But each is wealthy, technologically advanced, and brimming with human and social capital. These states' military capabilities have been unnaturally constrained by domestic opinion, moral hazard, and American support. The world, when viewed this way, suddenly seems decidedly more multipolar.

If the unipolar moment—the period of largely unchecked U.S. dominance that followed the collapse of the Soviet Union—is truly ending, the biggest question is what will replace it. This chapter explores global secular trends in economics, technology, and demographics to build a more holistic picture of where we might be headed.

Measuring Power

At its heart, the debate over whether the United States is headed into a multipolar or bipolar world is a debate about power. Here, we almost immediately run into measurement issues, as the measurement of power is one of the oldest—and most challenging—questions in the study of international relations. Power is hard to observe in action, few agree on exactly where it springs from, and the ability to turn that power into concrete outcomes is heavily dependent on context. As Joseph Nye memorably put it, "Power . . . is like love; it is easier to experience than to define or measure."[7] Indeed, measuring power requires answering almost laughably big philosophical questions: Does power flow from the barrel of a gun (that is, should we measure direct military capabilities)? Can it be purchased by a sufficiently wealthy state (that is, should we look at gross domestic product or gross national product)? Or is it the result of people (that is, does power derive from deep societal virtues, from human capital, or from mere demographic dominance)? Throughout this chapter, we will explore a variety of these metrics; all the basic economic data is drawn from the World Bank's databases, and other indexes and metrics are introduced as needed.

All we can really say for sure is that power—and thus polarity—seems to derive from some combination of these factors. As one recent report from the Rand Corporation puts it, "Nations rise and fall, succeed or fail in rivalries, and enjoy stability or descend into chaos because of a complex web of factors that affect competitive advantage."[8] To be a great power— a pole in the international system—requires strength in more than one area, including economics, military capabilities, industrial capacity, population, or technical know-how. As Monteiro describes it: "No state can be a great power if its endowment in any of these elements of power is vastly outmatched by the most powerful states in the world in that particular domain."[9] It is perhaps no surprise, then, that scholars most commonly rely on observable factors to build an "elements of national power" approach.[10] These factors can be economic or population metrics, measures of military spending or capabilities, natural resource endowments, or some index measure that seeks to incorporate all of the above.[11] The most widely used of these metrics is undoubtedly the Correlates of War Project's composite index of national capability (CINC) score, which provides a value for a state's share of the "power resources" in the international system at any given time. But though they are frequently used in quantitative analyses of international relations, CINC scores are also understood to be somewhat problematic. It just isn't clear that a CINC score, which relies on traditional metrics such as population and steel production—things essential for twentieth-century mechanized warfare—is necessarily good at capturing the strengths or weaknesses of modern, technologically advanced militaries. More modern indexes, such as the Lowy Institute's Asia Power index, attempt to achieve a better result by incorporating technological and alliance-based factors.

Given the weaknesses of CINC scores, some scholars instead favor the use of simple economic metrics (such as gross national income or gross domestic product), on the basis that economic power can be easily translated into military power with sufficient time. Indeed, if you assume that power is relatively fungible, economic measures are an excellent way to assess latent power. Consider the United States itself, which in 1939 had the nineteenth-largest military in the world. A mere five years later, it possessed by far the most powerful military in the world, thanks to the simultaneous destruction of many of the world's other major economies and the transformation of America's own industrial base into military production.[12] Measuring latent power is also an excellent way to account for the fact that different states make different choices when it comes to the traditional "guns vs. butter" trade-off. Over a medium to long time horizon, economic measures are a much better measure of potential or latent power than military spending or capabilities.

Yet as with technological and military prowess, there are no straight-line correlations here. Not all states have the capacity to turn economic success into military power, given constraints in population or size. One of the world's wealthiest states on a per capita basis, for example, is the natural-gas-rich Qatar, which has only a few hundred thousand citizens. Even with the use of expatriates and foreign contractors, Qatar would find it difficult to maintain a large military. It's also the case that today's modern postindustrial societies may find it harder to retool their civilian industries for wartime in a hurry. In short: It's easier to turn an automobile factory into an airplane factory than to turn a call center into any kind of factory. There is likely some minimum acceptable level of industrial base required to maintain a strong military, even in a post-industrial society.

Meanwhile, some economic measures tend to overstate latent power. As the political scientist Michael Beckley highlights, a large population also comes with liabilities, something gross domestic product (GDP) doesn't explicitly account for. Think about it this way: Even the ancient Romans couldn't just turn peasants into soldiers. They also had to figure out how to feed, clothe, arm, and—perhaps most important—train their new recruits. Beckley thus favors a measure of GDP multiplied by per capita GDP to capture some sense of both the size of an economy and how efficient it is.[13] Another alternative is to rely on measures that try to account for these liabilities; the World Bank, for example, produces an index (the Changing Wealth of Nations) that attempts to measure a state's true wealth, a combination of human capital, natural resource endowments, and foreign investments.[14]

At the end of the day, however, no measure of power is perfect, and none is ever likely to be. The best way to approach this problem is holistically: not declaring that one specific metric is the best, but rather summing up a variety of measures to ascertain how power is currently distributed in the international system. To obtain military victory, states must have sufficient technology, personnel, and economic might, along with access to critical natural resources. Economic and technological might can also be used in other ways to gain an advantage in international rivalries. In short, as Randall Schweller has observed: "States are not placed in the top rank because they excel in one way or another. Their rank depends on how they score on all categories of capabilities. They must have a complete portfolio of power capabilities."[15]

The United States vs. China

Taking a holistic approach to power suggests that we should consider some combination of economic, demographic, and military factors to assess relative American and Chinese power (figures 3–6). Michael Beckley's GDP × per capita GDP measure suggests a strong case for optimism among U.S. policymakers (figure 4). If he is correct and this metric accurately captures a better picture of economic strength, efficiency, and liabilities than more traditional metrics, it would suggest that the United

States has little to worry about; the United States has left China in the dust with little hope of catching up. Yet the extent to which this metric diverges from almost every other measure of national wealth or power is notable; we should be skeptical of any measure that so neatly confirms the assumption policymakers already make, that American power remains, as Beckley puts it, "unrivaled." Indeed, as one reviewer of Beckley's work notes, this argument relies heavily on an implicit assumption that the data "does not hide some inherent malaise in the U.S. socio-economic system."[16] The turbulent politics of contemporary America do not suggest confidence on that front. A recent Rand report on the sources of societal competition concurred: "The United States might have begun to take on the familiar and disturbing aspect of a great power whose engine of social dynamism is being encumbered by stagnation and social instability."[17] We should therefore treat Beckley's measure—and its wildly optimistic conclusion—with caution.

Indeed, on almost every other metric, the picture is more mixed. In terms of gross national income (GNI), China either has already surpassed the United States, if GNI is calculated using the purchasing power parity, or PPP, method (figure 3), or is rapidly closing the gap, if the Atlas method is used.[18] Likewise, if one measures economic performance as GDP (calculated using the PPP method, which accounts for differences in the prices and goods of services in different economies), China and the United States are within spitting distance of each other. Calculating GDP in current U.S. dollars instead shows more of a difference: in 2023, U.S. GDP was $27 trillion, whereas China's GDP was only $17 trillion. In demographic terms, China has always had a significantly larger population than the United States; China has thus had a higher CINC score than the United States since the early 1990s. Even the geometric index of national capabilities (GINC) score—a modified version of the CINC score that is more effective at measuring relative power during potential power transitions—suggests that the United States has already been overtaken by China (figure 5).

Of course, one reason why CINC scores are so widely disdained is that few observers could genuinely believe that the United States had been overtaken by China at the height of the unipolar moment in the 1990s! Pure population and economic figures are misleading; on a per capita basis, for example, China remains well behind the United States. But although

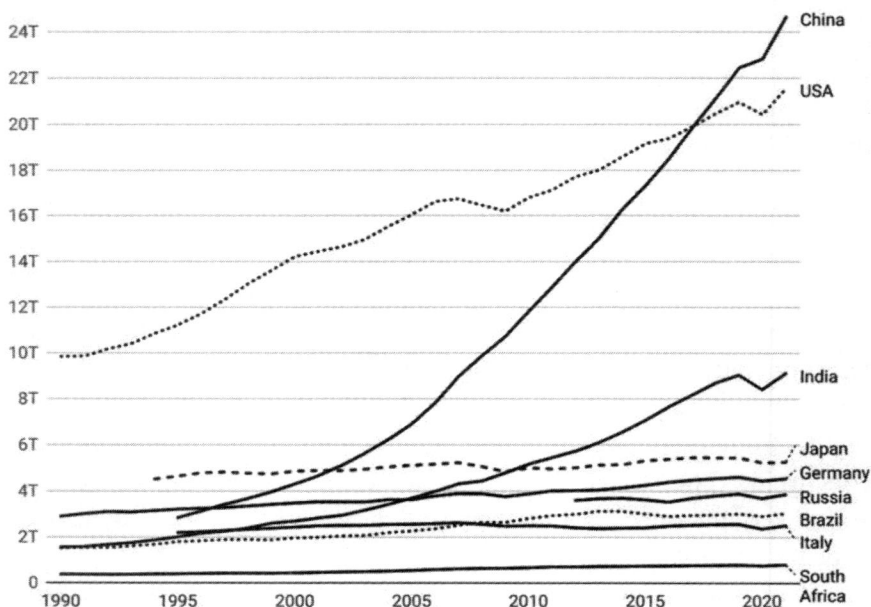

Figure 3. Gross national income (GNI), using purchasing power parity (PPP) method, given in current international dollars (Data from the World Bank)

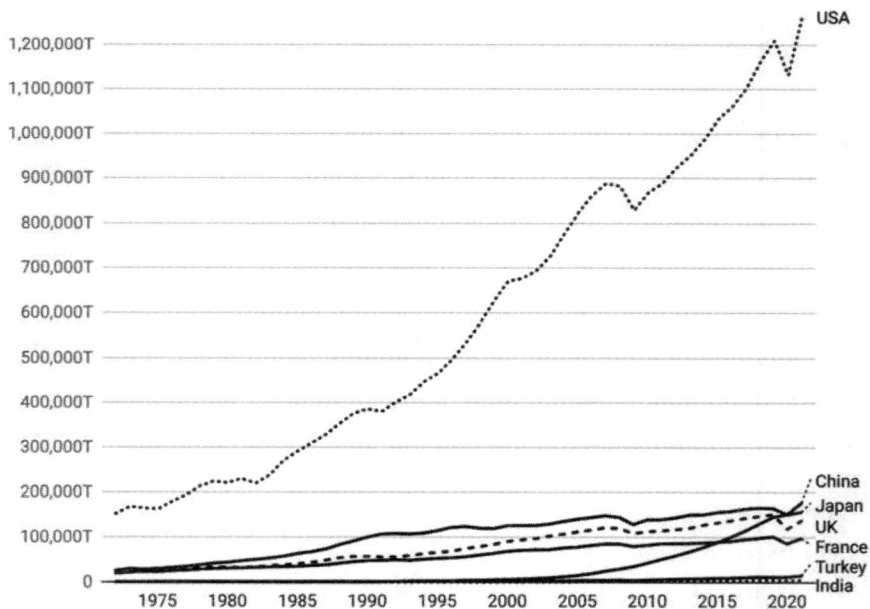

Figure 4. Gross domestic product (GDP) multiplied by per capita GDP, in current U.S. dollars, as in Michael Beckley's *Unrivaled* (Data from the World Bank)

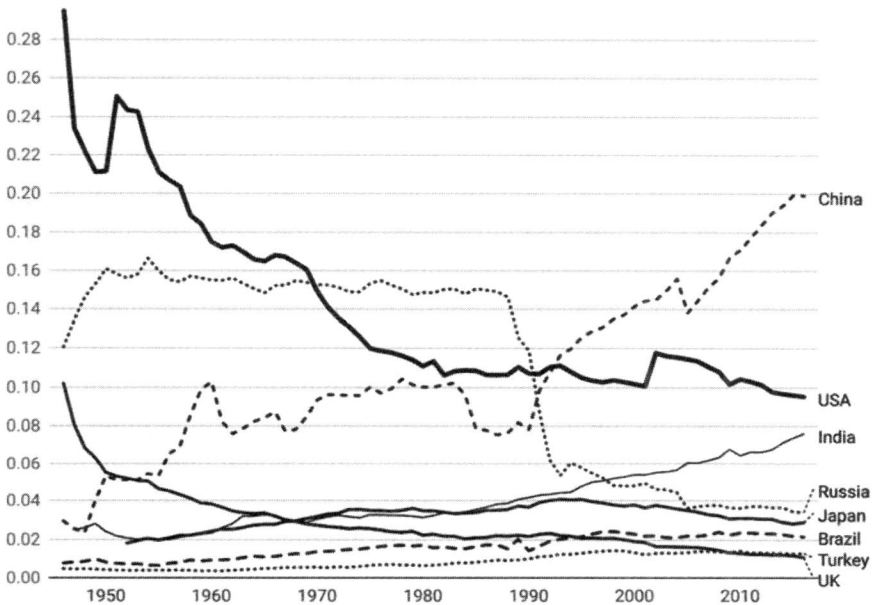

Figure 5. Comparative national capabilities, as measured by the geometric index of national capabilities (GINC) score, which is derived from the comparative index of national capabilities, or CINC (Data from the Correlates of War Project)

Chinese citizens still enjoy lower standards of living, it is notable how dramatically poverty has decreased in China in recent years. Even in terms of per capita GDP, the trend is one of relative decline for the United States: The U.S. economy is still growing, but China's economy is growing far faster. The World Bank's measure of total national wealth (which includes human capital and natural resources) shows a similar trend: China is closing the gap with the United States (figure 6). The Lowy Institute, an Australian think tank, produces an Asia power index, which includes measures of economic and military strength along with resources, alliance networks, and cultural influence; this shows the United States and China remaining relatively constant in power terms, and of fairly similar rank in power.[19] Each of these indexes relies on some combination of material resources to make its assessments, accepting—at least in theory—that economic and demographic trends are the raw resources that feed into economic leverage, military capabilities, and diplomatic clout.

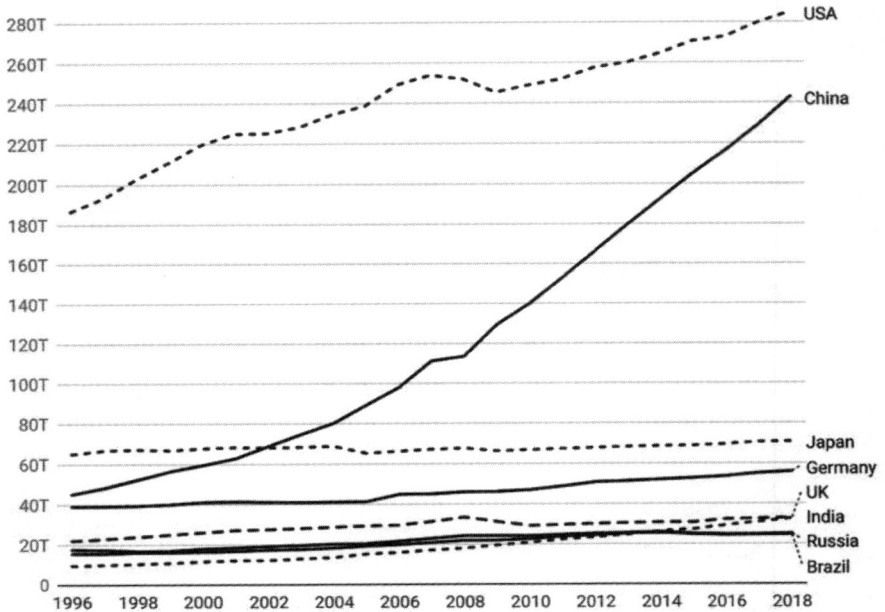

Figure 6. Total national wealth, according to the World Bank's measure of total societal wealth, which includes traditional measures such as GDP alongside measures of human and natural capital, measured in constant 2018 U.S. dollars (Data from the World Bank)

With respect to existing military capabilities, the gap between the United States and China remains somewhat wider. This is particularly true of military spending, where the United States remains ahead not only of China but also of the next seven or eight countries combined.[20] China itself spends a smaller percentage of GDP on its military than the Soviet Union ever did.[21] Comparative military spending can also be misleading; China benefits from cheaper personnel and domestic military procurement costs. Mark Milley, as the chairman of the Joint Chiefs of Staff, put it to the Senate in 2018, "The cost of Russian soldiers or Chinese soldiers is a tiny fraction [of the U.S. cost]. . . . Chinese and Russian investments, modernization, new weapons systems, etc., their R&D . . . is all government-owned and also is much cheaper."[22]

It's beyond the scope of this book to engage in detailed force-on-force assessments of the United States and China; such comparisons are in any case far too context-specific to be useful in understanding the broader balance of power between China and the United States. U.S. and Chinese military capabilities may be roughly equal in the Taiwan Strait, for example, but far less balanced off the coast of Hawaii. And at least for today, the gap in overall military capabilities remains wide; in the Lowy Asia power index rankings, for example, the United States and China are almost 30 points apart in terms of military capabilities, even as they are neck and neck in economic capabilities.[23] This is driven by a profound mismatch in expeditionary military capabilities: Only the United States can easily intervene in any region of the world. Over time, however, that story is still likely to be one of convergence. The U.S. Defense Intelligence Agency concluded in 2020 that China is likely to "develop a military by mid-century that is equal to—or in some cases superior to—the U.S. military."[24]

The trends that we see today thus suggest that we are in a period of flux in the international system. China is rising to meet the United States; history suggests that the next few decades will involve intense geopolitical competition between the two.

The Rest of the Story

From a look at the headlines—or from the analysis above—you might be forgiven for thinking that the world is headed back to an era of bipolar superpower competition akin to that of the latter half of the twentieth century. Yet there are many differences between these periods. As Ali Wyne points out in his book on the return of great power competition, the Cold War took place in a fundamentally different environment. World War II had destroyed significant chunks of the prewar international system, and the formation of ideological blocs resulted in a largely bifurcated economic system in developed countries, along with a small group of poorer, "nonaligned" states.[25] During the Cold War, the two superpowers were by far the most powerful entities in the international system; on the basis of CINC scores, for example, they controlled more than half of the world's systemic power resources, a proportion that increases when their respective alliance blocs are included. Today, the data suggests a different picture, one in which power is held not only by the superpowers but also by a variety of capable, dynamic middle powers that will help shape the international environment in coming decades (figure 7).

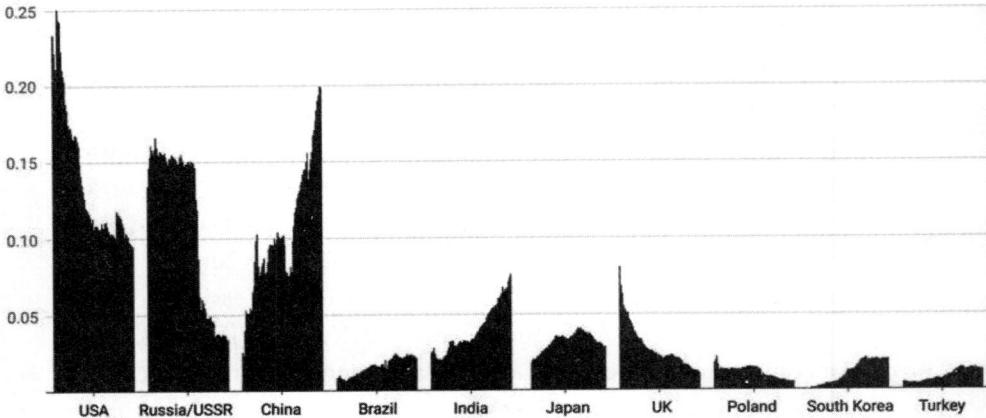

Figure 7. Comparative national capabilities, shown over time from 1946 to 2016. For each country, the change in geometric index of national capabilities (GINC) score is derived from the comparative index of national capabilities (CINC) score. (Data from the Correlates of War Project)

It is not simply that the United States is in relative decline, or even that China is rising, but rather that compared with earlier decades, power is held more widely and by a variety of powers in different regions. The United States and China are ahead of the pack, but by far less than their Cold War counterparts. Today, China and the United States together make up only 42 percent of the global economy measured in GDP and only 37 percent of total power resources as measured by CINC. They do not make up a majority of the world's total wealth—coming in at only 46 percent combined—and represent only about a quarter (28 percent) of global GNI.[26] It is the middle states—from Germany and France to Japan, Iran, Turkey, and India—that are more akin to classic regional great powers, possessing significant economic, demographic, technological, and latent military power.

Of course, how to define a "great power" has long been a point of contention in academic writing. In previous eras, despite the lack of data, it was often easier. One could simply define great powers as those with the defensive capabilities to survive against any attacker. But the nuclear revolution undermines that definition, as any country with nuclear weapons can defend itself in a last resort, no matter how weak its conventional capabilities. The rise of the superpowers—nations with genuine global reach—during the Cold War also makes this a more challenging problem. Can a nation be a great power if it is simply a strong regional player? Or must it have global interests and reach? Many observers now argue that to be considered a great power, a state must possess global expeditionary capabilities akin to those of the United States at the peak of its power.

Yet this raises the bar too high. There are several states that could achieve this level of military capability if they chose to: Britain, France, and Russia all possess some level of global expeditionary capabilities today. They are undoubtedly great powers. Nuno Monteiro coined the notion of "major powers" to accommodate those states that are not expeditionary superpowers but nonetheless possess the capabilities to resist other states and to inflict serious harm on interveners or other states *within* their home region. The Lowy Institute likewise separates states into "superpowers" and "major powers."[27]

This approach is not actually an innovation in international relations; the classical realists used to divide great powers into ranks. Randall Schweller, drawing on this approach in his book on the interwar period, distinguishes between "poles" and "lesser great powers" in the international system. As he puts it rather acerbically, "Most states, even of the great power variety, must ultimately serve someone: only 'top dogs' can expect otherwise."[28] In the absence of an external intervener, it is these second-rank states that occupy the traditional role of great powers: able to dominate and compete within their region given a chance. The data suggests that we may wish to return to this mode of thinking about international relations, as it is the middle powers to which much of the power in the international system is diffusing. The system that is emerging might thus be described as "unbalanced multipolarity"—to use Mearsheimer's definition—or perhaps "mixed multipolarity," where a relative bipolar parity between the United States and China is nested within a multipolar system.[29]

One other element bears discussing here, however. Despite their growing share of the global concentration of power, these middle powers are typically heavily dependent on economic prowess to achieve this rank and are notably underpowered in military terms. Most of America's Asian and European allies, for example, have the economic, demographic, or technological basis for military power but neither invest significant resources in their military nor maintain high levels of troops under arms. Their military capabilities have been suppressed over time by the peculiar structure of the U.S.-backed alliance system, which suggests that these states have significant headroom to rise further. In short, they have the potential to turn their economic prowess into military capabilities and thus move the system closer to true multipolarity. These second-tier great powers are discussed later in the context of U.S. strategy toward their broader region.

The Horizon

The biggest remaining question is whether the trend lines described here can be assumed to continue along a relatively consistent trajectory. Will China continue to grow? Will the United States be able to maintain its lead in military power? For both countries—and for the broader pool of second-tier powers—there are undoubtedly factors that could halt or stall their progress or, conversely, could drive a revival in their fortunes. We cannot predict specific events. We can, however, attempt to provide as complete a picture as possible of the factors that could, over time, alter the trajectory of current trends, reshape power dynamics, and make certain events, such as great power war, more likely. This method—sometimes called "horizon scanning"—would not have predicted the peaceful dissolution of the Soviet Union. But it might have highlighted the negative domestic economic trends and political calcification that contributed to that collapse. Horizon scanning likewise would not have predicted the Covid-19 pandemic in 2020, but it would probably have suggested that the world was overdue for a pandemic and that respiratory diseases were a likely vector.

In short, horizon scanning is more focused on trends than events, enabling us to understand gradual change over time—something that makes it perfect for the study of relative power dynamics. As a recent European Commission report put it, horizon scanning is particularly useful because in focusing on long-term changes, it "enhances resilient policy-making . . . and prepares society for less expected or rapid changes."[30] Here, we consider trends in five key areas: military, economic, demographic and human capital, technology, and domestic politics (table 2).

Perhaps the most obvious of these is demography; it is also the factor that—thanks to the generational nature of demographic change—can be

Table 2. Horizon scanning: Examples of potentially relevant trends or discontinuities

Military	Technology and industry	Economy	Demography and human capital	Domestic politics
Western underinvestment in military procurement	Semiconductor decoupling slows Chinese technology growth	Prospects for de-dollarization of global economy grow	Chinese demographic cliff undermines economy	Domestic political unrest in United States grows
Failures of arms control produce arms races	Continued congressional dysfunction undermines defense innovation	Chinese real estate debt bubble undermines Chinese growth	Africa's youth bubble raises economic prospects	India continues to backslide democratically
Major war	Move to industrial policy in the West upends industry	Decoupling drives fragmentation between regional trade blocks	Climate change leads to increased north-south migration pressures	Death of Vladimir Putin creates diplomatic opening with Russia
European Union gains greater authority over defense procurement	Climate pressures yield improved renewable technologies	EU fiscal integration accelerates post-Ukraine	College costs act as a growing debt burden on U.S. economy	Continued nationalist trends across Europe weaken the European Union
Nuclear proliferation accelerates				

forecasted most effectively. As we discussed briefly, China is facing not merely demographic decline but an extreme demographic cliff created by the Communist Party's one-child policy during the latter part of the twentieth century. Even the median estimates of China's population decline in coming decades suggest that we are likely to see China's overall population decline by 7 to 10 percent by 2050. Perhaps more worrying is China's population distribution, which is set to become ever more skewed toward the elderly in coming generations.[31] Short of some major disaster, there is no question about the direction of Chinese demographics.

Yet it remains open the extent to which this will affect Chinese economic and military power. Some experts have argued that China faces a steep decline because of this demographic shortfall—in particular, the drag that a large elderly population will exert on the Chinese economy.[32] Others, however, are less pessimistic. Economists at the IMF, for example, have argued that "although challenging, the working-age population decline need not presage a dramatic drop in the labor force."[33] Most societies experience population decline as they advance from developing to developed economic conditions; China's birthrate decline has simply been more pronounced than usual. And by taking steps such as raising the retirement age and improving workforce efficiency, the Chinese government could, at least in theory, mitigate the worst of these effects on economic growth.[34]

Few countries face China's extreme demographic obstacles, but the problem of declining population and economic growth is one faced by most of the world's advanced industrialized democracies. In 2021, for example, U.S. population growth was only 0.1 percent, the slowest rate of growth in the nation's history.[35] A decline in immigration, falling life expectancy, and a dramatically lower birth rate than in previous decades will make it difficult to address this challenge.[36] Countries across Europe have resorted to pro-natal campaigns to encourage births (with minimal success), and Japan—a country long skeptical of the cultural impact of immigration—has become far more friendly to immigrant workers in recent years to combat its own demographic mismatch between workers and retirees.[37]

In the economic space, several trends have the capacity to shift global power and influence in coming decades. China's economy has grown extremely rapidly in recent years, and many suspect that it will overheat at some point and suffer a recession or financial crisis associated with the Communist Party's excessive infrastructure spending. Any such crisis could slow China's economic growth; it is highly unlikely that the country will continue its high levels of economic growth into the middle of the twenty-first century. Yet a financial crisis remains a potential threat to the United States and Europe as well. The subprime mortgage bubble that created the Great Recession in 2008 is unlikely to reoccur thanks to the policy changes put in place in the 2010s. But the potential remains for bubble dynamics and crises in other spaces, particularly in the over-leveraged U.S. higher-education market.

Notably, however, the most concerning potential trends of coming decades carry risks for all of the leading economies. A global shift toward protectionism and decoupling in trade will produce an economic slowdown. Regardless of whether this occurs as part of a trade war (the Trump administration) or a more scalpel-like approach to disengagement in strategically important sectors (the Biden administration), it will affect countries around the world. And although much of the literature on economic decoupling assumes that lost ties to China or Russia will be replaced by "friend-shoring" or "ally-shoring," thus far there has been little appetite in Washington for trade even with fellow democracies. Ironically, it is sanctions—liable to continue over the long term—that may push Russia and China into a "friend-shoring" arrangement more effective than that of Western democracies. If managed poorly, decoupling could slow global growth and contribute to a general fragmentation of global trade into more self-contained blocs over time. Climate change and the political economy of decarbonization are intrinsically tied to this dynamic. With China—and Chinese innovation—now a key cog in the manufacture and design of green technologies, decoupling could slow the transition to less-carbon-intensive technologies.

In the military space, many of the non-economic factors that could substantially alter today's trend lines will be driven by state choices and their threat perceptions. A dramatic increase in military spending by America's European allies in the aftermath of the war in Ukraine, for example, has the potential to shift the distribution of power in Europe—particularly if Eastern European states like Poland spend more than their Western European neighbors. The same goes for increased military spending in Asia as China is perceived as more threatening, a trend already emerging in Japan. For both China and the United States, the failure of strategic arms control during the past decade could encourage arms races and place military spending on an upward trajectory over time.

More broadly, bureaucratic and institutional drags on defense budgets and innovation may become a problem, particularly in advanced industrialized democracies. In the United States, for example, it has been understood for some time that the sclerotic defense-procurement process tends to impede—not reward—innovation. Consolidation among defense contractors since the end of the Cold War makes it more difficult for the U.S.

government to hold companies to account for failures like the F-35. A dysfunctional federal-government budgeting process has often led to an overreliance on short-term budgetary measures (for example, "continuing resolutions") rather than dedicated long-term funding. If reform cannot be achieved, this stagnation of the military-industrial complex is likely to undermine the long-term military potential of the United States. This is not a problem restricted to America: Consider the difficulties experienced by Australia in attempting to manage the logistics of the AUKUS submarine deal or the obstacles faced by the European Union in trying to reconcile its desire to create more cooperation among member states. Protectionism, regulatory hurdles, and bureaucratic inertia all pose significant threats to the ability of Western nations to maintain their military and technological edge.

But perhaps the most important thing to note about future trends in military capabilities is that many of these potential shifts are well within the bounds of what one might reasonably expect to see going forward. We are relatively unlikely to see dramatic shifts in the military space—such as the emergence of a major new military power—and far more likely to simply see existing powers experience shifts in their existing military capabilities. There are two potential exceptions to this. One is India, where a choice to increase military spending could yield significant dividends. India is emerging as a middle-income country, but it has not yet made the investments in its defense sector that would allow it to wield a first-rate military.[38] Yet as China's rise in the past few decades has shown, a strong industrial base can be turned toward military ends; a country as large as India has the potential to dramatically increase its military capabilities through targeted spending and by building ties with other innovative states. The second exception would be a major war, whether between the United States and China or between China and states in East Asia. A major war that destroys substantial military capacity is perhaps the only thing that could dramatically undermine U.S. military power or halt China's military rise in coming decades.

The last of our categories is domestic politics, which is always a wild card. A variety of domestic factors could cause various powerful states to stumble, from further domestic political unrest in the United States to popular unrest against the Communist Party in China. Then there are factors like growing nationalism and continued democratic backsliding in India, which may make the country a less attractive partner for Western nations. In Europe, the spectrum of possibilities is wide, ranging from further Brexit-style departures from the European Union to substantive integration of Europe in the defense space or in fiscal policy. Either would have a significant impact on the ability of European states to coordinate on questions of defense and foreign policy; further dissolution of the United Kingdom into its constituent nations would decrease its ability to play a major role in European defense.

In short, there are too many potential domestic political factors to mention them all here—every state has its own domestic political idiosyncrasies!—but we will continue to explore the impact of domestic political shifts throughout the book. This section has sought to provide a general overview of the trends or major events that could potentially shift the direction of global power dynamics, but we will continue to use the horizon-scanning technique to address relevant nations—and the challenges or tailwinds they might experience—in the regional sections of later chapters.

Why Does Polarity Matter?

We now have some idea of the power distribution in today's international system, the current trend lines, and factors that might shift these trends. But we don't yet have a theoretical understanding of whether these dynamics are good or bad for U.S. interests. To develop this understanding, we must dive into the literature on polarity and stability, because although it is undoubtedly interesting to know whether the United States or China is marginally more powerful, it is the structure of the global distribution of power that is likely to be far more influential in shaping future outcomes.

International relations scholars have for centuries focused on polarity as one of the core independent variables that can explain why an international system is stable or unstable (that is, whether we see lots of wars in any given system). Without at least an intuitive understanding of polarity, one could not, for example, understand why the Spartans—in Thucydides's famous phrasing—so feared the rise of Athens. The emergence of another pole in the international system, produced by the long, slow shifting of demographics, economic power, or military capabilities, is among the most pressing concerns for states in recorded history and may presage a potential power transition in the international system. At the most basic level, polarity is a function of the distribution of capabilities and resources in the international system; that is, it reflects how power is distributed among the many actors in the international system at a given time. As power shifts over time, new poles and new patterns of polarity emerge in the international system. They are typically divided into three types:

Unipolarity is a system in which one state is far and away the most powerful in the system and it is nearly impossible for other states to challenge that state. *Unipolarity* typically refers to the period of American global dominance since the fall of the Soviet Union in 1991, but it could also be said to have existed regionally during periods of the Roman Empire in the Mediterranean or Chinese dominance of Asia in antiquity.

Bipolarity is a system in which two powers are relatively evenly matched and between them dominate the international system. It is commonly associated with the Cold War standoff between the United States and the Soviet Union. The eighteenth-century rivalry between Britain and France is another such bipolar system, in which the two European empires played out their rivalry across the Old and New Worlds.

Multipolarity is a system in which three or more great powers jockey for position in the international system; there is no upper limit on the number of states that can be poles in multipolarity, though in practice we typically see between three and seven states. This type of system can be *balanced*, with power distributed relatively evenly among several states, or *unbalanced*, with a few states clearly leading the pack. Multipolarity is by far the most common system in history, particularly from the Reformation in Europe to the pre–World War I era. Indeed, the historical dominance of multipolarity suggests one reason why it can be difficult to study the question of stability in the international system; we have surprisingly few non-multipolar systems to draw insights from.

In practice, however, the study of polarity contains more than a whiff of Justice Potter Stewart's old canard about pornography: "I shall not today attempt further to define the kinds of material I understand to be embraced within that shorthand description, and perhaps I could never succeed in intelligibly doing so. But I know it when I see it."[39] There are certainly studies that attempt to quantify polarity using explicit metrics. By these standards, unipolarity typically requires one state to hold 50 percent of the system's power resources (an amalgam of military and economic factors, industrial capacity, and demographics). Bipolarity would require two states to jointly hold 50 percent of the power resources, and multipolarity, three or more states to do so. Yet most studies of polarity rely instead on qualitative assessments of the international system: How strong do states seem in comparison with each other in historical case studies? It is almost inevitable that such subjective ratings lead to conflicting assessments; across just three analyses in the literature, the year 1919, as one example, has been variously described by scholars as unipolar, balanced multipolarity, and unbalanced multipolarity. It all depends on your point of view.

Today's debates about multipolarity are no less discordant. The scholars William Wohlforth and Stephen Brooks argued in a recent edition of *Foreign Affairs* that multipolarity is a myth and that we are still in an era of unipolarity. Other states are not yet balancing sufficiently against the United States, in their view, and the U.S. lead over other states has shrunk but not significantly enough to call unipolarity into question. Wohlforth and Brooks are increasingly in the minority, however. "To conclude that multipolarity is a myth," argues Bilahari Kausikan in response to Wohlforth and Brooks, "is to conceive of multipolarity in superficial, overly formalistic, and largely obsolete ways."[40] Scholars may disagree over whether we are entering a period of bipolarity or multipolarity, but there are now few who would dispute that some kind of power shift is occurring.

Scholars likewise disagree over which kinds of power distribution tend to be more peaceful or violent on average, a debate that, as one study of the causes of war puts it, goes back "at least as far as the Treaty of Westphalia in 1648."[41] Kenneth Waltz, the father of modern neorealism, argued that bipolarity is an inherently stable system, whereas multipolarity is unstable. Bipolar systems, he posited, are more conducive to the effective balancing of power because they contain fewer opportunities for great powers to fight each other and fewer opportunities for misperception. His stance was heavily influenced by the period in which he wrote: The Cold War, though dangerous, had congealed into something more stable and less dangerous than great power war, and the wars of the early twentieth century—both of which had emerged from chaotic multipolar systems—were relatively recent in memory.[42]

Today, many in Washington subscribe to a similar viewpoint. Indeed, the historical anomaly that the Cold War ended peacefully only tends to add to our intuitive suspicion that multipolarity is dangerous and bipolarity is more stable. But this tendency to rely on a single historical case as evidence of more general rules is problematic. Is multipolarity inherently less stable because of the sheer number of participants? That is the conclusion that many historians draw from the onset of World War I. Or perhaps we could extrapolate from the lack of direct power conflict during the Cold War to conclude that bipolarity is more stable? Citizens of Vietnam, Cambodia, or Korea might dispute that the Cold War was peaceful. As the late Bob Jervis put it, the Cold War, "the era of Great Power peace, . . . coexisted with an extremely large number of wars in the Third World, some of them extremely bloody."[43]

Indeed, despite Waltz's assertions, equally plausible arguments suggest that multipolarity may be less dangerous than bipolarity. Karl Deutsch and David Singer, for example, argue that arms races are less likely to escalate to war in multipolar systems, while Dale Copeland points to the increased wariness of great powers to start wars they may lose in a multipolar system.[44] There have certainly been peaceful multipolar systems in history: The Congress of Vienna in 1815, for example, created an entente between the major powers that lasted for almost a century. And some predictions based on the idea that multipolar regions are always unstable have proved highly inaccurate—for example, Mearsheimer's infamous "Back to the Future" article, in which he argued that post–Cold War Europe would descend back into fratricidal conflict with the return of multipolarity.[45]

Still other scholars argue that unipolarity is the most stable, as it has the potential to suppress nascent conflicts before they pose any real threat—or as Donald Trump so memorably put it to the journalist Bob Woodward: "I'd rather fight them over there than fight them over here."[46] It was notable that Trump was in effect quoting his own generals to Woodward, implicitly accepting their argument that America's global power base and military infrastructure had the potential to suppress conflict—or at least keep it far from the American homeland. Such arguments form the back-bone of much of the "primacy" school of U.S. foreign policy, whose proponents often argue that the unipolar moment was a unique opportunity for the United States to use its bounty of power to maintain a more peaceful international system. As the columnist Bret Stephens put it as late as 2015, "The alternative to Pax Americana—the only alternative—is global disorder."[47]

We can point to three core reasons for the big disagreements about polarity. In the first place, scholars often have different conceptions of "stability." Most tend to agree that stability is the absence of too much war and violence in the international system. But although some scholars suggest that their preferred system prevents war broadly, others argue merely that their preferred polarity prevents *great power* wars. That's a qualitatively different assertion. Indeed, it seems logical that a system that suppresses certain kinds of wars may encourage other kinds. As Nuno Monteiro points out in his book *A Theory of Unipolar Politics,* unipolarity is likely to encourage one specific kind of war, that of "recalcitrant minor powers"—that is, insurgents that object to the hegemon. This is certainly a trend we've seen in recent years as the United States has engaged in crusading campaigns in the Balkans and the Middle East. And the data backs it up: For at least the past thirty years, there's been a substantial drop in interstate war but a marked rise in civil wars.[48]

A second problem is that polarity itself may be little more than an in-tervening variable. As Joseph Grieco puts it: "There are very few empirical or logical grounds to believe the polarity of the international structure influences the incidence of war or the chances for peace."[49] Instead, polarity should be thought of as interacting with other variables to form out-comes. Consider the work of Glenn Snyder on alliances, which highlights the substantive differences between alliance politics under multipolarity and under bipolarity. Under multipolarity, for example, there's a much broader choice of alliance partners than under bipolarity, where structure determines alignment for all but a few states. In practice, this means that one of the most basic state behaviors in international relations—alliance formation—looks exceedingly different in a multipolar system than it does in a bipolar or unipolar one.[50]

Other core issues of international relations also vary by polarity. Rising or falling states are treated differently by their rivals depending on whether there are other threats in the system; balancing behavior becomes substantially more important under multipolarity, and wartime coalitions can look very different in multipolarity or bipolarity.[51] Some factors appear to make multipolarity more stable—most notably, coalition politics, which tend to produce defensive coalitions that make conquest far more difficult. Under bipolarity, in contrast, these tend instead to produce military spending and arms races, creating a far riskier environment in which misperception or miscalculations can more easily lead to war.[52]

The final problem when it comes to assessing whether multipolarity is less stable than bipolarity or unipolarity is that almost every analysis of the question relies on the Cold War as its central case. Yet it is unclear whether the Cold War can really be likened to other periods of history that came before, thanks to the game-changing existence of nuclear weapons since 1945. The Cold War may not have ended in a great power war. But it also took place under a set of circumstances quite unlike any in previous eras, in which both the United States and the Soviet Union knew that direct conflict could easily escalate out of control. At the same time, with mutually assured destruction providing an ultimate deterrent, nuclear weapons took the prospect of state death through conquest off the table and thus provided the superpowers with some reassurance that their state would survive.

In short, the nuclear balance of terror after 1945 represents a giant confounding variable for any understanding of polarity and stability in the international system. We have not yet seen a multipolar system in the nuclear age; it is possible that it too would be more stable than previous iterations of multipolarity thanks to the deterrent effect provided by nuclear weapons. Much of the recent writing about nuclear weapons suggests that they alter how states think about competition in fundamental ways.[53] Indeed, Waltz himself alluded to this possibility when writing about bipolarity, noting that "multipolarity abolishes the stark symmetry and pleasing simplicity of bipolarity, but nuclear weapons restore both of those qualities to a considerable extent."[54]

Ultimately, the evidence for the dangers of multipolar systems turns out to be somewhat circumstantial: a coincidence of historical recency bias and the potential confounding effects of nuclear weapons. Theory, meanwhile, suggests a more balanced picture. Some risks may be higher under multi-polarity (low-level conflicts), but others are higher under bipolarity (arms races). Likewise, there are benefits to both systems. Under multipolarity, buck-passing and free riding become more difficult, which gives great powers greater freedom of maneuver. Under bipolarity or unipolarity, the great powers may be able to shorten wars through increased leverage on their client states. On average, though, it seems that a multipolar system may be no worse than a bipolar one.

Embrace a More Diverse World

Thus far, we've talked mostly about facts and theories in this chapter: how power is distributed in today's international system, the pros and cons of different forms of polarity, and whether existing trends are likely to continue or diverge. But these questions are not merely academic navel-gazing. They are not even—to return to the opening of the chapter—mere *naval* gazing, as the simple comparison of military strength today tells us relatively little about how the future might look. Thinking closely about latent power and future patterns of influence in the international system is imperative if we are to address how the United States should think about navigating the developing twenty-first-century landscape. This is the topic of much of the rest of the book. We are entering a moment of shifting polarity; whether the United States can turn this to its advantage will depend on its strategic choices.

The data explored in this chapter suggests that—contrary to the popu-lar narrative that China's rise heralds a new bipolar competition—the world is entering a period of "unbalanced multipolarity," an international envi-ronment in which two major powers (the United States and China) are preeminent but other second-rank powers (for example, Japan, Germany, India, Turkey, or France) are important players. The United States cannot *create* multipolarity or bipolarity, but in this situation of unbalanced mul-tipolarity, it can, through its actions, either promote and emphasize the more multipolar characteristics of the international system or elevate the more bipolar U.S.-China competition. Despite the narrowing power gap between China and the United States, America's current strategy both embraces open competition with China and resists multipolarity, suppressing the capabilities and influence of these middle powers. It is, in short, a strategy for a bipolar world, not a multipolar one.

Indeed, the Biden administration's approach to a shifting global balance of power was clear: bolster American leverage by building an anti-China coalition, emphasizing closer military and technical cooperation between allies across Europe and Asia, and attempting to build a global bloc of democracies—or at least of "like-minded" countries—oriented against authoritarian revisionists. As the 2022 national security strategy document puts it: "We need to produce dramatically greater levels of cooperation. The key to doing this is to recognize that the core of our inclusive coalition are those partners who most closely share our interests. America's treaty alliances with other democratic countries are foundational to our strategy."[55] This is then paired with economic statecraft to contain China economically—undermining China's access to key global markets, restricting the transfer of advanced technologies, and promoting "ally-shoring" to move supply chains away from China. Under Biden, in short, the United States planned to re-run the Cold War playbook, championing a bipolar competition with China, attempting to restrain China's rise, and hoping that the backing of America's allies and partners can make up for its waning relative power.

It's a problematic strategy; China is no autarkic Soviet Union. Aside from some trade in commodities, the USSR was largely cut off from global trade; it relied heavily on internal connections within the communist bloc. In contrast, China today is a key hub of the global economy, with spokes connecting it to every region and every type of regime. Politically, China may have few friends that fully share its ideology or repressive governance. Yet Chinese trade and investment are welcomed—and potentially indispensable—in many parts of the world, even among America's closest allies. Worse, this "bloc"-based strategy still relies on the provision of American hard power for its primary military strength. In practice, this lessens the ability of allied states to contribute to offsetting Chinese power. It links every issue with the question of China, fails to prioritize, and is likely to make American relations with other countries China-centric, thereby making it more difficult for policymakers to handle bilateral or regional interests that may be as important.[56] And perhaps most problematically, it will push countries to "take a side" in a contest in which many states would rather not. Though the Biden administration tried to deny this—noting in the national security strategy that "we do not seek conflict or a new Cold War"—there is no real way to stop disagreements over China from bleeding into other areas of international politics.[57]

In contrast, the benefits of embracing the world's burgeoning multipolarity and attempting to build a strategy around it are significant. First and foremost, if the research on multipolarity explored in this chapter is correct, embracing multipolarity rather than trying to reassert a bipolar competition should lower the risk of direct great power war, albeit at the cost of potentially increasing the number of lower-stakes conflicts. Since avoiding a great power war that could rise to an existential threat is among the most important goals of American foreign policy, this is a worthwhile trade-off.[58] A multipolar strategy—one that is not built entirely around containing China—also allows the United States to hedge against a possible future decline in its power or against a further rise in Chinese capabilities. A strategy for multipolarity like the one proposed in the latter half of this book would implicitly recognize that putting all our eggs in one basket—relying solely on the United States to provide the military force necessary to monitor and manage all the world's major regions—is a significant risk to take. Other capable actors, particularly in Asia and Europe, must become a backup for American power, making it less likely that China will run the global table should the United States falter. And the embrace of multipolarity helps the United States hedge against a future in which it is China that falters. By maintaining flexibility and increasing the number of available partners, this approach can prepare the United States for other challenges that may emerge.

The United States should foster multipolarity in three specific ways. Each of these is covered in more depth in the following chapters; each encourages the growth of other capable actors in the international system and stronger networks of interconnectedness among a wide variety of states. First, the United States should embrace and promote burden-shifting to capable U.S. allies, allowing their latent economic power to emerge more fully as military capabilities. In the early years of the Cold War, Washington often compensated for its allies' relative weakness and poverty by providing direct military support. This pattern continued even after 1991, as U.S. policymakers emphasized allied reassurance over burden-sharing. As a result, even wealthy and technologically advanced U.S. allies are still largely dependent on the American security umbrella. These states are thus brimming with latent power but remarkably underperforming in terms of military capabilities. Promoting burden-sharing by allies will begin to redress this balance, allowing American allies in Europe and Asia to carry their own weight and enhance their role as "middle powers" in the international system.

Second, policymakers should seek to maintain flexibility in America's bilateral and multilateral partnerships. Rather than building formal, closed alliance structures as it did during the Cold War, the United States should seek flexible working partnerships with a variety of states. Consider NATO: For all the benefits and triumphs of the formal Cold War–era alliance, its bureaucratization and formalization meant the alliance persisted long after the threat it was meant to combat—the Soviet Union—had collapsed. In the aftermath of the Cold War, the organization underwent a prolonged period of searching for new missions, from counterterrorism to human rights promotion, most of which were ill-suited to existing membership and structure. In contrast, flexible partnerships or alignments on different topics can help hedge against future threats more effectively because they do not lock the United States in if circumstances change. They also allow for greater flexibility to build distinct coalitions on different topics, ranging from arms control or nonproliferation with clear adversaries to cooperation on economic or defense issues with friendlier states.

And finally, the United States should attempt to increase economic openness by resisting the use of coercive economic statecraft and instead focusing on resilience and diversity of global markets. In recent years, America has become somewhat addicted to the negative applications of economic statecraft, particularly the use of economic tools of coercion (that is, sanctions, export controls, and tariffs) to achieve foreign policy goals. These weapons will produce diminishing returns, especially if the dollar becomes less dominant in the future. Where there has been discussion of positive economic statecraft, it has focused on ideas like "ally-shoring," a walled-garden approach to international trade that will ultimately lead to a less interconnected, more bifurcated, and poorer global economy. Instead, policymakers should build a positive agenda of economic statecraft that improves ties between the United States and other regions of the world. This does not necessarily mean a return to the full-blown globalization trends of the post–Cold War period, but more trade openness on the part of the United States would help build goodwill among developing countries and increase global resilience.

Power Proliferates

Turkey is neither a military superpower nor an economic powerhouse. It ranks comfortably in the middle of the so-called middle powers. Indeed, Turkey is a quintessential upper-middle-income state: It is relatively populous, its GNI falls somewhere between that of Poland and Australia, and its GINC score places it close to South Korea and Germany in the power rankings.[59] But for much of 2022 and 2023, Turkey enjoyed outsize influence around the world. Despite its membership in NATO, Turkey refused to join sanctions against Russia after Russia invaded Ukraine, which enabled Turkey not only to benefit from a new influx of trade and tourism from Russia, but also to act as a crucial conduit for travel, trade, and diplomacy between Russia and the West. The country simultaneously continued to sell drones and other military equipment to Ukraine. This hedging approach allowed Turkey's president, Recep Tayyip Erdoğan, to play a pivotal role in brokering a grain export deal between Russia and Ukraine that allowed vital supplies to leave the war zone and resulted in an overnight fall in global food prices of almost 8 percent.[60] Turkey's geographically significant position atop the straits linking the Black Sea and the Mediterranean Sea allowed it to prohibit transit by warships from all sides.[61] Turkey's very status as a middle power with broad-ranging global ties has allowed it to play a pivotal role in this conflict.

Recent history suggests other examples of middle powers making their preferences known and their impact felt in global politics. Consider the Comprehensive and Progressive Agreement for Trans-Pacific Partnership (CPTPP), the successor to the Obama administration's coveted Asia trade deal, the Trans-Pacific Partnership (TPP). After the Trump administration withdrew the United States from the treaty, the other member states—a coalition of middle powers and developing states—worked together to resuscitate the deal in a new form. The irony of the situation could not be more pronounced. The United States abandoned the TPP even though it was designed to emphasize U.S. leadership in the Pacific; its partners—from Canada to Vietnam—chose to proceed regardless. Or consider India's choices since 2022. The government of Narendra Modi has hedged diplomatically and capitalized on economic turmoil by buying Russia's discounted resources to gain an economic boost. India remains concerned—experts say—that isolating Russia could end up driving it closer to China in a way that will hurt Indian interests over the long term.[62]

Each of these developments is a sign of burgeoning multipolarity. As we have explored in this chapter, the world is generally trending in a more multipolar direction, albeit one of *unbalanced* multipolarity in which the U.S.-China rivalry is nested in a broader, more diverse international system. Contrary to much of the common wisdom, it would be a mistake for the United States to ignore—or even try to curtail—this nascent multipolarity. The United States has an interest in promoting a more multipolar world by helping transform the latent power of its closest allies into military capacity. In general, multipolarity appears to be no more volatile than bipolarity; it also may be a safer environment in which to hedge against riskier outcomes. A scenario in which the United States finds itself incapable of keeping up with China in a head-to-head competition would be disastrous under bipolarity, for example, but far less of a problem in a truly multipolar world where allies can leverage their own assets and where policymakers increase their freedom of maneuver by refusing to put all their eggs in one basket.

PART

II

Finding Our Place

4

Realist Internationalism

The 1990s were a boom time for Hollywood; the U.S. entertainment industry pumped out blockbuster films and exported them around the world. Hollywood was seen as a core component of U.S. soft power—yet another way that America could shape the world to think more like it. The films themselves reflected the zeitgeist of the unipolar moment. From *Independence Day* to *Armageddon,* the United States and its military were in the lead, saving the planet from invading aliens, incipient natural disasters, and evil terrorists. When Bill Pullman, as the American president, rallied the world in *Independence Day,* there was little question in viewers' minds that his appeals to freedom and independence—to American values and ideals—would resonate around the world. Other films reflected America's image of itself as the world's policeman. In a few cases, this was self-referential; *Team America: World Police,* for example, presented a puppet- and expletive-filled satire of American foreign policy. But in many other cases, it was earnest, reflecting the widely held notion that America could solve any problem it set its mind to and was indisputably a force for good around the world. So deeply entrenched was this mindset that Harrison Ford, playing an embattled president in *Air Force One,* could unironically give a speech arguing that American self-interest should be secondary to its commitment to justice: "Real peace is not just the absence of conflict; it's the presence of justice. And tonight, I come to you with a pledge to change America's policy. Never again will I allow our political self-interests to deter us from doing what we know to be morally right.

Atrocity and terror are not political weapons. And to those who would use them: Your day is over. We will never negotiate. We will no longer tolerate and we will no longer be afraid. It's your turn to be afraid."[1] Even historical films—from *Apollo 13* to *Saving Private Ryan*—presented glossy, Hollywood-style versions of history in which the moral dilemmas of the past were not present and U.S. power could move mountains.

The dividing line between that era and the more cynical Hollywood of today is murky. The post-9/11 turn to gritty, dark products such as *Zero Dark Thirty* or *The Hurt Locker* reflected the primal fears of the war on terror. But a broader shift also took place. Today's films are as likely to look to superheroes for salvation as they are to look to America, and those heroes frequently come into conflict with cynical or corrupt U.S. government officials. When the world does need to be saved, it isn't always Americans doing it—at least not alone. The sequel to *Independence Day*, in 2016, featured a multinational coalition taking on the alien menace. And unlike in *Apollo 13*, when Matt Damon needed saving in *The Martian* in 2015, it took the American and Chinese governments, working together, to bring him home. Indeed, if anything demonstrates the rising market power of China, it is the fact that Hollywood movies are increasingly written so as not to offend Chinese viewers (or Chinese censors).

The stories that we tell ourselves are fundamentally a reflection of how we see our place in the world. The changes in Hollywood narratives since 1991 mirror the shifts in power that we have seen in the world and the resultant changes in how many Americans now think about foreign policy. Americans certainly continue to value freedom and justice; they still approve of the use of military force in many cases. Although poll numbers have declined in recent decades, most want to maintain an active role in world affairs.[2] But the failures of the post–Cold War period have added a cynical touch to how many Americans view their role in the world. By more than a two-to-one margin, Americans now believe that their country is becoming weaker, not stronger, in global affairs; more than half believe that the United States is doing too much in the world.[3] This shift mirrors shifting power dynamics in the international system. Today's world looks markedly different from both the post-1991 unipolar moment and the Cold War that preceded it. Trends in the international system generally point in one direction: a diminution of America's lead in economic and military might over the rest of the world, coupled with the rise of other state and non-state actors, resulting in a more multipolar world.

This section of the book shifts from analysis to prescription, from trying to understand the changes that have occurred both in the world and the emergent U.S. foreign policy debate to exploring how America can best respond to these shifts. What grand strategy—which approach to maintaining U.S. security and interests—is best in a shifting world? One thing is clear: Our current strategy may have been sufficient for the unipolar moment, when America's vast preponderance of power helped compensate for liberal internationalism's costly foreign policy failures. But it will not suffice for the world that is emerging, where America's margin of error for strategic mistakes is rapidly shrinking.

This chapter begins to lay out an alternative approach, proposing a more pragmatic realist grand strategy—*realist internationalism*—that better integrates American resources and national interests. In doing so, it presents a broad framework to which the following two chapters will add specific regional and functional details. First, we briefly explore why, despite its flaws, realism remains a viable and effective foundation for U.S. foreign policy. Then we lay out the core principles around which policymakers should think about restructuring U.S. foreign policy. And finally, we discuss a few of the most problematic practical questions for a realist foreign policy: how to define U.S. interests; the appropriateness—or lack thereof—of spheres of influence in U.S. foreign policy; how to think about hegemony; and the proper role of alliances.

Realism and Its Flaws

There are four core problems with advocating that realism should form the bedrock of U.S. foreign policy. First, many in Washington proclaim themselves to be "realist" when it suits them. This is perhaps inevitable when one considers that realism is a philosophy that claims to view the world and respond in a "realistic" way. As the historian John Bew puts it, "There are few foreign policy practitioners and thinkers that would style themselves as 'unrealistic.'"[4] Idealists—those who place ideology, from communism to democracy, at the center of foreign policy—are often quick to cloak their own concerns in the language of realism. Bob Kagan, a noted neoconservative, has argued that idealists are the *true* realists—those who see a bigger vision than mere parochial "national interest" concerns. Yet Kagan's version of Washington realism—characterized by proponents who argue that American security is dependent on expanding American-backed liberal and democratic values and that America's global military footprint is a bulwark for peace and stability around the world—is so distinct from the classic understanding of that term as to be an absurdity. It is, in short, fundamentally transformative, even as it pays lip service to the language of power.

Likewise, many grand strategic approaches, including deep engagement and liberal internationalism, start from a realist baseline, assuming that the national interest matters and that power is key in the international system. Each, however, departs from that realist baseline in radical ways, assuming that the international system can be transformed into something better, whether through the application of U.S. power or through the power of ideas, norms, or values. In part, these misreadings or misrepresentations of realism explain why many scholars or practitioners with realist inclinations today brand themselves in distinct ways, from "restraint" to "responsible statecraft"—or simply resist categorization altogether.

The second problem is the exact opposite: Declaring that U.S. foreign policy should abide by realist principles is sometimes regarded as a theoretical straitjacket. The dominance of structural neorealist theories in academia is often taken to imply that realism is concerned only with military power and that it ignores domestic politics, the quirks of bureaucratic decision-making, the psychology of leaders, global norms, and international institutions. The dominance of structural theories also results in constant criticisms that realists are violating their own principles if they discuss other variables in a policy context. Indeed, as Jonathan Kirshner has persuasively argued, by stripping realism down to a model this parsimonious, structural realists have left us with a theory that cannot fully explain, for example, why and when wars happen.[5]

Yet structural realism or neorealism—the school of thought most undergraduates are taught in International Relations 101—is just one variant of realism. More important, it is one that was never intended to serve this kind of prescriptive purpose. Ken Waltz, the godfather of neorealism, noted that his theory is one of international affairs, not of foreign policy; that is, it is focused on the grand sweep of history at the most abstract level. For anything else, it is necessary to seek additional sources of insight. Other variants of realism do not share these constraints: Classical and neoclassical realists have long accorded importance to all levels of analysis, from human emotions to domestic political constraints; their theories are far better suited to use in a foreign policy framework.

A third core problem with placing realism at the heart of foreign-policy making—and the one most heard in D.C.—is that realists are very good at criticizing but never offer specific solutions or policy proposals. As Stewart Patrick of the Council on Foreign Relations recently put it, "Apostles of restraint have their work cut out for them. . . . They need to clarify what restraint actually means, . . . what their proposed strategy means for American intervention, international cooperation, U.S. alliance commitments, regional and global power balances, and the promotion of deeply held values."[6] Jonathan Kirshner makes a similar point, arguing that, "probably as a function of the fact that it is so well attuned to avoiding foreign policy blunders," realism "has much less to say about the wisdom of positive steps a country might productively take."[7] But these criticisms are largely unjustified. It might be true that realists or restrainers have in recent years been prominent critics of existing U.S. policies—for example, arguing against the war on terror—but simply supporting existing U.S. policy does not make one a profound or innovative thinker either. Indeed, this criticism of realists is too often a way of conflating U.S. *engagement* with forward-deployed military missions. Realists and restrainers have in fact offered policy alternatives in many realms of U.S. foreign policy, from Ukraine to the Middle East to the defense of Taiwan.[8] Many are ardent proponents of U.S. diplomatic or economic engagement around the world. This book is an attempt to tie many of these threads together in a coherent strategy, but there is no denying that the groundwork is already there.

Finally, the association of the term *realism* in the public imagination with relatively crude practitioners of *machtpolitik* such as Kissinger—whom Michael Desch aptly describes as "neither a consistent nor a profound realist thinker"—also produces an impression that realists are heartless and amoral.[9] This misperception goes some way toward explaining why many label Donald Trump's foreign policies as "realist"; his foreign policy choices rely heavily on military means and economic coercion. They often have a crude transactionalism to them, unencumbered by morality. Yet morality, as discussed further below, can be the foundation of realist thinking. It is a situational, bounded, and consequentialist morality, rather than one driven by absolute rights and wrongs. For many classical realists, the creation of a moral foreign policy should be intrinsically constrained, as Hans Morgenthau once put it, by the "sharp distinction between the desirable and the possible—between what is desirable everywhere and at all times and what is possible under the concrete circumstances of time and place."[10]

Core Principles

Realism's strength as a theory—and the reason it has endured for centuries—is that it rightly centers power and security at the core of the international system. It is not a monolith. As William Wohlforth puts it, "The most important point is that realism is not now and never has been a single theory." Colin Elman, meanwhile, describes it as "a 'big tent,' with room for a number of different theories."[11] For my purposes, I adopt a purposefully ecumenical understanding of realism, one that sees it not as a rigid theoretical construct of international relations, but rather as a loose model of the world against which one can formulate foreign policy. In the interests of making assumptions explicit, I would argue that three core notions from the realist canon should form an essential core for U.S. policymakers. Each of these diverges in important ways from liberal theories of foreign policy.

1. States are guided primarily by security and the imperative of state survival. Although structural factors—particularly the balance of power in the international system—tend to be the most important forces in international relations, that does not mean other factors are meaningless. As proponents of neoclassical realism have long pointed out, domestic political constraints, the psychology of leaders, and ideological frameworks can all act as a "transmission belt for systemic impulses."[12] In practice, this means that states with internal partisan polarization may find it difficult to manage a coherent foreign policy, and for dic-

tatorships, regime security may at times prove more important than national security. At the same time, other factors are unlikely to overcome systemic threats. International institutions, for example, may help lower transaction costs between states but will not constrain states that genuinely believe their interests are imperiled from acting. Socialization within alliances may drive states to make commitments that are not necessarily in the national interest, but they are far less likely to follow through on those commitments in the event of actual conflict.

2. Foreign policy should be driven primarily by the *national* interest, construed in the broadest terms: the security and prosperity of the citizens of the United States. Realism is fundamentally a nationalist rather than an internationalist philosophy. This does not imply that realists should be jingoistic or that a realist foreign policy should be explicitly oriented in opposition to other nations. To put it another way, realism does not preclude cooperation or alignment with other states and does not oppose solidarity with the citizens of other states—so long as this does not conflict with core national interests. Realism does, however, require that foreign policy not be driven by collective notions of global good, such as preserving alliances for their own sake, or of protecting nebulous concepts like the liberal or rules-based order.

3. Anarchy is a persistent factor in the international system. Teleological notions of history—that is, the idea that states can overcome anarchy and achieve a more enlightened world order—are a recurring feature of history, from the cosmopolitanism of the pre–World War I period to Marxist visions of world communism to the modern embrace of a "liberal international order." Yet to paraphrase the old military saying, none of these visions have survived contact with the enemy. Idealized visions of international cooperation often end in tragedy. Lord Palmerston's proverb is as relevant today as it was in the 1840s: States have no eternal allies, and no perpetual enemies, but rather eternal and perpetual interests. It can be a costly mistake indeed for a state to ignore this dictum.

To this core set of assumptions—on which virtually every stripe of realist would agree—I would add two other points that are likely to provoke more disagreement.

4. States are primarily defensive in their approach to security. The brutal and incessant territorial revisionism predicted by offensive variants of realism—which suggest that states constantly seek power at almost any cost—is rarely seen in practice. Revisionism is clearly a cause of international conflict; rising states are often tempted to challenge others to revise the existing status quo. Yet those challenges are usually less absolute than offensive realists suggest. Revisionist states can often be bought off or accommodated. As Bob Jervis puts it, "Our memories of Hitler have tended to obscure the fact that most statesmen are unwilling to pay an exorbitant price for a chance at expansion, . . . [and] . . . more moderate leaders are apt to become defenders of the status quo when they receive significant concessions."[13] On balance, states are defensive in their approach to the world; they primarily seek security. This implies that foreign policy should be focused primarily on preventing misperceptions, deterrence failures, security spirals, and other forms of accidental conflict, an assumption at odds with some more hard-edged forms of offensive realism, which see all nations as intrinsically expansionist and violent.[14]

5. Military force is a necessary but insufficient tool for states as they seek to protect their national interest. Another common misperception about realism is that realist foreign policy frameworks rely solely on military tools of power. But although realists often highlight military means, other tools of statecraft are also important. If anything, historical cases of successful offshore balancing demonstrate that—in the absence of an onshore military presence— diplomatic wrangling, economic statecraft, and even espionage take on vital roles in balancing emerging threats. Consider, for example, nineteenth-century Britain, which relied heavily on diplomatic and economic tools to maintain a viable offshore posture to the European continent. The same is liable to be true today. A realist approach to today's interconnected world will require policymakers to better integrate a range of tools of statecraft into their strategic approaches and to engage deeply with the world through non-military means.

Realist Internationalism in Brief

These core assumptions form the basis for a prudent, yet non-doctrinaire, realist foreign policy that I call *realist internationalism*. Each of the principles and ideas underlying this approach to the world are further expanded upon in the following chapters. But in a nutshell, realist internationalism takes as its core goals the maintenance of American security and prosperity, the creation of a manageable balance of power among key states in the international system, the prevention of the rise of a regional hegemon in core global regions, and the avoidance of catastrophic great power war. This is a substantially more limited set of interests than those claimed by some other grand strategic approaches to the world. For example, realist internationalism eschews the notion of humanitarian intervention and does not seek to prevent conflict around the word as liberal internationalism does. Yet in its inclusion of American prosperity as a core interest, and its outward-looking focus on the United States as a player in world affairs, it also accepts a broader notion of American interests than strategies that focus primarily on the physical security of the continental United States.

To achieve this narrower set of interests, realist internationalism would shift U.S. military emphasis significantly, focusing not on military primacy (the goal of American foreign policy since the end of the Cold War) but rather on military sufficiency—that is, creating and maintaining the forces needed to defend the United States and its core security interests. This would imply not just a somewhat smaller U.S. military, but one that is structurally different from today's force, with a substantially heavier emphasis on naval and air forces. Although this would necessitate some level of global retrenchment, the United States should maintain a smaller network of military bases abroad focused on protecting access to the global commons.

Military sufficiency would jettison the current attempt to maintain a force designed to overmatch any foe or combination of foes in the international system, and focus instead on the core military capabilities needed to deny adversary superiority in key areas. In addition, it would seek to maintain capabilities that themselves enable the development of increased defensive capabilities among allied and aligned nations. Indeed, a core emphasis of a strategy of realist internationalism is the goal of dramatically increasing military burden-sharing among capable states in Europe and Asia—and a purposeful attempt to accelerate the shift toward multipolarity in the international system. In Europe, that would take the form of ending the U.S. presence and working with European states to backfill and bolster homegrown capabilities to deter states like Russia. In Asia, it would resist further buildups and focus heavily on building up the capabilities of local allies in Japan, South Korea, and Australia. The importance of burden-sharing under multipolarity is explored in greater depth below, and the military implications of this strategy for the core regions are explored in greater depth in chapter 5.

This strategy would also necessitate rethinking some of the thorniest ideas in international relations: how to define hegemony; how to think about collective global problems like climate change and nonproliferation; how to think about spheres of influence; and the appropriate role for alliances. Each of these is explored further in the sections below.

America in the World

Narrowing American Interests

At the heart of every grand strategy is an assessment of interests. Just as Abraham Maslow's hierarchy of needs runs from the essential and physical needs of a human being (for example, food and shelter) all the way to more metaphysical needs (for example, a sense of belonging), grand strategies can run the gamut from extremely narrow interests centered around state survival and territorial integrity to much broader notions like spreading ideology. Grand strategy, as Barry Posen has described it, is a state's "theory of how to obtain security for itself"; one's theory of security necessarily informs what you think your interests *are*. Like most realists, I adopt a narrow view of American interests. The best way to create security for Americans is to focus on defending the homeland, enabling Americans to maintain their domestic prosperity, and preventing the rise of any state that could conceivably threaten that condition.

The first—and by far the most important—interest is protecting the physical security of the American homeland against attack by other states or non-state actors. As others have previously noted, the United States is remarkably fortunate in this regard. As a country that covers most of a continent, the United States enjoys large ocean barriers to the east and west, and weaker, generally friendly neighbors to its north and south. This does not mean that it is entirely immune from attack, as both Pearl Harbor and the September 11 attacks attest. But such attacks are rare, and they are exceedingly challenging to undertake, both for states and for non-state actors; foreign terrorist groups have had few successes in undertaking large-scale terror attacks on American soil since 2001. Nuclear weapons pose a unique threat to Americans: Though they are far less likely to be used than many other weapons, they offer the potential for widespread death and destruction if ever used. Indeed, nuclear weapons are perhaps the only existential threat to Americans. Protecting the United States from these threats is the most basic role of government.

The second core interest that policymakers must seek to ensure is American democracy and prosperity at home. Economic strength is to some extent dependent on access to global markets and resources. Although the United States could undoubtedly survive an autarkic economic system—particularly since the advent of the shale revolution in energy production—disconnecting the country from the rest of the world economically would leave it substantially poorer. Indeed, this was the question that animated some of America's top strategic planners before its entry into World War II: What proportion of world markets did America need to retain access to in order to remain prosperous? It is even more relevant today; the United States is now the world's largest goods and services trading nation. This interest in prosperity does not supersede all other national security concerns; the United States can adopt some form of trade protectionism or make free-trade exceptions to build resilient supply chains and maintain the defense-industrial base. Yet to remain prosperous, it must retain access to a variety of critical resources and inputs for manufacturing, and the American population should have access to foreign exports. More important, retaining access to the global maritime commons—the sea lanes along which international trade runs—is a core national interest.

Defending American liberalism—in the classic political sense of the word—is a trickier interest to define. There is little doubt that policymakers will have failed if they allow foreign policy to undermine liberal democracy at home. Indeed, though sometimes overblown, the concerns of many libertarians about the impact of America's foreign policy at home have often proved prescient. Domestically, America's expansive post–Cold War foreign policy, most notably its war on terror, has undermined core rights in the realms of privacy and press freedom; the excesses of the war on terror contributed to the populist authoritarian turn in right-wing politics.[15] A knottier problem is the efforts of states such as Russia and China—feeling threatened by U.S. foreign policy choices and seeking to undermine a rival—to exploit political divisions in domestic politics. Policymakers must balance their foreign policy desires against the risks that these choices may produce domestic political backlash.

A third interest, shared with most offshore balancers, is managing the balance of power. Both globally and in three core regions—Europe, Asia, the Middle East—the United States should aim to prevent the rise of any state or combination of states that could challenge either its physical security or its prosperity. In practical terms, this means that no state should achieve the ability to exclude America, either militarily or economically, from that state's own region, a concept explored more thoroughly below. This kind of offshore strategy generally served the United States well during the Cold War. It does not require America itself to maintain hegemony in each region, but rather to use economic statecraft, diplomacy, and other means to induce regional states to create a more even balance of power and prevent unfriendly states from amassing too much power. It requires the development of appropriate metrics and monitoring of threats, which suggests a much stronger role for diplomacy and intelligence in U.S. statecraft, as well as maintaining the appropriate military capabilities needed to engage in each region if necessary.

There is also a fourth interest that cuts against the first three interests and requires policymakers to find balance in how they pursue policy: avoiding a catastrophic great power war. Although this argument flies directly in the face of traditional Clausewitzian notions of war as a continuation of politics, it is far better suited to the nuclear era, when any direct conflict between nuclear powers could escalate to a planetary catastrophe. Put simply, the nuclear revolution means that policymakers cannot afford to fight direct great power wars over relatively minor interests; the risks most often outweigh the stakes. This carries with it some risk that Russia, China, or others will engage in what some have described as a form of "nuclear blackmail," suggesting that they might "go nuclear" if the United States opposes their attempts to expand territorially. For this reason, it is important for leaders to be cognizant of where revisionism by other great powers is truly damaging to U.S. interests and where the stakes are lower; policymakers should have clear red lines in mind, even if those lines are not publicly declared. Meanwhile, the United States should seek to avoid destabilizing arms races or security spirals that could inadvertently lead to a conflict. Ultimately, avoiding a great power war will necessitate a hedging strategy toward Russia and China, accommodating some lesser revisionism—or opposing it primarily through non-military or indirect means—while preparing for the possibility that war may become necessary if these powers continue to push into core areas of interest for the United States.

These four principles are limited, purposely so. They stand in stark contrast to America's post–Cold War policies, which were transformative. Since the end of the Cold War, U.S. grand strategy has been exceedingly expansive in its understanding of American interests. For liberal internationalists, deep engagers, or those who favor primacy, America's interests are not merely physical security but a much deeper set of philosophical and transformative goals that would ultimately serve to create a more secure world. American global military primacy, humanitarian intervention, democracy promotion, counterterrorism, promotion of international institutions and order—each came with a theory that explained how it would ultimately make America more secure. Indeed, although the problem with American foreign policy is often portrayed as one of "over-militarization," the problem is as much about ends as it is about means.

Consider U.S. sanctions policy. In recent years, America has imposed punitive sanctions on countries from Russia to Venezuela to Iran. Economic statecraft, whether sanctions or trade policy, is an important component of the foreign policy tool kit. But America's sanctions are often aimed at truly maximalist, transformative ends: regime change in Venezuela, the return of conquered territory from Russia, or Iran's abandonment of proxy warfare. The failure of these sanctions to produce the sought-after policy change is less about the utility of sanctions and more that the goals set for them are entirely unrealistic. Indeed, the few cases of successful policy change by sanction are the result of realistic goals, such as the Bush- and Obama-era sanctions that preceded the negotiation of the Iran nuclear deal. Our military interventions too often share the same problems. The post-9/11 military campaign to topple the Taliban in Afghanistan, for example, was remarkably successful until it became a broader campaign to reshape Afghanistan into a modern nation by force. And even when military actions are described in the language of deterrence—as Erica Borghard, a professor at West Point, recently noted—they are still coercive and transformative in nature: We somehow expect that assassinating a senior Iranian general will compel Iran to change its foreign policy or that stationing more troops in the Asia-Pacific will force China to abandon its maritime claims.[16]

Those who are inclined toward a more realist foreign policy should not abandon values or the rhetorical defense of liberalism and democracy where possible; U.S. foreign policy cannot and should not be truly value neutral. The United States benefits from working toward cooperative endeavors in the international system.[17] Americans undoubtedly benefit from a relatively peaceful world, from the existence of fellow democracies, and from a useful set of global institutions and norms that can facilitate trade, diplomacy, and cooperation in resolving global crises. Retreating behind its walls entirely—as some among the nationalist wing of the Republican Party would have America do—would render Americans poorer and the world a less friendly and safe place. But it is important to be clear: These are not core interests for the United States. These values, norms, and institutions are valuable only *so long as they do not significantly undermine* the four core interests. As the past three decades have shown, the best way to defend liberal democracy at home is not militant liberalism abroad. Though values are important, the primary responsibility of policymakers is not to build a better world but to ensure the security of the United States and its citizens through the military, diplomatic, and economic means available to them.

Another non-core interest is the prevention of nuclear proliferation. A common theme in many grand strategic visions of the post–Cold War period is a heavy emphasis on nuclear proliferation as a primary threat to the United States; such concerns were often coupled with a fear of non-state actors or terrorist groups.[18] These concerns have turned out to be substantially overblown. As with other terrorism-related issues, intelligence—not forward military presence—is the best way to handle threats from non-state actors. Meanwhile, the ranks of nuclear-weapons states have grown only slowly in recent years, and at least some of that growth—in North Korea and potentially in Iran—was driven by concerns about U.S. regime change. One commonly heard area of concern about U.S. retrenchment is that it may prompt proliferation by U.S. allies in states, such as South Korea, that are facing increased security risks.[19] Others suggest that multipolarity will increase the risks of proliferation and that the world is increasingly reaching a "nuclear tipping point." The historian Frank Gavin, however, describes most of these arguments as "nuclear alarmism," noting that the Cold War was hardly the nuclear paradise that many proclaimed it to be, and arguing that a more "nuclearized environment need not be more dangerous."[20]

What are the risks to the United States of limited nuclear proliferation?[21] Research suggests that nuclear weapons are useful primarily for deterrence; states typically cannot use them to coerce or threaten their non-nuclear neighbors.[22] Broadly speaking, nuclear deterrence works. Nuclear states tend to shy away from direct conflict with each other, and even when they have come to blows—as in the Kargil War between India and Pakistan—the nuclear balance has held.[23] We should not be sanguine about significant proliferation, but the primary risk arises mostly from misperception, miscalculation, or accidents. Even in the U.S.-Soviet nuclear relationship, there were several near misses due to technology failures or human error; the potential for miscalculation will likely only rise in a multipolar nuclear era. In short, the United States should not embrace unfettered proliferation. It should use secondary tools of statecraft, such as sanctions or multilateral diplomacy, to dissuade states from proliferation. It should engage in aggressive arms control and deconfliction measures with other nuclear-weapon states. But as with democracy promotion, preventing nuclear proliferation is not a core interest of the United States, and the United States should neither maintain significant overseas forces nor engage in armed conflict to prevent proliferation.

Conceptualizing Regional Hegemony and Spheres of Influence

Hegemony—a concept often used but seldom well defined in discussions of foreign policy—is a way of thinking about order in the international system. At the simplest level, the international system could be organized in three ways: States could jockey among themselves, with the balance of power determining their relative standing in the system. States could accept hegemony and the idea that there is a hierarchical order in which some states are dominant and others subordinate. Or states could agree to some type of constitutionalism in which they overcome the state of international anarchy to embrace a rules- and law-based order.[24] It should go without saying that the first two are substantially more common across history; it remains unclear whether the third has ever existed.

Hegemony has been particularly common. Indeed, world politics can be characterized to some extent as a historical succession of different orders imposed on the world by the leading states in the system, whether the Roman legions or the sunset-defying British Empire. Traditionally, the relationship of the hegemon to other states has been thought of as a violent one—so much so that some scholars have questioned whether the United States can even be classed as a global hegemon given that it does not possess the military might to enforce its will on every state.[25] As John Mearsheimer puts it, "A hegemon is a state that is so powerful that . . . no other state has the military wherewithal to put up a fight against it. . . . Hegemony means domination of the system."[26]

But hegemony is not necessarily reducible to a purely military or violent relationship; states do not always conquer their way across a mountain of skulls to exert hegemony. Hegemons can instead exert control through various instruments of coercion: political, military, and economic.[27] As Robert Gilpin puts it: "The strong version of hegemonic order is built around direct and coercive domination of weaker and secondary states by the hegemon. But hegemonic orders can also be more benevolent and less coercive—organized around more of a reciprocal, consensual, and institutionalized relationship."[28] American hegemony is built at least partly on the dominance of the U.S. dollar and on the country's control of the central nodes of the interconnections that tie together the globalized economy.[29]

This bears on how we understand hegemony as a concept in grand strategic thought. Offshore balancers have long argued that America's core geopolitical goal should be to prevent regional hegemony by any other state in the three major regions of the world: Europe, the Middle East, and Asia. As a regional hegemon—holding by far the predominant position in the Americas—the United States itself exemplifies why realists fear re-

REALIST INTERNATIONALISM   127

gional hegemony: It has used the relative freedom of action created by its regional dominance to roam around the world, causing trouble in other regions. It was even able to establish itself as a hegemon in the Middle East for about twenty years, albeit at a cost.

Today, as many have noted, there is little risk of an emerging hegemon rising in either the Middle East or Europe. China's rise, however, poses serious questions for U.S. policymakers: How far does China have to extend its ambitious foreign policy before it becomes a threat to U.S. interests? What criteria could we use to understand the prospect of Chinese regional hegemony? It seems unlikely, for example, that China could succeed in conquering its way across Asia in today's defense-dominant world. By some other standards, particularly economic ones, however, China's ability to build an interconnected, hierarchical political and economic network in Asia—with China at the center—is far more plausible. This suggests that we must frame concerns about Chinese hegemony in broader than purely military terms and think about the implications for economics and politics.[30] In these areas, the risk to the United States is not simply that China may become so preeminent that it can leave Asia and project power across the oceans, but rather that it may come to possess the capacity to write the rules in Asia and exclude the United States from regional trade or politics altogether. As chapter 6 explores, Chinese hegemony in Asia must thus be construed more broadly than mere military control.

A related concept that merits attention is the idea of a "sphere of influence." Like hegemony, this concept is often painted in a largely military light. It also has a strong normative connotation, almost inevitably prompting discussion of Yalta and the arbitrary elite division of Europe after World War II, or of Chamberlain conceding territory to Hitler at Munich. Spheres of influence—detractors contend—are morally indefensible, the great powers condemning smaller countries to suffer at the hands of their larger neighbors. Indeed, since the end of the Cold War, American policymakers have railed against the concept. As Secretary of State Condoleezza Rice put it, America instead sought a world "in which great power is defined not by spheres of influence, or zero-sum competition, or the strong imposing their will on the weak."[31]

Yet this is a poor way to frame the issue. Spheres of influence are not a moral choice; they are instead a way of describing how geography interacts with the balance of interests. In plain English: A sphere of influence is a geographical area where one great power determines that its interests are not sufficient to risk challenging another power whose interests appear to be greater. A sphere of influence is a place where one state asserts dominance and another is afraid or unwilling to challenge it. As such, it is a measure of the practical limitations of a state's military power and political influence. Sometimes the borders between spheres of influence are stark, as in the Cold War division of Germany into East and West. And sometimes there are gray areas and countries that fall in no sphere of influence, as the Austrian case demonstrates. Geography matters a lot: The question of spheres of influence arises more often at the periphery of a great power's territory, or where one power's expansion runs into another's interests.

Throughout history, great powers often engaged in a delicate diplomatic dance to try to determine which steps might—or might not—be considered a violation of another great power's sphere of influence. This can be seen in one of the earliest uses of the phrase itself, in 1869, when the Russian foreign minister reassured his British counterpart that Britain might safely intervene in Afghanistan, which lay "completely outside the sphere within which Russia might be called upon to exercise her influence."[32] Such openly imperialistic horse-trading would be frowned upon today, but great powers still engage, more subtly, in this kind of assessment. Consider the diplomacy between the United States and Russia, in the early years of the war on terror, over whether the United States would be able to build logistics hubs and military bases in the sovereign states of post-Soviet central Asia to support the war in Afghanistan. The United States itself continues to abide by the Monroe Doctrine—maintaining the Western Hemisphere as its own privileged sphere—and has intervened often, both during the Cold War and after, to prevent political and ideological encroachment by other great powers.

Commentators tend to suggest that the West—or at least the United States—has moved past antiquated, colonialist ideas like spheres of influence and into a more enlightened era, but the truth is more mundane. During the post–Cold War period, America's predominance of power simply made the point moot. As the political scientist Graham Allison points out, "U.S. policymakers had ceased to recognize spheres of influence . . . not because the concept had become obsolete. Rather, the entire world had become a de facto American sphere."[33] But as multipolarity re-emerges, policymakers will have to learn to again live with the reality of spheres of influence. Indeed, spheres of influence are likely to be the subject of increased contestation during shifts in the balance of power. In the case of Russia, this has been expressed as protracted disagreement over the extent of NATO—and European Union—expansion and the fate of the "in-between states," the former Soviet republics now stuck in the no-man's land between Russia and NATO. This contestation has produced at least three wars, including Russia's invasion of Ukraine in 2022. Russia continues to resist Western encroachment in its historical area of influence, and Washington has long insisted that all states must retain the right to choose their political and alliance orientation, resisting the notion of either a Russian sphere of influence or a neutral gray zone in Europe.

Yet in practice, Washington has already accepted the idea that Ukraine falls outside America's no-longer-global sphere of influence. In refusing to intervene with direct military force in the current war—or, indeed, in the 2014 war—U.S. policymakers are implicitly drawing a clear boundary between current NATO members and Ukraine. Of course, the ultimate irony of this conflict is that Russia's poor military showing in the war is also proving that Ukraine is no longer within Russia's sphere of influence; Russia cannot impose its will militarily on the smaller state. China will likely present a greater challenge. In Washington, the question thus far has centered largely around the extent to which Taiwan will be permitted to be drawn into a Chinese sphere of influence. America's Cold War–era policy of strategic ambiguity was designed to place Taiwan in a gray zone where neither Beijing nor Taipei had the incentive to push the issue. The growth of Chinese power in recent years, and apparent growing determination in Beijing to achieve reunification with the island, poses similar questions for the United States as those raised in Ukraine. Should the United States maintain its long-running ambiguity on this question and risk being unprepared for Chinese action? Or should it adopt a firmer stance to demonstrate support for Taiwan—what some have described as "strategic clarity"—and risk a Chinese response? As in Ukraine, the attempt to clarify that Taiwan is outside Beijing's sphere of influence—and to deter military action by China—could end up provoking the war that we wish to avoid.

What is often missing from discussions of spheres of influence is the fate of the smaller states that are the subject of great power contestation. Indeed, a common refrain against the idea of spheres of influence is that it elides the agency of small and medium powers to make their own choices. To a significant extent, smaller states close to great powers will always have more limited options in foreign policy than others. Consider the example of Finland, whose success in the Winter War was enough to avoid annexation by the Soviet Union but was not enough to escape the USSR's gravitational pull in foreign policy. Finland spent most of the twentieth century abiding by a circumscribed form of neutrality as a result. But the Finnish example also suggests that we must be clear that even within the frame of "spheres of influence," small states retain agency. They can resist a great power's efforts to include them in its sphere, often by appealing to another great power for support, as the Viet Minh did during the Vietnam War. And they may be able to effectively build deterrence and use support from other countries to make themselves an unappetizing meal for their neighbor. This is something that Ukraine has demonstrated in stark terms over the past three years. As discussed in later chapters, the United States can embrace a similar approach in Taiwan and elsewhere.

The embrace of spheres of influence necessarily places smaller states at the pointy end of the spear. But the reality is that there is an extremely narrow path between asserting U.S. interests in areas geographically close to other great powers and avoiding great power war. Embracing the concept of spheres of influence can help smooth and expand that space; adopting less provocative and more hands-off approaches to helping small states protect themselves can lessen the risks of war.

Moving Past American "Leadership" in Alliances

Since 1991, the United States has been the world's sole superpower. Yet even after the Soviet collapse, U.S. policymakers continued the Cold War–era practice of building large networks of formal alliances and informal security partnerships. Today, alliances remain a core component of American grand strategy, a choice that looks very different from the historical practice of alliance management. Indeed, today's alliances are not short-term marriages of convenience against a common foe, but are often permanent or semi-permanent. Compare the rapidly shifting alliances of European states during the Napoleonic era—when countries would often shift back and forth between different coalitions—with today's more stable set of formalized, bureaucratized treaty organizations. These more formalized alliances have their advantages, including enabling military interoperability, but also their downsides, as permanence can serve to decouple strategic needs from institutional arrangements.

Perhaps more importantly, alliances today are rarely partnerships of equals. Instead, they typically comprise a set of American security guarantees to lesser powers, commitments at least ostensibly intended to buttress American power and security. Indeed, some credit alliances with helping the United States weather the Cold War and foster global peace and stability. The scholar-practitioner Mira Rapp-Hooper describes America's Cold War alliance building as "a genuine strategic innovation" compared with what had come before, "a peacetime alliance system intended to neutralize threats before they reached the nation's shores, to protect partners, and to foster control over them."[34] This simple and widespread belief has become almost totemic in Washington. As the Biden administration's 2022 national security strategy document put it: America's "alliances and partnerships around the world are our most important strategic asset and an indispensable element contributing to international peace and stability."[35]

From a realist standpoint, this is a puzzling statement. As Glenn Snyder puts it, "Alliances have no meaning apart from the adversary threat to which they are a response."[36] Many in Washington nonetheless apply a pseudo-realist logic to their support for America's alliances. A draft defense planning document from 1992—perhaps the best single exposition of American foreign policy logic since 1991—describes the theory thus: "In the absence of effective defense cooperation, regional rivalries could lead to tensions or even hostilities that would threaten to bring critical regions under hostile domination. . . . As in the past, such struggles might eventually force the U.S. at much higher cost to protect its interests and counter the potential development of a new global threat."[37]

By maintaining alliances and security commitments, proponents thus suggest, the United States can deter regional conflicts that could ultimately prove costly. Yet even putting aside the somewhat circular logic at play here—that the United States must militarily commit overseas to prevent the need for future overseas military action—there is limited evidence to suggest that the United States has been successful in doing so. During the past thirty years, alliance networks have failed to prevent major wars, from the Balkans to the Middle East. Saddam Hussein was an informal ally of the United States when he chose to invade Kuwait; Israel continues to use American-supplied weapons to wage war in Gaza, Lebanon, and Syria. Saudi Arabia and the United Arab Emirates reportedly considered invading neighboring Qatar in 2017; all three countries are U.S. security partners and host major U.S. bases.[38]

It is also an open question whether alliances have done more to deter or to precipitate security competition in some regions. NATO expansion, for example, has clearly provided some of the impetus for Russia's attempts to create "frozen conflicts" in Ukraine, Georgia, and Moldova. In the Middle East, Iranian asymmetric capabilities have only increased as the U.S. military role there has grown. Perhaps the most persuasive argument in favor of America's alliance commitments is that they may constrain nuclear proliferation. If allies are placed under America's nuclear umbrella, the argument goes, they are more likely to forgo their own nuclear deterrent. Even here, however, recent research suggests that "alliances are less useful than often presumed with respect to the prevention of nuclear proliferation among their members."[39] And the classic Cold War–era debates about extended deterrence also suggest that there are limits to how credible U.S. commitments to use nuclear weapons on behalf of an ally can be.[40]

Ultimately, many of the arguments about alliances boil down to a notion that only American leadership can resolve global collective-action problems. As the draft defense planning document from 1992 put it: "Only a nation that is strong enough to act decisively can provide the leadership needed to encourage others to resist aggression."[41] Yet even if that is true, it remains unclear why forming permanent alliances is better than simply dealing with threats as they arise. And the collective-action problem also works the other way: In Europe in particular, U.S. military presence has served to smooth over disagreements between European states about which defense capabilities to prioritize, which threats are most acute, and how much to spend on defense. It is far easier to simply rely on American capabilities than it is to get the thirty-some states of Europe, encompassing more than a million square miles of territory and myriad institutional structures, to find a consensus on difficult questions.

If this logic is questionable, why have U.S. policymakers committed so many resources to alliance building? One plausible explanation is elite socialization. Alliances, particularly formalized ones like NATO, tend to produce socialization among policymakers, in which the interests and policy goals of one country can come to approximate the policies of its allies. Though more commonly discussed in the political science literature on entrapment and war, this socialization can also have more general effects on how policymakers regard their own national interests. As Jennifer Lind puts it, perhaps "alliances entangle because they begin to be seen as ends in themselves; alliance preservation itself, and thus a reputation for keeping commitments, becomes seen as a vital national interest."[42] It is hard to look at Washington debates—in which reverence for alliances is treated as a shibboleth and questioning alliances is regarded with distaste—and not sense that this dynamic might be at work.

Given the power differential between the United States and most of its allies, the notion that alliance socialization might be driving U.S. foreign policy goals is a worrying one. Yet at the same time, alliances are neither useless nor uniformly problematic. They provide American policymakers with diplomatic leverage over partners and permit the United States to set the agenda in its negotiations with other countries. And if they are kept lean and efficient, alliances can provide a forum in which like-minded states can coordinate and build unified responses to common problems. They can create the capacity for military interoperability and shared resources, which, at least in theory, can reduce the costs and burdens of security across all alliance members.

All that this suggests, however, is that alliances are merely a tool of statecraft: a means, not an end unto themselves, and no more untouchable or sacrosanct than any other tool of statecraft. Liberal internationalists may argue that the maintenance of an alliance system is a core interest of the United States, but alliances are not an unalloyed good for U.S. national interests. For Americans, the most visible cost of alliances is monetary. Presidents as far back as Dwight Eisenhower have bemoaned the unwillingness of NATO states to share in the burden of common defense. As John F. Kennedy put it, other "NATO states are not paying their fair share and [are] living 'off the fat of the land.'"[43] NATO itself estimates that U.S. defense spending makes up about two-thirds of total alliance defense spending today. Such an imbalance was perhaps justifiable in the 1950s, as Europe rebuilt from the ravages of war. Today, it is absurd. The GDP of the United States is only 82 percent of the combined GDP of European members of NATO, and its population is less than half that of European member states.[44]

Alliances also carry opportunity costs. America's provision of defense capabilities in Europe has inhibited the development of a European defense-industrial base.[45] American presence—and the demands of interoperability—has led European states to underinvest in specific military capabilities or the ability to manufacture them, which has required the United States to step in during crises. And faced with the rise of ISIS and the Russian seizure of Crimea, the Obama administration found itself unable to successfully fulfill both its commitments to allies and its proposed "pivot to Asia." The Biden administration faced a similar dilemma. The distribution of military capabilities within U.S. alliances remains horribly uneven; even faced with a rising China and a revanchist Russia, America cannot rely on its allies to shoulder some of the burden.

Indeed, even if the risk of formal entrapment in war may be less common than realists have traditionally suggested, the growing shift within U.S. foreign policy to viewing alliances as an end rather than a means is a form of entanglement with other states that can be corrosive to the national interest. Policymakers too often focus on providing allies with U.S. guarantees and capabilities and fail to fully assess whether such steps yield benefits for Americans. And they often focus too much on "reassuring" allies and too little on rebalancing partnerships to compensate for new strategic realities. Consider, for example, the Persian Gulf, where America finds itself providing costly security commitments to one side in a regional dispute, even as core U.S. interests in the region have dramatically decreased. Recognizing this shift, the Obama administration tried to normalize relations with Iran and build a less lopsided regional approach. But the administration found itself unable to break free of path-dependent security partnerships with Israel and the Gulf states.

For realist-inclined policymakers, this suggests a core dilemma: how to maintain the more limited benefits of alliances globally—particularly those in strategically important areas—without falling into the alliance trap. Two specific policies can help.

SET CLEAR LINES AND CIRCUMSCRIBE EXISTING COMMITMENTS Policymakers should make efforts to draw clear lines around existing U.S. security commitments. The United States may struggle to formally downsize its alliance commitments. But it can avoid further expansion of security guarantees to new states, a process that dilutes the benefits of security commitments and increases the risks that extended deterrence will fail. As the political scientists Jennifer Lind and William Wohlforth have argued, ending U.S. alliances or continuing to expand them each pose serious risks; instead, "the United States and its partners should consolidate the gains the [liberal] order has reaped."⁴⁶ The United States can also clarify the scope of these guarantees to be less all-encompassing, whether that is clarifying that NATO's Article V does not necessarily require direct U.S. military intervention or that existing security guarantees to Asian states do not include the contested maritime features most likely to spark a conflict with China. Maintaining existing alliances while accepting that not every guarantee is necessarily "ironclad" reduces the potential for security dilemmas in other regions and offers a path forward that maintains the limited benefits of alliances while avoiding more catastrophic paths. It also brings U.S. paper commitments into closer alignment with actual interests and thereby reduces credible commitment concerns.

In addition, U.S. policymakers must also begin to more clearly differentiate between "allies" and "partners" in both rhetoric and practice. These two words have become synonymous in Washington parlance but are in fact legally and strategically distinct: Allies enjoy a formal security treaty with the United States, whereas partners enjoy a variety of more amorphous relationships ranging from arms sales to training programs to military basing agreements. American policies since the end of the Cold War have often blurred the lines between these two statuses, and leaders have often used the terms interchangeably. Some of the best-known U.S. allies—notably, Israel and Saudi Arabia—are not truly "allies" in a legal sense.

The embrace of "partners" as a core component of U.S. defense is problematic because it implicitly commits the United States to protect countries it may not intend to fight for. Consider the rhetorical difference between the Biden administration's statements before the Ukraine war—in which Defense Secretary Lloyd Austin described America's commitment to Ukrainian sovereignty as "ironclad"—and the administration's actual policy response to Russia's invasion. The response was significant—sanctions, arms shipments, financial assistance—but involved no direct U.S. military action. This contrasts strongly with the U.S. response inside NATO member states like Poland, where troop deployments have massively increased.

But the clear and unambiguous difference in actual policy toward NATO members versus non-NATO members that the war in Ukraine revealed has not been the norm. Programs like the Partnership for Peace, in acting as a gateway to NATO accession for many states in Central and Eastern Europe, also made it less clear which states American security guarantees applied to. It has become commonplace to talk about "allies and partners" with little differentiation, blurring the boundary between formal and informal allies. This approach also implicitly extends the U.S. nuclear umbrella to almost everywhere in the world, diluting the credibility of that commitment and making deterrence failures more, rather than less, likely. Eschewing further expansion of NATO and pulling the United States back from that organization, combined with a clearer elevation of closely delineated formal alliances, can help reduce the risks of U.S. alliance policy going forward.

PROMOTE BURDEN-SHARING Second, and more important, policymakers must focus their efforts within existing alliances on the need for swift and substantive burden-sharing. The United States should always be the balancer of last resort, not the first responder. Though U.S. policymakers have often bemoaned the unwillingness of allies in Europe and elsewhere to contribute to the common defense, the fact is that Washington itself has often been schizophrenic. Obama's defense secretary, Robert Gates, made headlines in 2011 for his scandalous statement that "if current trends in the decline of European defense capabilities are not halted and reversed," NATO would face "a dim, if not dismal future."[47] Yet just a few years later, that administration would commit to the near-Orwellian-sounding "European Reassurance Initiative," increasing the U.S. presence in Europe by as much as ten thousand troops on a semi-permanent basis. Even the first Trump administration, notorious for its loud and repeated insistence that allies should do more, fell into this pattern. President Trump himself would lambaste European states as "delinquent" on their contributions to NATO, leading some to conclude that the United States might pull back from NATO. Yet from 2016 to 2020, the United States tripled the amount spent on the European Reassurance Initiative (renamed the European Deterrence Initiative in 2017) and increased the number of troops in the region.[48]

Washington has traditionally emphasized allied reassurance over burden-sharing. When faced with new crises, U.S. policymakers are quick to respond with increased commitments to allies. Even in the face of Europe's post-Ukraine *Zeitenwende* ("turning point") on foreign policy, the Biden administration chose to supply more than one hundred thousand troops to the continent and to downplay the question of burden-sharing. The implicit theory underlying these choices is that if the United States does not constantly and sufficiently reassure allies, they may instead choose to bandwagon with China or Russia, aligning with and appeasing these states rather than continuing to oppose them. Yet traditional theories of alliances suggest that the United States has vastly overestimated the likelihood of its allies abandoning it. As Glenn Snyder notes, the risk of abandonment depends not just on the degree of direct military dependence—that is, U.S. forces and boots on the ground—but also on the "explicitness of commitment, disparity of interests in conflict with the opponent, and the behavioral record."[49]

In short, though many administrations talk about their desire for burden-sharing, they rarely seek burden-sharing in practice, finding it more attractive to maintain influence over allies than to promote independent military capabilities among them. This should not be surprising. After all, there's an inherent contradiction between the notion of American "leadership" as it is embraced in Washington and the implementation of burden-sharing: If America is to be successful in shifting some of its military burdens onto allies, it will necessarily have to relinquish some control over the ways those allies use their increased military capacity.

There are always policy disagreements among U.S. allies, though these disagreements are often concentrated in the economic space. But with increased European defense capacity, we may well see disagreements on issues in the security space too. Indeed, though the French-proposed catchphrase "European strategic autonomy" met with general derision in D.C., it is most likely an accurate way of describing how the process of promoting independent allied capabilities will unfold; the process will increase autonomy and accentuate some differences with U.S. policymakers. This is, however, a manageable risk and far preferable to the existing trend toward U.S. overextension globally. Many of the states that are best situated to boost their own defense capabilities are advanced industrialized democracies that share a general tendency toward liberal values with the United States. Other small states benefit from access to world markets and international forums facilitated by the United States. They are unlikely to turn on the United States, even if there are more disagreements in some policy areas.

The promotion of burden-sharing will require policymakers to actively work with states elsewhere to identify suitable targets and timelines for the transition to non-American forces. This process will undoubtedly require some tough love; if allies balk at investing more in defense or show no signs of progress, policymakers may well have to consider taking unilateral steps to draw down forces or place limits on cooperation. At the same time, however, the United States cannot apply too many conditions to this process of building and enabling allied capabilities; states must be free to develop their own industrial base rather than being pushed toward U.S. systems. And where collective-action problems prevent large groupings of states—particularly in Europe—from working together, the United States should act to facilitate smaller, minilateral groupings of states that can cooperate on specific defense and defense-industrial issues.

This process will not occur overnight. But within the next two decades, the United States could aim to build a heavily networked set of global military partnerships that are able to handle basic regional problems without substantive U.S. involvement. Ultimately, America's role in its alliances should shift from one of leader to one of facilitator, convener, and guarantor of last resort in critical regions.

What About Existing Grand Strategic Debates?

The last significant round of grand strategic debates occurred in the early to mid-1990s, beginning as the Cold War wound down and intensifying after the collapse of the Soviet Union, as foreign policy elites in Washington sought to formulate a new strategy for a new international environment.[50] As one contemporary pointed out, "Kennan having set the standard, it was only natural that after the Soviet Union collapsed foreign policy pundits of all views would offer their own 'unified field theory' describing the post–Cold War era and prescribing a grand policy for dealing with it. Thus, we have in effect been watching the running of the George Kennan Sweepstakes."[51] These debates continued throughout the post–Cold War period, most notably after the failures of the war in Iraq.

Today's debates are similar to those of the 1990s, precipitated by similar—though less dramatic—factors: a shifting global balance of power, a growing sense that the unipolar moment is ending, and the incipient shift toward balancing against the United States by some regional states.[52] We have so far avoided significant discussion of existing grand strategic debates. In part, this is to avoid getting bogged down in debates that may be dated: A strategy for the unipolar moment will inevitably look different from one for a multipolar or bipolar world. Strategy can be expressed only in context; today's context is different from that of the 1990s. Nonetheless, it is worth a brief discussion of existing grand strategic debates, if only so that we can better understand where the strategy of realist internationalism proposed in this chapter fits among them.

In 1996, Barry Posen and Andrew Ross provided a typology of emerging grand strategic options. Although the strategies they identified varied across several dimensions, these strategies could be mapped on a rough spectrum by how ambitious they were.[53] A similar approach can be applied to debates since that time. How much forward presence does a grand strategy prescribe? To what extent is it trying to shape global order rather than manage it? What level of "insurance" is deemed necessary to prevent negative outcomes from harming American security in the future? These are not identical questions, but they all suggest a similar rough hierarchy of grand strategic options, from the least ambitious—requiring less U.S. commitment overseas—to the most ambitious strategies that require active and engaged military presence in every region (figure 8).

The boundaries between grand strategic approaches are often minutely precise in theory and highly nebulous in practice. Policymakers rarely explicitly embrace a named grand strategy, which makes it hard to tell whether an administration represents one or another of these approaches; many grand strategies blend into each other in practice. For this reason, some scholars favor simply lumping together approaches into "do more"

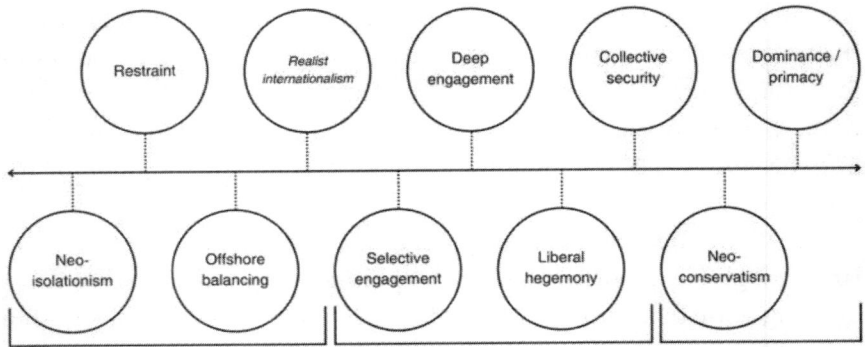

Figure 8. The most widely discussed grand strategic options from the past three decades. Existing grand strategy proposals range, left to right, from extremely modest to extremely revisionist.

or "do less" camps, as "maximizing the differences between alternative grand strategies brings out their differences most clearly."[54] In this sense, there are three groupings worth highlighting here.

The left end of the spectrum encompasses approaches to grand strategy that are less ambitious than America's current approach to the world. These run from neo-isolationism, which advocates a complete drawdown of U.S. forces around the world and no overseas military presence, to restraint to offshore balancing, both of which prescribe minimal forward presence as needed in critical regions.[55] For each of these strategies, the goal is not to change the world but rather to achieve security within the existing order. The strategy advanced in this book, realist internationalism, falls on the edge of this group.

In the center of the spectrum are the approaches to grand strategy that most closely approximate U.S. strategy in recent years. From selective engagement to deep engagement, liberal hegemony and collective security, these grand strategies advocate some substantial level of U.S. forward presence in key regions of the world; each supports the use of U.S. military power to prevent nonproliferation, protect human rights, and tamp down incipient conflicts among both U.S. allies and adversaries.[56] All prioritize order building through international institutions or alliance networks. These approaches are distinguished largely by how expansive they believe U.S. interests are, their beliefs about the conditions under which the United States should use force, and how they think about international institutions and norms. Each is, to some extent, attempting to shape the future of the international system; they differ mostly on the extent and means of that revisionism.

On the right end of the spectrum are grand strategies that are highly unilateral and revisionist, unconstrained by any notion of international norms or rules. Although the United States has implemented elements of these strategies at certain points during the past thirty years—most notably, in the George W. Bush administration's invasion of Iraq—they represent the extreme, radical end of the grand strategy spectrum. Neo-conservatism (or "deep engagement plus") and primacy (or "dominance") both seek to use U.S. power in unfettered ways to reshape the global environment in favor of the United States.[57] They advocate significantly greater U.S. military commitments overseas—the war in Iraq, for example, involved almost half a million American troops in the Middle East—and significantly higher defense spending. These approaches differ primarily on the question of democracy and values, but for both, U.S. military and economic power should be used to confront and contain any potential challenger to the United States and smother the abilities even of U.S. allies to challenge the United States.

The summaries above are a dramatic oversimplification. Indeed, in such a short space it's impossible to do justice to the nuanced and lively debates on grand strategy that characterized this period. Many of the grand strategies discussed above differ across other dimensions, such as the breadth of U.S. interests or whether they believe that international institutions and norms can become self-sustaining over time. Many of these strategies also have deeper roots than the 1990s: Liberal hegemony (or liberal internationalism) has its roots in the anti-Soviet coalitions and global institutions of the Cold War; a form of neo-isolationism characterized the U.S. approach toward Europe during the first century or so of the United States' existence; and offshore balancing was a central component of British grand strategy before being co-opted by American thinkers in the twenty-first century. A wide variety of works delve into each of these strategies in depth and can contextualize them far better than this brief overview.[58]

It is perhaps most useful to simply explain where realist internationalism sits relative to these options—in the space between offshore balancing and selective engagement. Militarily, this book advocates a similar approach to that of offshore balancing, but with some exceptions for the practical difficulties of downsizing existing U.S. commitments. It also embraces a substantially broader focus on non-military tools of foreign policy. Indeed, one might think that realist internationalism, in its emphasis on engagement, is more similar to selective engagement. Yet as Posen and Ross noted back in 1996, "Selective engagement is not as selective as its advocates would have us believe."[59] Realist internationalism proposes a significantly more limited set of U.S. interests than selective engagement, whose advocates argued that in addition to its central security goals, the United States should aim to pursue such diverse goals as preventing the spread of weapons of mass destruction, fostering the spread of democracy whenever possible, and protecting the environment. Engagement—but for far more limited ends—is the watchword of this book.

Here, we largely look forward rather than backward. There are clear through lines of continuity between some of the grand strategies proposed in the 1990s—or indeed those proposed in the 1950s or 1970s—and the options available to the United States today. But faced with a different global environment, we should not necessarily frame our discussions of U.S. grand strategy in terms of past debates.

No One Loves a Political Realist

Ironically, despite the clear resurgence of power politics in the international space, the mid 2020s are not a great time to be a realist. In particular, realist arguments about the war in Ukraine—and about the limited interests that the United States has in that conflict—have not sat well with a commentariat populated by those who idolize the liberal ideals of the unipolar moment. As Edward Luce of the *Financial Times* put it in a recent essay, "the 'realist' school of foreign policy . . . has had a terrible press recently, most of it richly deserved."[60] Tom Nichols, a professor at the U.S. Naval War College, took it even further, arguing that the war in Ukraine proves that "realism is nonsense."[61] But in many ways, this tension is not new: Realism has a long and somewhat conflicted relationship with U.S. policymaking. Perhaps the most famous of all American strategists—George Kennan—was a self-proclaimed realist but spent much of his career in the policy wilderness. America's most infamous realist—Henry

Kissinger—was more politically savvy and far more inconsistent about his views in practice.[62] As Robert Gilpin once put it, "no one loves a political realist"; skepticism about transformative change and a pessimistic view of human nature are unpopular.[63] But during periods of significant shifts in the international system, American leaders have often fallen back on the principles of realism. A generally realist approach, for example, allowed Dwight Eisenhower to manage the early years of the Cold War; Richard Nixon's realism allowed the United States to navigate oil crises, Middle Eastern wars, the end of the gold standard, and the opening of Mao's China.

Today's world is likewise in transition, from the post–Cold War period to something else. It is a time ripe for a more pragmatic, realist approach to U.S. foreign policy, even if the domestic political landscape may be less than welcoming. This chapter focused on laying out the foundations of a realist internationalist approach to U.S. foreign policy. It suggests a more circumscribed set of American interests and makes explicit the assumptions underlying the grand strategy proposed here. In doing so, it argues that realist principles—broadly and ecumenically construed—present the most viable and effective option for U.S. foreign policy going forward. But a broad framework is not sufficient to help guide policymakers in the implementation of this strategy. The next two chapters therefore explore the practical ramifications of this framework: What would a realist internationalist approach mean in specific regions? And how can policymakers best chart a path that takes us from today's overextension to this more limited and pragmatic approach to foreign policy?

5

Pull Back

For almost seventy years now, Germany has been Europe's most cautious power. The aftermath of two world wars, occupation, and state dismemberment left the country's ruling elite with an imperial hangover. Even after the Cold War, German leaders remained wary of military power and fearful of overreach, pursuing instead a foreign policy heavy on diplomacy, economic cooperation, and European integration. Yet all of that seemed to change in March 2022, when Chancellor Olaf Scholz gave a much-anticipated speech to the Bundestag in which he described a "*Zeitenwende*" in German foreign and defense policy. No more would Germany cower behind purely diplomatic or economic tools, Scholz argued: "What is needed to secure peace in Europe will be done. Germany will contribute its share to these efforts in a spirit of solidarity. . . . It is clear that we must invest much more in the security of our country. In order to protect our freedom and our democracy . . . we will now—year after year—invest more than two percent of our gross domestic product in our defense."[1]

Zeitenwende translates roughly as the "turning of the times"—or perhaps "watershed." Either way, it signaled a massive shift in Germany's defense outlook, committing the government to spend $100 billion to improve defense. Germany sent Leopard tanks and other weapons to Ukraine. This was matched with a pronounced shift in Germany's commercial relations. Previously an obstacle to Russian-energy sanctions—and the focus of the fight over the Nord Stream 2 pipeline—Germany suddenly become willing, even eager, to implement harsh European Union sanctions against Russia and committed to ending its reliance on Russian gas imports. This was a costly shift: By the time the next winter ended, nearly one in six industrial firms in the country had reduced production or shuttered entirely.

For a brief time, even Germany's Eastern European neighbors seemed happy with the monumental changes German leaders were willing to undertake. But then the *Zeitenwende* began to fizzle out. Details emerged: The promised $100 billion was a smaller commitment than expected. It would be split over multiple years. It was time-limited, with no guarantee of renewal after the first four years. And rather than being funneled into native European capabilities, or into Europe's defense-industrial base, it would instead be used to buy American-made F-35s and Chinook helicopters, which would increase reliance on U.S. platforms, a choice that— as Jeremy Shapiro and Jana Puglierin put it—would "create dependencies that will last for decades."[2] After all is said and done, the *Zeitenwende* barely caused a ripple in the stagnant pond of European defense. This has in many ways been the true irony of the war in Ukraine: Russia's invasion awakened European countries' sense of threat, pushing them to make promises on defense that would have been unthinkable just months earlier. But Russia's failure to achieve its military goals—combined with the Biden administration's reassuring commitment to U.S. military presence in Europe—once again smothered that nascent sense of threat in the crib, undermining the political will to actually follow through on those promises. Instead of bringing radical change, the *Zeitenwende* continued the broad sweep of U.S.-European relations in the post–Cold War period, in which the promise and necessity of burden-sharing is loudly heralded but always remains just around the corner.

This chapter explores what U.S. military commitments would look like under a strategy of realist internationalism in two regions that have become less strategically significant over time: Europe and the Middle East. In each, U.S. policymakers must seek to break the cycle of path dependence and inertia. In the Middle East, this will require tough choices and a willingness to stick by them, no small feat to be sure. In Europe, by contrast, this will require a concerted effort to promote burden-shifting to allies. If done right, the United States can break the cycle of primacy and build a more sustainable posture—without sacrificing its security.

Geopolitics Matters

Before we dive in, a few words on the relationship between geography and strategy are in order, in part to explain the organization of this chapter and the next. Realism has always been rooted in geopolitics, and to the extent that most other grand strategies in the U.S. tradition borrow at least some of realism's basic assumptions about military force, those strategies are also based in geography. But there are several significant challenges to adequately incorporating the importance of geography in modern strategy.

The first is that much of what today is called "geopolitics" is a bastardization of the term. Certainly, the fathers of geopolitics (and they were *all* fathers) were prone to over-formalizing models of the world and to treating geography as causal rather than as some intervening variable for state success or failure.[3] But the pendulum has swung almost to the other extreme; rather than referring to formal Heartland and Rimland models of the world, "geopolitics" is more widely used today as a generic synonym for great power politics or relations between states. When Ursula von der Leyen, for example, used her first speech as president of the European Commission to advocate for a "geopolitical commission," it was widely interpreted to mean little more than an increased focus on security and external affairs.[4]

But as Jaehan Park has eloquently put it, "If everything is geopolitical, nothing really is."[5] The result is a functional—though not necessarily conscious—disconnect between the realities of geography and the policy prescriptions assumed to arise from them. Consider discussions about NATO today, which often rely on vague Cold War rationales about the U.S. need to maintain security in Europe, but which typically fail to account for the geographical differences between Cold War–era NATO and today's alliance. To policymakers from the Eisenhower or Truman era, for whom NATO was intended primarily to prevent Western Europe's industrial capacity from falling into Soviet hands, the idea that Estonia is somehow essential to U.S. security would make little sense.[6] Or take Middle Eastern oil: Washington has yet to adapt in strategy terms to the revolutionary shale-oil transition of recent years. Old geopolitical assumptions underlie a lot of today's foreign policy decisions but are often applied incorrectly.

Greater clarity about the actual geographic constraints on U.S. strategy is another concern. As Patrick Porter notes, there is often a widespread assumption that technology has shrunk the world and enabled countries to overcome many of the obstacles associated with geography.[7] There is some truth to this assumption. Certainly, technology has made it easier to communicate and even travel between regions. As Daniel Immerwahr puts it, much of America's ability to maintain overseas bases results from what he calls "empire-killing technologies," which make "movement easier without direct territorial control."[8] But the world has not actually shrunk, and technology cannot fully compensate for geographic obstacles, particularly when it comes to military force. In our modern, technologically sophisticated world, the U.S. army still needs to cross the Pacific Ocean to get to Asia; the distance of an air base from a target dictates how long planes can remain in the air over the target without refueling; and Turkey's control of the Dardanelles still means that the country can prevent ships from entering the Black Sea. In Ukraine, much of the fighting in the past few years has revolved around train depots or interchanges crucial for physical logistics. Even technology itself is often dependent on geography. As Henry Farrell and Abe Newman point out, it is the physical location of undersea cables, internet switches, and banking infrastructure that grants the United States much of the leverage that it possesses today in imposing sanctions and conducting espionage.[9]

Passing the Baton in Europe

The case for a substantial U.S. military presence in Europe becomes weaker by the year. Russia has become an increasingly obvious threat to Eastern European states, but the balance of power in Europe simply does not favor Moscow. Despite this, there are significant political obstacles to a transition from American to homegrown European security. The key questions are how to overcome those obstacles, the extent of American retrenchment from Europe, and how fast any transition could realistically take place.

An Ideal World: A Strong Europe

Realists are in broad agreement that America is overcommitted in Europe. Indeed, the fact that the U.S. military remained in Europe after the end of the Cold War seems profoundly at odds with realism's assumption that alliances are primarily a response to threat.[10] But whether bureaucratic politics or simple path dependence are to blame, the fact is that, thirty years after the collapse of the Soviet Union, America is still largely responsible for protecting Europe. And the geographic scope of the commitment has expanded to encompass all of the former Warsaw Pact countries. As a result, NATO's membership has doubled. The United States currently has around one hundred thousand troops stationed in Europe. Troop levels increased after the start of the war in Ukraine in 2022, but even in more normal times, the U.S. troop commitment to the continent has hovered between fifty and seventy-five thousand. Existing base structures—and the slowly dying Treaty on Conventional Armed Forces in Europe—keep the majority of U.S. personnel based in Germany, Italy, and the United Kingdom, but growing numbers are now stationed in Eastern European states on a rotational (but in practice permanent) basis.[11] Perhaps more important than the raw number of troops is America's role as a technological and logistical enabler for European forces, which often lack key capabilities in intelligence, surveillance, and reconnaissance (ISR), airlift, or refueling. The Libya intervention in 2011 is perhaps the clearest example of American centrality to European force projection; though initially intended to play the primary role in the intervention, European forces were not able to sustain operations alone. The United States ended up providing ammunition, air-to-air refueling, and significant intelligence support. As one observer at the time put it, "Europe flew the planes and attack helicopters, but most of the time they were firing US munitions at targets identified by the US, in operations coordinated by US technology."[12]

Ten years from now, the United States should have no significant troop presence in Europe. There may be specific niche capabilities—particularly in the intelligence space—that the United States continues to provide in Europe. Most existing capability gaps, however, should be filled by European nations, whose forces must be capable of responding to crises without immediate American assistance. In particular, European forces should be sufficient and appropriately postured to deter Russia, which remains the most obvious external security threat. They should also have sufficient naval capabilities to manage security in the Mediterranean and Baltic Seas. Shifts in U.S. troop presence in Europe should be matched by shifts in rhetorical and practical commitments to European states' security. The United States does not need to formally withdraw from NATO unless no other choice presents itself. But in pulling back, the United States should make clear that it intends to fulfill the role of a guarantor of last resort— providing arms and assistance rather than direct military support—in almost all cases. The United States should maintain its nuclear guarantees to Europe for several years until an acceptable European substitute emerges, but it should also exert strong pressure to encourage either the European Union to develop a joint nuclear deterrent or France and Britain to extend guarantees to their neighbors. It is possible that this move could prompt Polish or German proliferation if British or French extended deterrence is perceived to be non-credible.[13] But it remains highly unlikely; after all, why would a suitable British nuclear commitment be less credible than an American one? Ultimately, the risk of a limited amount of proliferation in the European context is not a significant threat to U.S. interests.

There is no inherent contradiction between America's Article V commitment to NATO and a declaration that the United States intends to avoid the direct use of force in the region. Article V only commits states to take whatever action they deem necessary to support an attacked state; as the case of Ukraine highlights, a more hands-off approach that prioritizes arms, intelligence, and economic assistance can be highly effective in bolstering the abilities of partner states to defend themselves. An American role as a final guarantor of European security—a balancer of last resort, willing to intervene only when Europe as a continent truly faces an existential threat—remains consistent with NATO membership. In fifteen years, in an ideal world, America and Europe should be relatively equal partners and allies, not security provider and dependent.

Barriers to Implementation

In the case of Europe, the problem is not convincing policymakers that Europe must do more to stand on its own two feet. In the past few years, a wave of publications and public discussions—many even funded by European governments—have sought to explore how Europe might cope if America pivoted to Asia or if the return of Donald Trump to the presidency were to cause the United States to withdraw from Europe. Some experts still favor a significant U.S. presence; a notable example is

Michael Mazarr of the Rand Corporation, who argues that the United States can continue to deter both Russia and China without significant changes in posture. But for others, this is excessively optimistic. Many now argue that shifting trends mean that change in the U.S.-Europe relationship is inevitable.[14] As Nathalie Tocci of the Italian think tank Istituto Affari Internazionali puts it: "The profound transformation of the international system has made European strategic autonomy necessary. The U.S. remains the only major power able to project its influence, including militarily, at the global level, but no longer represents the world's undisputed hegemon. . . . The EU cannot just assume it can rely on the U.S. as it once did."[15] Max Bergmann of the Center for Strategic and International Studies, meanwhile, notes simply that "there is no way Washington will be able to maintain the current level of diplomatic engagement, force deployments, and resourcing to Europe over the longer term. . . . The United States is overstretched."[16]

Burden-sharing is easier said than done, however. For Europe to do more for its own defense, it must overcome some fundamental problems. The most obvious of these is simple: There is no such thing as Europe. Though the European Union has successfully drawn together its members in commercial, regulatory, and monetary terms, it is not a unified political entity; decisions on security rest with national governments. Among other things, this means that there is no unified threat perception among European states. States in Eastern Europe are concerned about Russia, countries in southern Europe worry about the Mediterranean and migrant flows, and countries such as France have interests in Africa. There is a decided lack of trust between East and West on security issues, something that has become only more acute since the start of the war in Ukraine. As one paper from the European Council on Foreign Relations bluntly puts it: "The nations of Europe do not agree on what to do and do not trust each other enough to reach compromises on these questions."[17] The expansion of both NATO and the European Union since 1991 has made it significantly harder to build consensus on defense within Europe.

Power differentials are also problematic. Europe's most powerful players, France and Germany, are widely perceived as "bandwagoners" willing to compromise with Russia in order to maintain the peace. This stance is, of course, highly unpopular in Poland and the Baltic states, weaker countries where governments fear Russian attack. The departure of the United Kingdom—which is typically more hawkish—from the European Union has only worsened this problem. It is thus little surprise that countries in Europe are often unwilling to subordinate their defense to the supranational level. There is also no common understanding of "strategic autonomy" in European capitals. For some, it is little more than a reference to military capabilities; for others, it is about charting a multipolar course for Europe distinct from that of the United States. On his visit to Washington in 2023, the Polish prime minister, Mateusz Morawiecki, an opponent of strategic autonomy, told a think-tank gathering that they should fear the idea: "European autonomy sounds fancy, doesn't it? But it means shifting the center of European gravity towards China and severing the ties with the US."[18] The notion of strategic autonomy is increasingly loaded with geopolitical baggage and beset by tensions both among member states and between capitals and the Commission in Brussels.

Given this, a focus on capabilities is likely to be more successful in promoting burden-sharing than any attempt to knit together Europe's strategic thinking. But problems here run deeper than disagreement about strategy. It is true that European states spend too little on their defense; years of U.S. policymakers harping about European "free riding" on defense have made this point clear. It is also true that Europe's economic power has declined relative to that of the United States in the past few years, a trend driven in part by the impact of the war in Ukraine.[19] But European states will need to dig deep and spend more regardless. A clear approach to how the United States intends to disengage from the continent—consistently messaged across administrations—should help accelerate spending. This in turn will raise questions about how the money is spent. Experts generally agree that European forces have become hollowed out in recent years thanks to budget cuts. One obvious target for increased spending is thus the significant need to bring existing units and capabilities up to appropriate performance standards. But new weapons systems and investment in defense production capabilities are also needed. Even today, European states often purchase off-the-shelf weapons systems from the United States. This has much to recommend it for some European capitals: It is by far the quickest way to fill holes in European capabilities and has the benefit of tying the United States to European defense over the long term. But it also undermines the long-term development of an appropriate European defense-industrial base that can adequately produce arms and ammunition at a reasonable cost and thereby weakens future European defense capacity.[20]

Another spending problem is parochialism. When it comes to new capabilities, the same nationalist dynamics that govern strategic decisions by European capitals also govern their ability to spend wisely in a way that bolsters common defense rather than simply national priorities. It's not simply domestic protectionism and industrial policy—though that certainly plays a role. Rather, the memory of the eurozone crisis and years of disagreements over sanctions against Russia also weigh heavily, as policymakers worry about a similar period of internal disagreement and pressure being applied to states in the realm of defense. Some member states fear, very reasonably, that delegating security capabilities to other European capitals—or even to Brussels—might leave them in the lurch in the case of a hot war. This perhaps explains why various steps taken toward joint procurement and interoperability in recent years have not amounted to a significant shift in defense cooperation. One such initiative is the European Union's proposal to build a Rapid Deployment Capacity, which would attempt to build a common European capability to respond to crises in a modular fashion, applying plug-and-play units from different states.[21] The loosening of EU debt rules related to defense in recent months—a response to Donald Trump's second-term rhetoric—is likewise promising, but embryonic.

A final problem that has inhibited the development of homegrown capabilities in Europe is institutional. Should European defense be bolstered through the European Union or through NATO? This concern goes as far back as Madeleine Albright's famous "three D's," in particular, the idea that any homegrown European defense should not diminish or duplicate existing NATO capabilities, lest it undermine them.[22] Indeed, it is still common wisdom in some European capitals that bolstering the defense and security wing of the European Union might undermine NATO; countries in Eastern Europe in particular have long felt that empowering Brussels on defense might actually lead the United States to pull back. Today, it's increasingly clear that the causality points in the opposite direction: The United States may choose to dial down its presence at least in part over frustrations about burden-sharing. A poll by the Eurasia Group Foundation in 2023 found that half of all Americans want to either reduce the number of troops in Europe or withdraw all troops from Europe; almost half responded to questions about NATO's importance with concerns about burden-sharing.[23]

The institutional question is key. The European Union has a variety of institutional mechanisms that might help in the process of building out a joint European defense, particularly the development of a cross-continent defense-industrial base. It has been remarkably successful in building infrastructure for sanctions and economic statecraft in recent years. But it has never had a coherent defense and foreign policy apparatus and currently has no obvious means for joint command or decision-making in a crisis.[24] Any process to build a comprehensive EU defense will likely take decades. It may well look like the lengthy and messy processes of political compromise that eventually resulted in the Common Market and the euro. NATO, on the other hand, is substantially better positioned to defend Europe in a crisis—thanks to existing command structures—but remains heavily dependent on U.S. capabilities. Any viable path forward for European defense will need to include both an evolving role for the European Union and a gradual shifting of responsibility inside the existing structures of NATO.

A Program of Transition

The result of these myriad problems has been policy paralysis. European states remain bogged down in overarching debates about the form a common European defense would take—the recent release of the European Union's first Strategic Compass is one such example—and have failed to make real-world progress.[25] Since the start of the war in Ukraine, analysts from the London-based International Institute for Strategic Studies (IISS) have noted, "no major recapitalization of armed forces or large-scale procurement to address capability gaps have yet materialized."[26] Paradoxically, although Russia's stunning losses in Ukraine mean that there has rarely been a safer window for the transition of European security from American to European hands, it has remained easier to pass the buck to the United States than to overcome tough collective-action problems. As Sean Monaghan, an official in the British Ministry of Defense, describes,

European states face "entrenched, bureaucratic challenges to cooperation."[27] Any coherent attempt to implement this transition will require strong action from policymakers to overcome policy inertia.

The timing of transition from American to European defense responsibilities is perhaps the most critical question. A recent scholarly debate on the prospects for European defense put this problem into stark relief. A study from the IISS explored several scenarios, each of which assumed that the withdrawal of U.S. forces from Europe was sudden and would be followed by an almost immediate Russian intervention, and concluded that European states could not defend themselves. The scholar Barry Posen, however, called that calculus into question in his response, noting that it changes substantially if European states are given time to adapt to the U.S. withdrawal.[28] These debates suggest a long lead time for the transition, during which the United States gradually shifts the burden across various defense competencies to European states, rather than any sort of sudden shock. Of course, American leaders have been intimating a shift away from Europe for years now, most notably during the Obama administration's attempt to pivot to Asia.[29] It has done little thus far to bolster a European resolve to act.

For this reason, it is important for U.S. policymakers to be as clear as possible on the withdrawal process and timeline. Adding a set of concrete deadlines that are close enough to concentrate the mind, but far enough out to achieve real change, can help. Ten years is a plausible and eminently achievable target; even the IISS report—with its relatively pessimistic assumptions—argues that a sufficient recapitalization program across Europe could yield results in eight to twelve years for land-based forces, a decade for air capabilities, and fifteen to twenty years for maritime capabilities.[30] Land forces and certain air assets are the most important components of a credible European defense, particularly given that—in contrast to the IISS report's assumptions—the United States is highly likely to continue its general role as guarantor of the global maritime commons. Ten years, however, is a long time, and there will undoubtedly be questions about the credibility of American willingness to step back from Europe. This problem could not have been more clearly illustrated than by the U.S. withdrawal from Afghanistan in 2021: Many European states found themselves shocked that the Biden administration followed through on its promise to pull out of Afghanistan.[31] The U.S. commitment to dialing down its European commitments must thus be credible enough that it is taken seriously by European states; it cannot simply be a verbal rehashing of decades of burden-sharing debates.

For this reason, U.S. policymakers should commit to both a long-term drawdown of forces in Europe *and* a clear plan for how that withdrawal will be phased over time. The United States should withdraw the most easily replaced capabilities first and plan for a longer horizon on more complex capabilities. This would suggest the earlier withdrawal of U.S. infantry brigade combat teams (BCTs) and of logistics and sustainment for these forces; this should be accompanied by a transition to a European strategic allied commander. In the medium term, the United States should target the withdrawal of harder-to-replace armored BCTs, along with artillery as well as refueling and airlift capabilities. The capabilities that are the most challenging to replace—including missile and air defense and warning systems—would be among the last to depart; certain niche capabilities in the intelligence, surveillance, and reconnaissance space, along with strategic nuclear assets such as the Aegis Ashore ballistic missile defense system, may persist until or even past the fifteen-year mark. Pre-positioned matériel for U.S. forces can be repatriated, or can be sustained if U.S. policymakers wish to maintain maximum flexibility going forward.[32] This timetable should be made more credible by shifts in Pentagon spending and in the programs appropriated by Congress; defense budget documents should clearly specify what is being cut and when programs will become surplus to requirements. Perhaps most importantly, although there is room for give-and-take during this process, the United States should in general follow through with the withdrawal of appropriate capabilities regardless of whether European states step up by specified deadlines, which will increase the credibility of the overall process. At the end of this process, the United States should have relinquished almost all control over European defense, removed its ground and air forces from the continent, and returned to a largely offshore posture.

The next question is strategic. Both Europe and the United States have in recent years focused on European-level solutions to the problem of defense. Europe, in the aggregate, "has the security demands and interests of a great power," as scholars from the Center for Strategic and International

Studies (CSIS) recently noted.[33] But it is not a unified political entity. Top-down change in European defense has thus far proved disappointing at best. Instead, a viable program of burden-shifting by the United States should focus on encouraging bottom-up strategies for European defense, helping Europe's constituent states build a backstop of national defense capabilities and the structures that allow like-minded states at the sub-European level to pool those resources effectively. This is the only viable way to avoid a lowest-common-denominator approach to defense that fails to provide sufficient security for member states. This may sound counterintuitive—and for Europeans who are supportive of "ever closer union," it may be close to sacrilege. But much as the transition to the Common Market, or the transition to the euro, required European states to first reach specific levels of interconnectedness, economic development, and fiscal goals, a transition to a common security and defense policy that links European states can be based only on a foundation of strong *national* defense capabilities. Indeed, to the extent that the European Commission has built a more robust diplomatic presence in recent years, it has followed this path, building on—and co-opting—the strong diplomatic corps of its member states.

The most common criticisms of building up defense at the national level are twofold: first, that it is infeasible for Europe's smaller states to manage without French or German help, and second, that it will inevitably result in duplication and waste. But both concerns are surmountable. France, Germany, and the United Kingdom are Europe's behemoths, capable of mounting a comprehensive defense on their own. But groups of small and medium-sized states that share common threat perceptions and common interests can also be effective in pooling their resources to produce comprehensive defense capabilities. Poland, the Baltic states, and their Scandinavian neighbors form a natural grouping concerned about deterrence against Russia and about spillover of the war in Ukraine. The countries of the Black Sea region—Romania, Hungary, and others—already cooperate on maritime issues and have already engaged in cooperative work on energy and transit infrastructure through the Three Seas Initiative. Italy, Spain, Greece, Cyprus, and Malta form a natural axis concerned with migration, instability in the Middle East and North Africa, and the security of the Mediterranean Sea. And Britain, Germany, and the Scandinavian states share interests in Baltic and even Arctic security.

The idea of sub-NATO (or sub-EU) groupings based on geography and interests—which themselves tend to be strongly correlated—is not an innovation; during the Cold War, NATO used a geography-based command system. By building groupings around common threat perceptions and retaining capabilities locally—or at least subregionally—countries can mitigate some of the worst concerns associated with trying to solve the common-defense collective-action problem in Europe. Because the states involved share common threat perceptions, it is less difficult to win consent and to prioritize, and because capabilities can be pooled across countries, smaller countries are still able to benefit from economies of scale. It can also help mitigate the presence of unaligned states like Hungary and Turkey inside existing alliance structures by relegating them to a minor role and removing their veto capabilities. That said, there is also a strong role for both the European Union and NATO to play in coordinating and nurturing this process. NATO's standing bureaucracy is well equipped to help identify areas of common threat and strategic opportunity, to deconflict procurement between member states, and to avoid overlap or gaps in capabilities. The European Union, meanwhile, is well placed to encourage the creation and sustainment of a European defense-industrial base and to fund it through Eurobonds or other monetary innovations. As the authors of one recent report advocate, a process not unlike that which produced the common agricultural policy would be helpful in protecting national interests in the defense space while advancing broader European interests. The common agricultural policy may be no one's idea of a best-practice approach to governance, but when it comes to mitigating the worst impulses of nationalism to achieve broader comity on critical questions, it has been surprisingly effective.

The United States cannot ultimately be directly responsible for the choices European states make during this process. But the United States will be crucial to planning on the NATO side of this equation. U.S. policymakers can help encourage the formation of these blocs in several ways, especially through diplomatic engagement that seeks to identify appropriate partners and bring them together within the confines of the U.S. drawdown process. Perhaps more controversially, U.S. policymakers must also be willing to get out of the way of the European Union on defense-procurement issues, particularly in avoiding any insistence on a preference for U.S. arms suppliers over European suppliers during this process. Ideally, the process of building sub-NATO constellations for defense—and the involvement of both NATO and the European Union—would eventually lead to greater pan-European integration and contribute over time to a more coherent EU defense and security policy headquartered in Brussels. There is a clear public demand for this: 77 percent of respondents across Europe were in favor in one recent poll.[34] But even if this process does not result in broader supranational defense capabilities, it should still be capable of achieving homegrown European defense and deterrence at an acceptable cost—and without significant U.S. commitments. Throughout this process, policymakers should remember that American interests are best served by an effective defense of Europe; these interests do not require it to happen through any specific institutional forum. Building a common European defense may, as one author put it, be a "generational project," but the phased transition to European defense of Europe does not have to be.

Downgrading the Middle East

The Middle East has dominated U.S. foreign policy since 1991. As Andrew Bacevich, a historian and former military officer who spent much of his career in the Middle East, described in 2016: "From the end of World War II to 1980, virtually no American soldiers were killed in action while serving in that region. . . . Since 1990, virtually no American soldiers have been killed in action anywhere except in the Greater Middle East."[35] Over time, however, U.S. interests in the region have shrunk substantially, diminishing the region's importance. For almost fifteen years, policymakers have been openly acknowledging this shrinking strategic significance and attempting to "pivot" away from the region toward other global challenges.[36] But the United States is stuck in a cycle: drawing forces out of the Middle East every few years only to see new crises pull them back in. To escape this cycle requires getting back to basics: ending path-dependent deployments while clearly articulating how the United States can continue to protect its core interests in the Middle East with a primarily offshore posture. The biggest challenge in this process will be resisting the temptation to make the region a central zone of contention with China.

An Ideal (Non-)Posture

Arguments about whether the United States is over- or under-committed to the Middle East are typically obscured by the question of one's baseline. If your baseline case for American involvement in the region is 2007, at the height of the war on terror—when the United States had more than three hundred thousand troops in theater—you might well argue that America has already largely retrenched from the region. If, on the other hand, you take your baseline case to be America's posture during the 1980s or even the mid-1990s, you might well argue that the United States is still heavily militarily invested. Exact numbers are hard to come by, as Department of Defense data is notoriously opaque. News reports and press releases, however, suggest that the United States has between thirty thousand and fifty thousand troops in the region today. This number has proved remarkably resilient. Each of the past four presidents promised to retrench from the Middle East, but each has responded to crisis by maintaining or increasing U.S. commitments within this band.[37] For Barack Obama, for example, the Arab Spring and his choice to intervene in Libya undermined his ability to retrench; for Donald Trump, it was the escalatory tensions created by his "maximum pressure" policy on Iran. U.S. forces today perform a variety of missions in the region: Some train partner forces, as in Iraq, whereas others—notably deployments in Syria—are related to counterterrorism or to deterring Iran. Inertia remains a powerful driver of regional deployments, and the United States maintains major bases across the region, including an army base in Kuwait, air hubs in Qatar, Turkey, and the United Arab Emirates, and a major naval base in Bahrain, which houses the command headquarters of the U.S. Fifth Fleet.[38]

Over the next five to ten years, the United States should withdraw its ground and land forces from the Middle East and close most of its bases in the region. Some of these withdrawals can be accomplished in a short time, whereas others may require several years of coordination with local states to wind down facilities, transition out of training programs, or hand off responsibility to local forces. But there should be no conditions for these withdrawals. U.S. military planners may seek agreements with regional governments to consider transitioning a few bases to "cold" status or re-purposing them to store pre-positioned matériel for future contingencies, but this should be minimal.

When it comes to air and naval forces, the United States should also withdraw the majority of its forces but retain at least one base of each type. In the case of air forces, the purpose should primarily be transit and logistics (that is, the primary function of an air base should be U.S. global protection of the maritime commons, rather than a focus on regional contingencies). For naval forces, one mission should remain: a small force dedicated to maritime security and the protection of transit through the Strait of Hormuz and the Bab el-Mandeb Strait. Although both missions could technically be accomplished by fully offshore capabilities, there are minimal costs and risks to retaining smaller bases in these cases. The best place to maintain such bases is in the tiniest Middle Eastern states, where the governments' lack of direct military power creates a mutual interdependence between the United States and regime leaders and thereby minimizes the risks of reckless driving and entrapment by these partners. Most importantly, there are almost no cases in which the United States should directly re-engage in the region's conflicts. As discussed in the next section, many of America's goals in the Middle East are not likely to be achieved using military methods. In fifteen years, America's relationship with the region should be primarily political and economic, not military.

Appropriately Assessing U.S. Interests

By the latter half of the Cold War, America had two important priorities in the Middle East. One was preventing Soviet hegemony in the region; the other, securing the free flow of oil out of the Gulf. These two goals were fundamentally interlinked: America's ability to defend against the Soviet army in Europe and support allies elsewhere was heavily dependent on its ability to procure Middle Eastern oil, and American concerns about defending the sea lanes were linked to fears of Soviet or Soviet-allied action. The Carter Doctrine, for example—which committed the United States to repel any attempt to control the Gulf or its oil by military means—was initially a response to the Soviet invasion of Afghanistan, though it later became a justification for other uses of force.[39]

The USSR is now ancient history, and the energy question looks rather different from our early-twenty-first-century standpoint. Indeed, the landscape of global energy has shifted significantly in ways that strengthen America's energy security and undermine the energy security of our major competitor. The shale revolution and America's re-emergence as a global energy powerhouse, the advent of liquefied natural gas, the beneficial effects of NAFTA in linking regional energy infrastructure, and even the creation of national strategic oil reserves have all bolstered the U.S. position. Certainly, some American allies—notably, Japan and South Korea—remain highly dependent on Middle Eastern oil. And so long as oil is traded on global markets, America will remain vulnerable to fluctuations in oil prices. But America no longer must fear an actual shortage of fuel in a time of conflict; energy-security fears have diminished, though they will never entirely vanish.[40]

Over time, America's perceived interests in the region have grown to include a variety of other issues: nuclear nonproliferation, counterterrorism, democracy promotion, support for Israel, and maintaining regional stability. Some of these "interests" conflate means and ends. Others, including counterterrorism and democracy promotion, were added during the heady unipolar moment. As goals, they were in many ways laudable, but it would be a stretch to call them vital U.S. national security interests. It has also become increasingly clear that these goals cannot be achieved through military means; a significant body of research now shows that effective regime change and democracy promotion are extremely hard to achieve through force.[41] In some cases, America's goals have been worsened by the use of military force.

Take nonproliferation. As the Nobel laureate Thomas Schelling explained in 2006, U.S. policies designed to prevent proliferation—most notably the invasion of Iraq—have created regime-security fears that themselves are a prime driver of nuclear proliferation.[42] Dictators who see the fates of Saddam Hussein or Muammar Qadhafi are more likely to develop a nuclear deterrent and less likely to give it up. Or consider counterterrorism. The United States has enjoyed moderate military success against al Qaeda, ISIS, and other groups, but has also fomented regional backlash and has proved incapable of resolving the underlying societal causes of radicalization. Even non-military means of achieving these goals have often proved challenging—as the backlash created in states like Egypt by U.S. civilian democracy-promotion programs attests.

In short: The United States should continue to use diplomacy and other non-coercive tools to address humanitarian or economic concerns (for example, development, women's rights, or refugee policy), but such concerns cannot and should not form the core of our strategy toward the Middle East. In the case of nonproliferation, the United States should use a combination of moderate sanctions relief and multilateral diplomacy to push Iran to freeze its nuclear program and avoid a proliferation spiral in the region; pressure should also be brought to bear on more friendly states such as Turkey and Saudi Arabia to resist proliferation. More broadly, it is time for the United States to once again narrow its stated interests in the region to two core goals: maintaining the free flow of oil to world markets and preventing another state's hegemony in the Gulf, whether that state is a member of the region or an outside party like China. Fortunately, these are both relatively easy tasks.

As we have already discussed, energy security is a decreasing concern for the United States and one that scholars generally agree can be attained with low levels of military commitment to the region or even via an over-the-horizon posture (that is, with military forces stationed outside the region itself).[43] A small U.S. naval presence in the region, of sufficient size to manage threats to shipping, should be more than up to this task. At the same time, both the geography of the region and current politics suggest that the risk of a potential in-region hegemon is low. America's destruction of Iraq's military capabilities and the slow decline of Egyptian military capacity over the past few decades have removed two of the most notable threats to regional stability. Iran's network of regional proxies is effective at fomenting chaos, but the country is not capable of conquering its neighbors.[44] The petrostates of the Gulf—most notably, Saudi Arabia—are wealthy and exceedingly well armed but are not populous enough to be true military contenders, and other states are too isolated (Israel) or too distant (Turkey) to dominate the region. This doesn't imply that conflict will not happen—just view the post–October 7 chaos in the region—but rather that it isn't likely to be particularly consequential for the regional balance of power. As the political scientist Eugene Gholz describes it, the Middle East is "generally a region of low-competence conventional militaries."[45] In the absence of a significant U.S. troop presence, regional states will balance against each other.

The remaining concern is China, which in recent years has built commercial ties with Middle Eastern states on a strong foundation of energy links. This has enabled it to expand its regional political and economic portfolio from a relatively narrow focus on Iran to more balanced engagement with all states of the region.⁴⁶ Today, China's position vis-à-vis the Middle East increasingly resembles that of the United States in the 1980s: a heavy dependence on Middle Eastern oil, strong political and economic ties with regional states, and concerns about the ability of a rival to control the flow of energy. The U.S. position is far stronger and is more analogous to that of the USSR: strong domestic energy production bolstering security. For the United States, it is enough to retain a minimal military presence, along with more significant economic and diplomatic links in the region, to prevent Chinese dominance. This is particularly true given the potential for conflict if China believes that its energy supplies are excessively threatened by the U.S. military presence. Policymakers thus need to maintain a balanced approach to the region, one that does not create a significant threat to Chinese interests—and thereby spark a conflict—but that also maintains regional influence. Threading this needle will be the most difficult part of U.S. policy toward the region in coming decades.

Facing Facts

Attempts to reshape U.S. force posture in the Middle East into something leaner and more efficient are nothing new. The Obama administration in its second term focused on the development of what became known as the "light footprint" approach. The administration sought to rely on smaller deployments, more evenly spread across the region at small "lily pad" bases and with a strong focus on supporting Special Forces and intelligence, surveillance, and reconnaissance for counterterrorism. Donald Trump promised that U.S. troops would no longer engage in nation-building. The Biden administration, in turn, entered office promising to undertake a "global posture review," a core goal of which was to figure out how to "right-size its [America's] forward military presence in the Middle East."⁴⁷ Path dependence, however, has restrained these changes, and the number of troops in the region has remained relatively stable since 2014. Over time, it has become apparent that this low-cost light-footprint approach may in fact be worse than the alternatives, making U.S. troops on small bases a target for local militias and proxy groups, and leaving them vulnerable to Iranian missile attacks. This has rendered many of these deployments pointless at best, and actively harmful at worst. The majority of U.S. troops at some smaller bases in Iraq and Syria today are engaged primarily in force protection for *their own bases,* even as they face the routine risk of death.

Indeed, many of the functions that U.S. troops perform in the Middle East could be done from over the horizon or in conjunction with partners. Administrations, however, have balked at reducing these deployments, the Department of Defense seeing the maintenance of "presence" in the region as an end unto itself. This is a broader problem with more general implications for U.S. force readiness—even outside the Middle East. As Bob Work, a former deputy secretary of defense, put it a few years back: "A slavish devotion to forward presence has nearly broken the U.S. Navy."[48] Similar problems of over-exhaustion plague U.S. Special Forces and the U.S. Air Force.[49] The Middle East—as the region where presence yields the fewest benefits and carries the biggest potential costs—is thus also the most logical place to push back on the narrative that U.S. presence is a stabilizing force in and of itself. In fact, there's virtually no need for any ground forces in the Middle East; U.S. basing policy should reflect that. The United States should close its major army bases in the region, including those in Jordan, Turkey, Kuwait, and Iraq. U.S. troops should be withdrawn from Syria. To hedge against future conflict, policymakers might designate one or two smaller locations for the storage of pre-positioned matériel. But unlike in Europe, where the process of retrenchment will be lengthy and complex, in the Middle East the complete drawdown of American ground forces could be achieved in less than five years; indeed, some regional states such as Iraq might be keen to see the United States go.

Naval and air assets pose somewhat more complex questions, particularly given the role of the navy in protecting the flow of energy supplies. The United States currently maintains the forward operating headquarters of the Fifth Fleet in Bahrain, which includes a variety of naval assets, from strike groups to de-mining and intelligence capabilities. For much of the past few decades, the Fifth Fleet also included one or even two aircraft carriers, but that is no longer necessarily the case.[50] This naval presence should shrink further and instead emphasize the specific niche capabilities required to monitor, patrol, and keep key waterways open. Such capabilities would include intelligence assets, mine-clearing capabilities, air and surface patrols, and air defense systems.[51] Indeed, though he argues for a fully offshore presence, Gholz is essentially right when he argues that "the goal for U.S. strategy in the Persian Gulf should be to provide a few particular military capabilities that might tip the balance against an aggressor."[52] Maintaining this smaller naval force in the Gulf should be accompanied by a shift from a heavy focus on Iran and the Strait of Hormuz to a more general focus on the major regional waterways, including the Suez Canal and the Bab el-Mandeb Strait. Ideally, this would involve improved coordination—and perhaps even a joint command structure—with U.S. bases across the Gulf of Aden, particularly Camp Lemonnier in Djibouti, where a focus on anti-piracy is ultimately part of the same mission set. The connection to anti-piracy efforts might also help reassure Beijing that America is earnest in its assertions about free and open sea lanes.

When it comes to air assets, the question is less about the forces required for in-region strikes or reconnaissance and more about whether Middle Eastern bases are needed for global military logistics. Indeed, apart from the air assets required for the protection of sea lanes, there is no real need for any significant forward-deployed strike force in the region. But the United States does benefit from maintaining an air base in the Gulf that can be used as a transit point connecting Europe, the Indo-Pacific, and the United States. As Renanah Miles Joyce and Brian Blankenship, academics who study the politics of military bases, put it, "Because projecting power is logistically intensive, and becomes even harder when moving troops and materiel across bodies of water, great powers seek access to foreign territory to station, deploy, and resupply military forces."[53] Such bases are in many ways fundamentally different from most existing U.S. Middle Eastern—or even European—deployments in that they do not require a significant number of personnel or a significant amount of matériel to sustain. They are not home to "tripwire forces" that could spark a conflict, and they are focused not on regional contingencies but rather on the maintenance of U.S. capabilities globally. The United States should thus seek to retain one air base (or at most two) of this kind in the relatively stable states of the Gulf.

The locations of the remaining air and naval bases in the region are surprisingly flexible. Existing bases in Bahrain and Qatar are perhaps the most logical locations, but there is no reason why other options cannot also be considered. The key is to maximize U.S. utility while minimizing risk. Of course, as Joyce and Blankenship point out, foreign bases are a tool of geopolitics, on both sides.[54] Host states are often looking for benefits over and above monetary compensation, including the implicit guarantee of U.S. military protection. It would be best, then, to maintain bases in the smallest, most geopolitically independent states, where U.S. political leverage is likely to be greatest and the risks of being pulled into a conflict are smallest. Qatar and Oman are the most obvious candidates. Oman in particular would make an excellent host for a newer naval base; the Port of Duqm is located just outside the straits and is potentially deep enough to host an aircraft carrier.[55] It is also outside the range of most Iranian missiles. A shift over time from Bahrain to that port would be warranted; splitting the force is also a possibility.[56] Regardless, any host country should commit to not also allowing a Chinese base, something that has been problematic in Djibouti. The United States may not be able to prevent a Chinese naval presence in the Gulf, but it can at least avoid open competition for bases.

The Curious Case of the al-Tanf Garrison

Sometime in 2016, the U.S. military—then engaged in the counter-ISIS campaign—came into possession of a military base and border crossing at al-Tanf in Syria, an area at the intersection of the Jordanian, Iraqi, and Syrian borders. By 2018, though official information about the base was limited, a series of news stories reported that several hundred U.S. troops were at the base training Syrian rebels; that those forces had frequently engaged in skirmishes with Iranian and Syrian government proxies in the fifty-five-kilometer "deconfliction zone" surrounding the base; and that the base was serving as a launching pad for special operations forces on counterterrorism missions.

But as the campaign against ISIS wound down, questions about when the United States would be leaving al-Tanf were largely met with deaf ears. In the first Trump administration, the base—and America's broader efforts in Syria—became a point of significant contention between the president and his advisers. Trump himself was committed to withdrawing all U.S. troops from Syria, but Defense Secretary Jim Mattis, along with two of his national security advisers (H. R. McMaster and later John Bolton), sought to persuade Trump that U.S. forces at al-Tanf were vital for pressure on Iran, and—in perhaps the most ridiculous sleight of hand ever waged by staffers on a president—persuaded Trump that the base was helpful for his stated objective of seizing Syria's oil. His advisers argued that al-Tanf—with its critical position on major roads and borders inside Syria—could be a crucial part of U.S. opposition to the creation of an Iranian "Shia crescent" linking its forces in Iran, Syria, and Lebanon.

This rationale spread quickly. As General Joseph Votel, head of Central Command, put it at the time: "We don't have a counter Iranian mission here. We have a defeat ISIS mission. But I do recognize that our presence, our development of partners and relationships down here does have an indirect effect on some malign activities that Iran and their various proxies and surrogates would like to pursue down here."[57] By 2023, it had become clear that the base was effectively permanent. And yet no one could really explain why. As Colonel Dan Magruder of the U.S. Air Force put it in a Brookings Institution report, there are several potential reasons for maintaining the garrison at al-Tanf, including "interdicting ISIS remnants, disrupting the Syrian economy and Iranian influence," and taking advantage of it "for political leverage in negotiations."[58] These are not particularly persuasive rationales. Worse, the base has become a magnet for rocket attacks by militant groups in Iraq and Syria—"a bull's eye," as the *Economist* described it, "for Iranian-backed groups whenever they want to lash out at America."[59] One diplomat, quoted in the same article, described al-Tanf as little more than a "vestigial limb."[60]

The story of the al-Tanf garrison is in miniature the story of U.S. attempts to retrench from the Middle East: bureaucratic politics enabled by inertia; attempts to find new rationales to fit existing commitments when old rationales disappear; and policy continuity even when strategic realities suggest that a change is warranted. As we have explored in this chapter, in both Europe and the Middle East, alliances, partnerships, and deployments today resemble less a promising tool for policymakers and more a dead albatross weighing down the ability of U.S. policymakers to focus on pressing issues. Both regions have become less strategically significant over time, particularly in comparison with the Indo-Pacific. Yet American policy remains hobbled by path dependence. In both Europe and the Middle East, the key task for policymakers looking to create a more realist foreign policy is to break the cycle of inertia. This may require difficult initial choices, some of which may require confronting or challenging key bureaucratic or congressional constituencies. But these changes are necessary if the United States is to truly build a sustainable strategy that corresponds to global strategic realities. The alternative—as the curious case of the never-ending deployment at al-Tanf shows—is a world in which U.S. alliances or bases that were once strategic assets continue to transform over time into strategic burdens.

6

Lean Forward

National security strategy documents are rarely controversial. It's even rarer that they attract attention outside the D.C. bubble. But the 2017 national security strategy—Donald Trump's first real foray into the realm of strategy—was closely watched around the world for how it might seek to smooth the rough edges off the president's rhetoric and turn his often contradictory public statements into a coherent strategic vision of the world. It was no surprise to anyone that the document broke with its predecessors in several ways, reframing foreign policy not around win-win liberal internationalism but around the more hard-nosed concept of great power competition. The language in the document, however, went far further than many had expected. "It is increasingly clear," the national security strategy document argued, "that China and Russia want to shape a world consistent with their authoritarian model—gaining veto authority over other nations' economic, diplomatic, and security decisions." China, a related strategy document argued, seeks "Indo-Pacific regional hegemony in the near-term and displacement of the United States to achieve global preeminence in the future."[1] Previous administrations had been careful to frame relations with China in cautious and cooperative terms; for the new Trump administration, it was time to throw caution to the wind.

Unlike almost every other Trump initiative, this one was wholeheartedly embraced in Washington. Over the four years of Trump's first term, Washington's chattering classes made an almost 180-degree turn on the

U.S.-China relationship, its risks, and its promises. Ten years ago, the conventional wisdom in Washington held that engagement with China could undermine the risks created by a rising Asian mega-state. Some true believers posited a bastardized version of modernization theory, arguing that Chinese growth and openness to the world would precipitate political liberalization inside China. Others pinned their hopes on the entangling effects of economic interdependence as a constraint not only on China's bellicosity but also on its willingness to upset the applecart of international order. The fundamental bet at the heart of D.C.'s "responsible stakeholder" theory was simple: China, if sufficiently enmeshed in the existing web of postwar international institutions and trading arrangements, would come to support the existing order rather than challenge it.[2]

Today, that thesis has been almost entirely debunked, and there are few who do not see some kind of threat rising from Beijing's growing capabilities and economic power. Indeed, the concept of competition has become so integral to Washington that, as the *Atlantic* recently put it, we're now debating "whether or not to brand the competition with China a 'cold war' rather than interrogating our fixation on competition in the first place."[3] But the fundamental questions about the U.S.-China relationship—what threat does a rising China pose to the United States? and what should the U.S. role in Asia be?—remain contested. This chapter shifts from retrenchment to engagement and argues that America must step up in Asia if it is to provide a viable alternative to growing Chinese power in the region. Military and security engagement cannot be the only component of this strategy; America must find ways to offer plausible economic and diplomatic incentives to the states of the region. This chapter first explores the challenging military situation in the Indo-Pacific before zooming out to discuss the rise of geo-economics and its role in U.S. strategy toward China—and the world.

Walking a Fine Line in the Indo-Pacific

Asia—or the Indo-Pacific, as it has now been rebranded—is the most challenging region for U.S. foreign policy and our biggest priority. It is also the region where the prescriptions of many realists diverge from their more restrained counterparts and converge more with the mainstream. Indeed, America's policy priorities in the region should be maintaining a free and open Indo-Pacific and enabling regional states to resist Chinese hegemony, keeping America anchored in the region. Although this may sound superficially similar to the policies pursued by recent administrations, it should instead be a primarily non-military strategy, one that elevates economic and diplomatic tools of statecraft while policymakers take great care that their attempts to maintain a U.S. foothold in Asia do not unintentionally spiral into conflict with China.

An Ideal Posture Doesn't Trip the Security Dilemma

America's current approach to Asian security presents dilemmas similar to those the country faces in other regions, yet the context is radically different. As in Europe and the Middle East, the United States has been regionally dominant—even hegemonic—in Asia in recent decades. Unlike in Europe or the Middle East, however, in Asia the challenge of finding a new, post-unipolar normal is substantially complicated by the rise of a potential peer competitor in China. China's economic heft and its growing military capabilities suggest that it has the potential to become not only a regional hegemon but a global superpower competitor to the United States in coming decades. America's current posture in the region is not well suited to this emerging challenge; that is particularly so for American land forces in Japan and South Korea, which are primarily postured to deal with the threat from North Korea. America's current alliance structure is also challenging; it is significantly more fragmented than in Europe, where NATO, for all its flaws, provides a unifying framework within which U.S. policymakers can work. The primary areas of security concern for the United States in Asia, meanwhile, involve contested sea lanes, small islands, and multiple countries, where unclear boundaries and demarcations raise the risks of misunderstanding and conflict. Indeed, as Øystein Tunsjø has pointed out, Asia's maritime geography suggests that any great power competition there would necessarily be less stable and less predictable than the static lines of Cold War defense were.[4]

In this challenging environment, policymakers must thread the needle between pulling back too far—thus implicitly ceding Asia to Chinese influence—and leaning too far forward, thereby provoking security spirals and potential conflict. They must preserve maximum freedom of maneuver for America in the future without provoking war in the near term. This will be no easy task. Burden-sharing and a limited American military presence—with a heavy focus on the maritime domain—is the most plausible solution to this dilemma. In fifteen years, the U.S. posture in Asia should be built on a foundation of strong, self-reliant allies capable of deterrence. The United States should have fewer troops on the Korean peninsula, but potentially more maritime and air assets located on Guam, on Diego Garcia, and potentially in Singapore. Most importantly, policymakers must resist placing security at the heart of American policy toward Asian states, and must instead keep appropriate capabilities as a backstop for military contingencies while engaging economically and politically with the region, something we explore further in the second half of this chapter. America's primary security concern in Asia may indeed be China, yet that is primarily a function of our fear that China might be able to restrict our access to the rest of Asia. Given that context, there is no point in a strategy that antagonizes or alienates regional states simply to push back on China. American policy toward Asia could be viewed as a success if the next few decades see the United States maintain or expand its political and economic ties with the region—without provoking a major war.

Answering the Big Questions

The contours of Washington's approach to China have become sharper in recent years as the policy community has shifted from an approach that leaned toward accommodation—emphasizing China's rise as a "responsible stakeholder"—to one that is openly confrontational and has attempted to contain Chinese economic growth and global influence. This was a notably sudden shift. As Ryan Hass, who was China director on the National Security Council during this period, noted: "In the span of 24 months, the official policy of the United States shifted from viewing China as a potential partner with whom it would need to manage critical differences to an entrenched rival that seeks to harm the United States. Rarely, if ever before has U.S. policy on an issue of such strategic significance shifted so sharply in such a short period and in the absence of any form of militarized conflict."[5] This shift resulted from the conjunction of several distinct factors. Growing assertiveness from Beijing was undoubtedly one factor, but domestic American politics also played a major role.

The pandemic shock, which originated in Wuhan in 2020—where the spread of the Covid-19 virus was clearly enabled by a Chinese government cover-up—added to the general sense that China's leaders could not be trusted. Today, there is broad agreement in Washington that China poses some level of threat to the United States; the big question is what *kind* of threat a rising China poses, and more crucially, how the United States should respond. There is no consensus on these challenging questions.

At the simplest level, China poses the same threat that any rising power in a critical region poses to the United States: It could potentially become a regional hegemon and—eventually—pose a threat to the U.S. homeland. As discussed in chapter 4, however, the links between regional hegemony and an actual threat to U.S. interests are often fuzzier than assumed. Regional hegemons may gain significant "freedom to roam," and it is certainly conceivable that Chinese hegemony in Asia might allow it to build capabilities that could eventually give it a foothold in the Western Hemisphere.[6] Yet observers also generally acknowledge that Asia is not a conducive environment for territorial conquest; the predominantly maritime environment means that China will find it increasingly difficult to engage in territorial seizure as it moves away from its own borders. The conquest of Taiwan would be challenging, but feasible; the conquest of Japan or the Philippines would be an order of magnitude more difficult. China's ability to achieve territorial hegemony in Asia is thus sharply delimited by the stopping power of water; the country is no USSR, ready to roll across borders and seize the heartlands of industrial Europe.

For U.S. interests, therefore, the most pressing concern may be some form of "soft regional hegemony" that combines Chinese territorial control with political and economic coercive power. In past centuries, for example, China held a near hegemonic role in East Asia through a tributary system in which regional states acted as commercial and military vassals for Chinese interests. A key fear of more hawkish defense analysts in Washington is that—in the absence of a suitably assertive American posture in East or Southeast Asia—regional states will choose to bandwagon with China, recreating a modern version of this system and excluding the United States from the politics and economics of the region.[7] Though such an outcome is by no means assured, America's efforts to prevent Chinese hegemony in Asia must hedge against this possibility.

The extent of Chinese revisionism is also unclear. Like many rising powers, China is clearly revisionist in some areas of its policy, seeking changes in the regional and global status quo that better accommodate its own interests.[8] Taiwan and islands in the South and East China Seas are also clearly elements of Chinese revisionism. But outside East Asia, the extent of that revisionism is unknown. Some argue that it is limited to institutions and prestige and does not include territorial or extra-regional ambitions, but others—including a range of books from the scholarly to the conspiratorial—argue that Chinese leaders want regional or global domination.[9] They believe, as the Princeton professor Aaron Friedberg puts it, that "China is trying to replace the United States as the world's leading economic and technological nation and to displace it as the preponderant power in East Asia."[10] The most we can really say is that the question of Beijing's ultimate intentions remains open.[11] As Alastair Johnston describes, rather than seeking to overturn it, China has largely been challenging the existing system from the inside: "It is hard to conclude that China is a clearly revisionist state operating outside, or barely inside, the boundaries of a so-called international community."[12] This, in a nutshell, is the key dilemma facing U.S. policymakers: Simply assuming unbridled revisionism on the part of China shuts off a variety of plausible policy responses and risks overreaction and conflict, but assuming the opposite is also dangerous and leaves the United States potentially vulnerable in decades to come. Although most approaches to this question therefore attempt—implicitly or explicitly—to assess the extent of Chinese revisionism before defining an appropriate posture for the United States, drawing "inferences about a state's intentions from its military posture" is, as Bob Jervis has noted, a near impossible task.[13]

Ultimately, the only way to handle this dilemma is to be proactive about defining U.S. interests, rather than simply reacting to Chinese actions or our perceptions of China's intentions. As the scholar Jessica Chen Weiss points out, this has long been a problem in U.S.-Asia policy. "Without a clear sense of what it seeks," she notes, "U.S. foreign policy has become reactive, spinning in circles, rather than steering toward a desired destination."[14] The core purpose of U.S. foreign policy toward Asia is not to regain regional military hegemony, something that is in any case likely impossible. Nor should it be an obsessive focus on preventing any Chinese gains.

Instead, the U.S. focus must be on maintaining a favorable balance of power that supports core U.S. interests.[15] In crises, U.S. policymakers should avoid direct conflict when U.S. interests do not warrant the costs of war. In peacetime, they should focus on maintaining access, building good relationships across the region, and avoiding any suggestion that the goal of the United States is regime change in Beijing. Each of these will help hedge against the worst potential outcomes of China's rise and mitigate the risks of direct conflict.

Perhaps the most important component of this approach to the region is seeing it *as* a region rather than as a ground for U.S.-China contestation. Past administrations have at least nodded in this direction. Consider the Obama administration's negotiation of the Trans-Pacific Partnership, or the first Trump administration's embrace of the Japanese "Indo-Pacific" framework for the region.[16] Both of these, however, were really as much about China as anything else: building a regional trade bloc that would exclude China, and attempting to fold India—China's most obvious regional counterbalance—into the East Asian security order. Policymakers must engage with the region on its own merits too. Such engagement should include assistance to regional states in developing their own defensive capabilities and building connections among themselves, as well as economic and diplomatic engagement with existing regional forums such as the Association of Southeast Asian Nations (ASEAN).

This means that, despite our focus here on military questions, U.S. policy toward Asia cannot be only about security affairs. As Evan Feigenbaum of the Carnegie Endowment puts it, the United States has often been too focused on "reinforcing our security role while allowing the economic pillar of our leadership to atrophy." He refers to the potential for the United States to become the "Hessians of Asia," attractive only to regional states because of its military capabilities.[17] Such a narrow regional profile—one focused purely on security—is less durable and less resilient than a broad strategy of U.S. engagement with the region. In a nutshell, if the United States wishes to prevent Chinese hegemony in Asia, the best way to do so is to foster a vibrant multipolar regional order, an approach that has the added benefit of allowing the United States to hedge against the rise of future potential threats.

An Issue-Driven Regional Approach

In Asia, as in our other regions, U.S. force posture should be determined not by path dependence but by the role that military force or deterrence might play in specific contingencies. In general, America's posture in Asia should be built on a foundation of strong, self-reliant allies capable of deterrence, including a Taiwanese "porcupine" defense, a stronger, more resilient Japan, and an engaged Australia and India. Unlike in Europe and the Middle East, however, in Asia there is still an active role for U.S. military power. The United States should have fewer troops on the Korean peninsula, but it should have more maritime and air assets at existing bases on Guam and Diego Garcia and potential new bases in Singapore and elsewhere. Ultimately, however, the specifics of U.S. force posture in Asia are less important than answering questions about specific regional issues and how risks can be mitigated over time, through the development of either U.S. or allied capabilities.

In practice, much of the debate over U.S.-China tensions already centers on Taiwan, the one place where Chinese intentions to alter the status quo are clear and where U.S. interests are not necessarily sufficient to warrant a conflict. This is certainly not a new problem. As Ryan Hass and Jude Blanchette put it bluntly, "Taiwan has long been the issue that threatens to bring the United States and China into open conflict."[18] But in recent years, the balance of power in the Taiwan Strait has been shifting, and it is no longer the case that the United States would necessarily win such a war.[19] This has led some in Washington to argue that the United States must make a clear commitment to defend Taiwan and must improve U.S. military capabilities to that end; in effect, this would mean abandoning America's historic posture of "strategic ambiguity" toward the island. These advocates typically make one of two specific arguments to support their case.

The first of these is a loose kind of domino theory, the Cold War–era notion that the loss of a single state to communism could precipitate a wave of further losses. If Taiwan were to fall to Chinese invasion or blockade, proponents argue, other regional states would become fearful of U.S. abandonment and begin to cozy up to Beijing, making it harder for the United States to build or maintain any regional anti-China coalition.[20] They also contend that an uncontested Chinese takeover of Taiwan—which has an ambiguous status as a U.S. security partner—could be the first step in China's regional "salami slicing." During the Cold War, "salami slicing" referred to the idea that the Soviet Union might engage in small, relatively minor territorial aggressions, forcing Western states to either escalate over minor stakes or risk death by a thousand cuts. Some argue that an insufficient U.S. response to a Taiwan invasion could open the door for a Chinese conquest of parts of Vietnam or other non-U.S.-treaty allies. The second argument is more concrete and focuses on the military implications of allowing Taiwan to fall to China. Thanks to the island's central location on the edge of the first island chain, control of Taiwan would give China military advantages in the region's waters and make it more challenging for U.S. forces to secure the remaining states in the region.[21] In a nutshell: Chinese control would solidify Beijing's control of the seas inside the so-called first island chain, a geographic line that runs from Japan down toward Indonesia, and give China access to ports that can more easily reach the waters of the second island chain and the broader Pacific Ocean.

Neither argument is entirely persuasive. The first relies heavily on assumptions about credibility and the domestic politics of U.S. partners in the region. In many ways, this is emblematic of the way that many in Washington often talk about credibility: as a globalized phenomenon in which any failure or weakness by the United States anywhere around the world necessarily calls into question America's security commitments everywhere. Yet academic research suggests that this is not how credible commitments work in practice: States consider the specifics of each case when assessing credibility.[22] Thus, although one could argue that in the case of Taiwan, a relatively uncontested Chinese takeover might cause states near China to fear that the United States holds a similar view of their own independence, such fears are far from guaranteed. Views from within the region today suggest that although many regional states fear China, they nonetheless view Taiwan as a relatively ambiguous issue that raises questions of sovereignty. Major U.S. allies in the region would not necessarily contribute in their own right to the defense of Taiwan and are likely to be more hesitant to challenge a Chinese blockade.[23] As Mike Mazarr and Patrick Porter have argued, the idea that "the United States should consider the security of Taiwan a vital or even existential interest and promise unequivocally to defend Taiwan rel[ies] on implausible assertions about what will happen in the event an attack succeeds."[24]

The second argument is more persuasive. The waters within the first island chain are already contested between the United States and China; any Chinese action to seize Taiwan would cause significant disruptions to shipping regardless of the U.S. response. But there is a significant difference between the interior of the first island chain and the interior of the second island chain when it comes to trade and maritime access, which suggests that the primary concern of U.S. policymakers should not necessarily be maintaining contested waters up to China's shores, but rather maintaining freedom of navigation within the second island chain.[25] In this light, the fall of Taiwan might shift the regional military balance and undermine U.S. capabilities within the second island chain. "Chinese control of Taiwan," as one pair of analysts describe it, "would likely improve the military balance in China's favor because of reunification's positive impact on Chinese submarine warfare and ocean surveillance capabilities."[26] Yet fighting a war over Taiwan simply to preserve the ability to fight more effectively in the future is the antithesis of the logic of offshore balancing. Any attempt to defend Taiwan could easily escalate to a broader U.S.-China war; indeed, many analyses or war games conclude that the defense of Taiwan would likely require U.S. strikes on the Chinese mainland.[27] But America does not actually need Taiwan to fight its way back onshore in Asia, or even to defend other assets within the region. Such arguments also typically discount the potential costs to China of seizing Taiwan by force. To quote Porter and Mazarr again, "Even assuming a successful landing and breakout . . . an invasion would likely plunge China into complex urban warfare and counterinsurgency."[28] China might be in a more advantageous geographic position, but its overall military capabilities would likely be weaker for a significant time after any invasion of Taiwan.

Fortunately, the choice is not a binary one between war with China or losing Taiwan. Instead, there are a variety of middle options that seek to enable Taiwan to defend itself. The most promising of these is the "porcupine" approach, which would use a variety of low-cost air- and sea-denial capabilities—weapons that aim solely to make conquest more difficult—to turn Taiwan into an impregnable stronghold. The United States should restrict sales of relatively useless prestige and symmetric warfare capabilities such as high-end fighter jets or tanks to Taiwan, and instead push the island to stockpile armaments, build up its own domestic manufacturing capabilities, and focus its doctrine and training on denial and irregular warfare.[29] At the heart of this strategy is an unpleasant fact: Many of Taiwan's existing capabilities would not survive a first wave assault by China. Yet the island is naturally defensible, and as James Timbie and James Ellis have written, "distributed, survivable, and affordable defenses could greatly complicate an attempt to invade Taiwan by the People's Liberation Army."[30] Enabling Taiwan to defend itself could potentially raise the costs of invasion or blockade so high that China is deterred from action. U.S. policymakers—particularly those in Congress—should use their considerable influence and effective veto power over arms sales to push Taiwan toward more useful equipment and should make clear to Taiwanese leaders that the United States retains its commitment to strategic ambiguity.

Elsewhere in Asia, territorial questions are easier to answer. The United States would have a strong interest in defending Japan, the Philippines, or South Korea from China. These scenarios, however, are relatively far-fetched and are most likely out of reach of China's capabilities for at least the next few decades. The biggest challenges are in the maritime space. Chinese efforts to engage in island building inside the first island chain may expand China's air defense perimeter and its ability to project force. This is concerning even when it does not infringe upon the sovereign territory of other regional states. In the Spratly and Paracel Islands, for example, China has constructed half a dozen bases, several capable of hosting air strips and visiting ships, which has expanded its reach in the South China Sea.[31] Yet there is little the United States can do to push back on these developments other than continue to treat these waters as contested and reject China's assertions of its newfound maritime claims.

Potentially more troubling are the tensions between China and various U.S. regional partners over island features such as the Second Thomas Shoal (contested between China and the Philippines), and the Diaoyu Islands (contested between Japan and China). Here again, the question of alliance security commitments arises. The United States has existing commitments to Japanese, South Korean, and Philippine territory. It makes little sense to abrogate these commitments; if any of these countries *proper* were threatened by Chinese invasion, U.S. interests would compel it to act. But although U.S. security commitments are not technically assumed to apply to many of the contested territories above, they have often been interpreted as doing so by policymakers. The islands in question are almost uniformly unimportant in a strategic sense, but the active push and pull of Chinese and regional navies around them could easily act as a flash point for broader conflict. In conducting a broader recalibration of alliances, policymakers should be clear that U.S. security guarantees do not extend to disputed maritime features, and should be exceedingly cautious about supporting allies in the context of disputes over marginal territorial features. Ultimately, these features are not worth the risk of war; they would rise to the level of critical interests of the United States only if they suddenly enabled China to threaten Japan or to impede America's access to sea lanes.[32] Neither is likely.

Over the long term, the United States also needs to engage with regional states—particularly Japan, South Korea, the Philippines, and Australia—on bolstering their own domestic defense capabilities. Much as U.S. deterrence against the Soviet Union during the Cold War was significantly aided by the contributions of states such as West Germany, America's commitments to Asian states will be far more credible and plausible if accompanied by capacity building on the part of partners. Japan has begun to take promising early steps toward rebuilding its military capabilities, including making the necessary constitutional changes and increasing its military spending to a level that will soon place it third in global rankings. Japan's lengthy period of underinvestment leaves many capabilities missing or underdeveloped.[33] U.S. policymakers should strongly encourage the development of anti-air and anti-ship capabilities that are best suited for territorial defense, along with long-range strike and naval capabilities.[34] Thanks to geography, Japan is ideally situated to hinder China's ability to completely dominate the interior of the first island chain, and to complement America's regional presence.[35]

In South Korea, things are complicated by the legacy of the Korean War, which technically never ended, and the twenty-eight thousand U.S. troops that remain there as a result. These troops could easily be replaced by South Korean forces; the country already spends a significant amount on advanced defense capabilities. A U.S. withdrawal would not destabilize the situation on the Korean peninsula, and could reduce some of the risks that come from the presence of so many U.S. troops so close to China. Large, concentrated troop deployments in Asia offer few benefits in the case of future conflict and could even prompt a Chinese first strike.[36] Even as the United States draws down its ground forces in South Korea, however, it should continue to focus on building out and diversifying base access for its naval needs in the region, with a particular focus on Indonesia, Malaysia, and Singapore.[37] Policymakers should widely disperse U.S. forces across the region and seek to harden base infrastructure. They should also prioritize redundancy wherever possible.[38] Even within NATO, base access for certain military operations has proved to be problematic in recent decades (for example, Turkish opposition to the fight against ISIS). With many Asian states taking divergent stances on specific regional contingencies (for example, Taiwan), redundancy in bases may prove essential in the future.[39]

The question of India remains an interesting one. India is increasingly popular in the Pentagon as a potential regional bulwark against China. But many scholars with expertise in the politics and the security dynamics of the subcontinent are more skeptical of India's long-term trajectory as a U.S. partner and worry about U.S. "overconfidence in strategic alignment" with India.[40] The rise of a relatively virulent form of Hindu nationalism under the Modi government in India, combined with growing repression against Muslims, and the potential for territorial disputes with its neighbors all suggest that India is far from the ideal partner. And then there is the question of future growth. Although India is relatively far from being able to compete with major regional powers in Asia, it is a populous, fast-growing country whose potential growth trajectory could resemble that of China. Long-range forecasts suggest that India's economy could even overtake the U.S. economy by midcentury.[41] This raises the complex question for policymakers of what a rising Indian power might mean for regional security. Indeed, perhaps the worst decision that U.S. policymakers could make would be to engage in a multi-decade competition with China while supporting India's rise, only to face similar concerns about Indian regional hegemony. Policymakers should therefore be cautious in their reliance on India. The partnership should remain largely transactional, and the United States should be careful not to let military cooperation agreements—particularly the highly touted "Quad" arrangement—progress to the point of an actual defense commitment.[42] Indeed, this principle should be applied much more broadly: One of America's biggest assets in Asia is its continued flexibility. Unlike in Europe, where the U.S. must contend with an ossified and unchanging alliance system, in Asia the United States retains significant freedom to modify its partnerships to suit changing needs.[43] Policymakers should strive to preserve this flexibility.

A final area where U.S. military policy toward the region is sorely lacking is the attempt to develop some kind of confidence-building measures toward China (for example, increased track 2 dialogues, military deconfliction arrangements, or exchanges of military observers). Some have argued that reassurance is unlikely to work given that China views the United States as weak.[44] But as they were during the Cold War, low-level confidence-building measures can still be of use regardless of Chinese intentions. Indeed, although much of the debate on this question has focused on the importance of high-level arms control, it's important to note that U.S.-Soviet confidence building didn't start with nuclear or arms control. Instead, as Zdzisław Lachowski has explained, the successive crises in Berlin, Cuba, and Czechoslovakia in the 1960s encouraged both the United States and the Soviet Union to develop measures that might "avoid inadvertent major military conflict or nuclear annihilation."[45] Like those of the past, today's confidence-building measures should aim for small, incremental improvements that can reduce the risk of conflict in the long run. Indeed, the goal here is not cooperation per se but deconfliction and the avoidance of errors, something that both sides have a strong interest in. Allowing observers at military exercises—a tradition that goes back to European militaries of the nineteenth century—can provide transparency and a way for both sides to gain intelligence that tempers threat perceptions. Confidence-building measures focused on Taiwanese airspace are another promising avenue, as is the attempt to build a new variety of the Incidents at Sea (IncSea) agreement that helped decrease tensions between the United States and the Soviet Union over maritime interceptions.[46] Some recent studies have described this approach as "behavioral arms control," a set of "informal initiatives to reduce military risks by focusing on the actions, rather than the capabilities, that can lead to escalation."[47]

Ultimately, the goal of U.S. policy in Asia should not be to control the region or to regain lost hegemony. "Rather than maintain an ill-fated pursuit of primacy," as Jen Kavanagh and Kelly Grieco argue, "the United States should adopt a strategy that prioritizes balancing, not exceeding, Chinese power."[48] In short, the United States should seek to preserve freedom of maneuver and open trading and diplomatic structures in the region not only for itself but for regional states as well. The United States would benefit economically and in security terms from a vibrant, multipolar Asia, which would also serve to blunt China's ability to carve up the region and dominate it. This will require an engaged United States in a region of strong, capable countries.

A Free and Open Economic Order

Influence in Asia—and even global sway for the United States—is about more than just security or territory. And in recent years, America has in many respects fled the field of battle when it comes to active economic engagement with the world. Policymakers have turned decisively against free trade and have continued to enact a thoroughgoing agenda of coercive economic statecraft, from sanctions to export controls and tariffs. If America is to present a positive vision of an open world in which states can benefit from interaction and trade, and in which America is more than simply a supplier of security services, then policymakers must rethink their approach to economic statecraft.

China and the Backlash Against Trade

In recent years, the question of U.S. economic engagement has become intrinsically linked with the question of U.S.-China policy. As far back as the Obama administration, U.S. officials sought to create the Trans-Pacific Partnership (TPP), a regional trade organization in the Pacific that they hoped would tie the United States to the region in non-military ways. It was also a response to China's own growing use of economic statecraft, most notably the Belt and Road Initiative, which sought to build infrastructure ties with China's neighbors. The TPP was a relatively coherent and potentially effective idea, one that would help further integrate the countries of Asia into the U.S.-dominated global trade order, and even help diversify American supply chains, thereby diminishing the overall influence of China in U.S. trade. It is highly ironic that growing fears of China would ultimately help kill the initiative.

A backlash against trade gained momentum in the aftermath of the financial crisis of 2008. American pundits and reporters during this period were increasingly linking globalization to economic malaise and political dissatisfaction at home. This was not an entirely fair criticism. The central cause of the financial crisis was not the globalization of trade—which had in any case been ongoing since the 1970s—but rather the internationalization of financial markets, which allowed a crisis in American mortgage-backed securities to become a global economic calamity. And domestic economic dislocation was only partly the result of jobs moving overseas; most of the impact came from technological advances in automation and manufacturing. Workers were being replaced by robots, not foreigners. Yet with the glacially slow recovery of the American economy from the financial crisis, globalization would become a bête noire for both left- and right-wing politicians. The unorthodox presidential campaign of Senator Bernie Sanders drew heavily on this argument, insisting that "foreign policy must take into account the outrageous income and wealth inequality that exists globally and in our own country."[49] Donald Trump did much the same in his 2016 campaign, raving about globalization, promising to kill the newly negotiated TPP, and arguing that globalization had allowed China to take advantage of working-class Americans.[50]

In short, by the time the Obama administration had concluded its negotiations on the TPP, not even Hillary Clinton, the Democratic Party's presumptive nominee, would endorse the agreement, even though she had helped negotiate it as secretary of state. The surprise election of Donald Trump in 2016 only worsened the problem. Trump, as promised, withdrew the United States from the TPP and implemented a variety of tariffs and trade disputes against China, as well as against U.S. allies in Europe. On the left, meanwhile, the idea began to take hold that Hillary Clinton's electoral loss was largely the result of the party's failure to speak to voters economically affected by decades of globalization. The Covid-19 pandemic, and the resulting supply shocks to consumer goods, only added to the notion that trade was risky.

By the time the Biden administration took office in 2021, a number of high-ranking officials—most notably Jake Sullivan, the national security adviser—were committed to rethinking the neoliberal economic consensus and building a different kind of trade system that would favor workers over business interests. They tied this vision explicitly to security. As Sullivan wrote in 2020: "Today's national security experts need to move beyond the prevailing neoliberal economic philosophy of the past 40 years. . . . The foreign-policy establishment need not come up with the next economic philosophy; the task is more limited—to contribute a geopolitical perspective to the unfolding debate on what should follow neoliberalism and then to make the national security case for a new approach as it emerges."[51] The Biden administration's trade policy was largely a veneer of rhetoric superimposed over other priority issues; Katherine Tai, the U.S. trade representative, even went so far as to tell the assembled plutocrats at the World Economic Forum in Davos that the administration sought to midwife a "new economic order" focused on protecting workers, not consumers.[52] And although the administration claimed to be offering a successor agreement to the TPP in the new Indo-Pacific Economic Framework for Prosperity (IPEF), this agreement was oriented primarily toward standards, regulatory frameworks, and supply chain management; IPEF's trade pillar has been held up indefinitely thanks to domestic political opposition in Congress.[53] Likewise, the administration was vocally supportive of the idea of "ally-shoring" or "friend-shoring," but did not in practice pursue it.[54] If anything, U.S. trade and investment policies are becoming *less* liberal, even toward advanced industrialized democracies.

This could not be happening at a worse time: The peculiar period of Cold War bipolarity—when economies largely operated in self-contained blocs and thus could be more easily disaggregated from security choices—is long gone, and the world is re-entering a period of geopolitical competition in which economic ties can be manipulated for strategic ends. Most countries around the world do not view military and security affairs in a vacuum, and for many, it seems as if, in matters of trade, America has retreated from the world stage exactly when its presence is most needed. The Trump and Biden turn away from free trade has already begun to affect the global trading order; a recent WTO ruling pointed out that "geopolitical tensions are beginning to affect trade flows, including in ways that point towards fragmentation of trading relationships."[55] To put it another way, the Biden administration's embrace of democracy as a central litmus test for U.S. foreign policy also covered the retreat of U.S. support for market capitalism globally. Trade carries geopolitical benefits, not least its ability to keep the United States engaged and active in world affairs without requiring the direct use of military force. It is profoundly ironic that even as geo-economics is becoming more relevant for U.S. national security, this interconnectedness is being used by some to undermine an active American global economic role.

Coercion and Power

Although policymakers have backed away from trade in recent years, they have become only more attracted to the aggressive use of co-ercive economic statecraft to achieve policy goals. Policymakers—both in Congress and the executive branch—often reach for financial and techno-logical restrictions (sanctions, export controls, and the like) in furtherance of U.S. foreign policy goals. The political consensus around this use of economic statecraft is robust, in part because it offers policymakers an opportunity to appear invested in overseas crises at relatively low cost, and in part because America's centrality at the heart of global finance and technology innovation increases the tools available to policymakers.[56] But although these weapons can sometimes be effective in the short term, they produce diminishing returns over time. To put it bluntly: Once the United States has weaponized all the benefits of post–Cold War globalization, there will be fewer levers left to pull in the future, particularly if the dollar becomes less dominant.[57] This problem became particularly pronounced under the Biden administration, which—from decoupling to export con-trols and domestic industrial policy—wielded American economic strength as a cudgel.[58]

Perhaps the best-known tool in America's economic arsenal is sanctions. The use of embargoes dates to antiquity, but the United States has perfected the modern form of sanctions, combining complex financial and regulatory restrictions with America's central place in the global economy to bar adversaries from access to international markets. Indeed, from a relatively discredited status in the late 1990s, financial sanctions have had an astound-ing rebirth; since 2001, American policymakers have turned to sanctions to coerce and compel other states on everything from nuclear weapons to democracy promotion and human rights. The narrowest of these sanctions are aimed at individuals or single entities (for example, Bashar al-Assad); the broadest are aimed at whole economic sectors (for example, Russian oil and gas producers). The record of sanctions, however, remains poor. They can be effective in denying terrorists or dictators access to foreign bank accounts, and somewhat effective at preventing rogue states from accessing dual-use technology for nuclear-weapons development. They can be successful when narrowly targeted and multilaterally coordinated. But few U.S. sanctions programs meet these standards, and they are almost entirely unsuccessful at forcing regime change or compelling states to change their core policy goals. Indeed, with one major exception—the negotiations that led to the Iran nuclear deal—most of the sanctions levied by the United States in the past twenty years have failed to produce significant policy change.

What they have produced is backlash from firms, companies, and even countries caught in the blast radius. American sanctions typically rely on the extraterritorial application of U.S. financial restrictions to succeed. Banks and other companies overseas—though they may be headquartered in Ireland, owned by French investors, or doing business primarily in Malaysia—must abide by U.S. sanctions law if they wish to access U.S. markets, trade in dollars, or do business with American companies. In practice, this means that sanctions are enforced by U.S. allies and friendly states, which also suffer the economic blow. These restrictions have often been wildly unpopular with other governments. And policymakers have too often been tempted to use their power, as Henry Farrell and Abraham Newman put it, "not just to subdue villains, but to subjugate friends that had largely accepted interdependence as a source of market efficiencies."[59] The first Trump administration employed direct sanctions on European companies in relation to the Nord Stream 2 pipeline; the second imposed punitive tariffs on Canada, Mexico, and the European Union. The result has been increasingly creative forms of sanctions circumvention, such as the European Union's new blocking statute, which prohibits European companies from complying with extraterritorial sanctions. Other sanctions-circumvention strategies have included the creation of "shadow" tanker fleets to trade sanctioned oil, and the Russian government's push to trade oil and gas in non-dollar currencies. Although none of these are close to undermining American centrality in the global financial system—or dethroning the dollar—the direction of travel is unmistakable.[60]

It is perhaps no surprise that with sanctions yielding fewer results, American policymakers have begun to look for other policy levers. Both Trump and Biden embraced the use of traditional tools like tariffs, creating national security exemptions to WTO rules and placing restrictions on European steel and aluminum, along with Chinese washing machines, solar panels, and various manufacturing inputs.[61] Yet they also innovated. At the heart of this effort was a realization that what had made American sanctions so powerful was America's position at the central node of the global financial system.[62] And so the Trump administration—and later the Biden administration—began to cast around for other areas where the United States might exert control over global networks. They settled on a new use for an old tool: export controls. First developed during the Cold War to inhibit the flow of technology to the Soviet Union, export controls had been a backwater since 1991, used mostly to prevent the export of nuclear technology. But if applied correctly to critical advanced technologies in which America held much of the technical know-how, export controls could in theory be used to degrade the technological capacity of adversaries. By the middle of the Biden administration, export controls had expanded to become a central tool of U.S. economic statecraft, and the administration restricted the sale of American-designed advanced semiconductors—along with technology related to artificial intelligence and quantum computing—to China. Although the national security adviser Jake Sullivan was quick to argue that these restrictions were tightly focused on "technology that could tilt the military balance," in practice the administration had a more ambitious goal: inhibiting China's technological and economic development, thereby hobbling its ability to compete with the United States.[63]

These promising new tools of economic coercion, however, are already exhibiting some of the same defects as sanctions. Sanctions and export controls can push states to develop their own domestic industries further and faster than they would have otherwise, thereby accelerating trade decoupling and decreasing reliance on U.S.-produced components globally. This certainly seems to be the case with Chinese semiconductors; although restrictions are clearly having some effect on high-end uses of chips in China, Chinese companies have thus far been able to develop domestic alternatives for many of the embargoed products.[64] Circumvention is another problem. Chip-related export controls have already produced arbitrage through middle states; perhaps the most obvious example is the significant increase in chip-related products exported to central Asia in the aftermath of restrictions on trade with Russia.[65] There are likewise suspicions that China is sourcing advanced chips through middle states in the Gulf and elsewhere, which has led the Commerce Department to expand its restrictions to several dozen other states, where companies seeking access to these technologies are now subject to end-user monitoring and other restrictions. This expansion puts the lie to the argument that America can take a "small yard, high fence" approach to restrictions on critical technologies.[66]

Instead, as with sanctions, it has become almost immediately apparent that export controls must be extraterritorialized if they are to be effective. This raises significant alliance-management issues, as U.S. partners—in this case, the Dutch, South Koreans, and Taiwanese—are hesitant about export controls that could significantly affect the future market share of their biggest companies. The increasing centrality of trade restrictions to manage critical national security vulnerabilities poses similar problems and adds a contentious set of issues to U.S. diplomacy with both allies and countries in the Global South. American attempts to persuade other states to avoid using Chinese technology from Huawei in their transition to 5G cellular networks, for example, arose logically from the fear that these networks would enable Chinese espionage the same way that American spies have capitalized on prior generations of technology. But such arguments were widely unpopular among developing nations, which saw few affordable alternatives to Chinese technology and saw American coercion on the issue as unjust. Similar dynamics are beginning to play out in the realm of green technology, where countries face American pressure not to rely heavily on Chinese technology as they transition to cleaner forms of energy. Ultimately, for many countries, trade-offs look very different than for the United States; most do not appreciate being compelled to place American security interests over economic growth. If the United States continues to use these tools to coerce allies to abide by its own trade policies, it is likely only a matter of time before export controls and other tools of coercive statecraft end up creating a backlash, just as the excessive use of sanctions has.

A final point bears mentioning. To the extent that it has been successful in recent decades, American economic statecraft has relied heavily on leveraging U.S. economic power to compel other states to adopt America's preferred policies. But as we explored in chapter 3, global power has been shifting for some time, and America's dominance of global economic networks is declining. Some of this is pure economic heft. As Agathe Demarais describes, "In the early 2030s the Chinese economy will displace that of the United States as the world's largest. China's economic dominance will turn the threat of U.S. sanctions against Beijing into mere rhetoric."[67] But other challenges are likely to arise from the overuse of sanctions, export controls, and other coercive economic tools. The dollar is likely to remain the world's preeminent reserve currency for some time; no good alternatives exist. But other states are increasingly looking for ways to insulate themselves from sanctions; this trend will only escalate if the United States continues to use extensive unilateral or extraterritorial sanctions. Farrell and Newman put it more dramatically: "The United States was able to retain its empire so long," they argue, "because it was hidden in the shadows. Now that it has been exposed to the light, it will crumble, or worse."[68]

Rebalancing Positive and Negative

The overall picture is not pretty. With growing opposition to trade and economic engagement and the growing use of sanctions, American economic statecraft today is primarily coercive. In layman's terms: America is all sticks and no carrots. This will not serve to persuade other states of much at all. "The United States also needs to be for something," points out Dan Drezner, "something that is more appealing to the rest of the world than, say, Russian arms or Chinese cash."[69] Positive visions of economic statecraft have been offered in recent years—take, for example, progressive proposals to build a more equal and peaceful world through engagement on questions of economic justice overseas.[70] Though such proposals are more "blue-sky" thinking than practical policies, they are nonetheless a coherent vision of how America might use positive economic statecraft to improve its position globally. Or consider the proposals put forward to create a more secure set of supply chains among advanced industrialized democracies, better known as "ally-shoring" or "friend-shoring." This concept, which has been widely hailed in Washington, calls for the United States to focus on "sourcing essential goods and services with countries that share democratic values and a commitment to an open, rules-based international order," in effect building a democratic bloc for trade while decoupling from China and other authoritarians.[71] Although there are many obstacles to implementing such a policy—for example, European opposition to China decoupling and U.S. hostility to new trade deals—it is undoubtedly a clear vision for American economic engagement with the world.[72]

Another attempt to offer a positive vision of economic engagement was the Biden administration's promotion of industrial policy and joint military procurement among U.S. allies as essential components of its "arsenal of democracy" strategy. Industrial policy has been central to legislation such as the Inflation Reduction Act (IRA) and the CHIPS and Science Act, which seek to bolster American manufacturing in green technologies and in semiconductors, respectively, and thereby reduce reliance on risky foreign supply chains. The Biden administration also promoted defense-industrial cooperation among NATO allies, encouraging European states to step up their efforts in manufacturing. Both are coherent notions that solve significant policy problems. In practice, however, these two policies conflict. Industrial policy as written by Congress is characterized by "buy American" restrictions that inhibit inter-allied cooperation and by subsidies that undermine WTO regulations governing non-tariff barriers. It's notable that one of the biggest areas of contention between the United States and Europe under the Biden administration was the IRA and the ways in which it privileged American manufacturers over their European counterparts. In short, the parochialism required by democratic politics makes it difficult for policymakers to engage in managed planning of supply chains across industrialized democracies; allies and partners may have divergent interests in the economic space, even when they share common ground on security.

Perhaps the most plausible and popular way the United States could once again offer a vision of positive economic engagement with the world would be to re-embrace the value of global trade and integration, a policy much more in line with America's historic embrace of trade as a central pillar of foreign policy than today's equivocation about commerce.[73] This has been widely viewed as impossible in recent years, as the domestic backlash against trade and trade-related security risks has militated against any administration adopting a free-trade approach. The risk of embracing military power and rejecting economic integration is that it leaves the

United States to act as little more than a global mercenary force while China or other states gobble up the world economy. In contrast, trade integration remains America's most effective and promising avenue for reaching and persuading other countries that the United States is a better partner than China. Both U.S. allies and adversaries are hungry for increased trade ties with the United States. "Countries in East and South-East Asia," the *Economist* wrote in November 2023, "thrive on their economic ties with China, but want an American counterbalance. They fear that over-relying on the regional giant would erode their agency and sovereignty."[74] Policymakers in the region have been guardedly optimistic about the Biden administration's IPEF, but they do not hide their desire for a more trade-oriented agreement.

There are fewer domestic political obstacles to trade than commonly assumed. Certainly, there is concentrated opposition to trade in very specific sectors and among traditional labor-oriented pressure groups, for whom the primary concerns are manufacturing offshoring and job losses. The public, however, is broadly supportive of increased global trade integration; almost 80 percent of those polled view trade as an opportunity for U.S. businesses.[75] Businesses are also generally in favor of more trade openness, and it's notable that even with negative rhetoric on trade emanating from the Trump and Biden administrations, U.S. trade in goods remains high.[76] These figures are without policymakers making the affirmative case for trade, which overwhelmingly benefits the American consumer, particularly the poor. One study, for example, estimated that moving toward a more autarkic international trade system could decrease the purchasing power of the poor in America by up to 60 percent.[77]

Finally, and perhaps most important, many of the purported links between national security and trade are either tenuous or overblown. It has been a long-running article of faith among many liberal internationalists, for example, that significant forward U.S. military presence is necessary to tamp down overseas conflicts and prevent states from redirecting otherwise productive economic spending toward arms races.[78] As the scholars Eugene Gholz and Daryl Press note, however, "scholars and policymakers tend to overstate countries' reliance on particular trading partners, trade routes, and suppliers of natural resources because they conflate interdependence with vulnerability."[79] Research instead suggests that markets adapt quickly and with relatively modest costs to disruptions, something clearly visible in the economic upheaval and eventual stabilization that followed the start of the war in Ukraine in 2022. Likewise, U.S. alliances are often described as essential for trade relations or economic prosperity, but the actual evidence for this proposition is far more tenuous.[80] Market access does not appear to be linked to security ties, and although allies often exhibit higher levels of trade, the effects of regional stability and diversified markets appear far more important to U.S. economic prospects than any direct effect of alliances.

The same is true for supply chain vulnerability and access to critical minerals. It is true that in certain areas—high-end chips, weapons systems, critical minerals—dependence on a single supplier or fragile supply chain can undermine resilience and create unnecessary economic or security risks. Those who lived through the Covid-19 pandemic will forever be aware that supply chains can sometimes fail in times of unexpected global stress and turmoil. But in most respects, resilience is enhanced—not undermined—by a broader diffusion of trade around the world. This is a logical, but often poorly understood, point. More sources for goods—in effect, more supply chains—means that supply shortfalls are less likely to affect consumers or economies in a significant way. One might consider the global oil market, where a truly globalized trade in oil means that disruptions are typically resolved quickly with minimal economic costs.[81]

Global energy markets also provide a good model for how we might understand the security risks of trade in specific technological or natural-resource-dependent sectors. Scholars have done significant work on this problem in the context of energy, and the scholarship is clear: In most situations, markets are generally effective at providing necessary inputs in response to global demands. But policymakers must think carefully about the limited areas in which potential wartime disruptions could create significant economic damage or issues in sustaining a military campaign.[82] Certain high-tech products with military applications should not be manufactured overseas, and policymakers may wish to hedge against future shortfalls by stockpiling certain critical materials that are not available domestically. But these lists should be short. Most items can be manufactured domestically in extremis, as the sudden surge in domestic manufacturing of PPE during the pandemic highlights. And security concerns simply cannot offset the significant value of trade for the vast majority of goods, natural resources, and even services. Recent guidance from the WTO highlights the point: "Trade interdependence, open trade policies, and cooperation among economies through international organizations can reduce the probability of conflict and raise economic security."[83]

In short, perhaps the clearest and most effective vision the United States can offer the world is of an America that is an integral part of global economic networks, a vision that can be achieved while avoiding significant security risks from extended supply chains. Instead of creating a closed ecosystem of advanced Western democracies—a vision that will create a two-tier global system that insulates the United States and Europe from competition but leaves them disconnected from much of the rest of the world—the United States should seek to open trade broadly and widely, using the attractive U.S. market and the opportunities it creates to woo countries that might be on the fence. And instead of pouring energy into attempting to engineer specific, robust supply chains, the United States should seek diversity in its supplier relationships. It is undoubtedly true that when left to their own devices, companies and markets tend to prioritize efficiency over redundancy or security, and there will be specific areas in which the United States may need to hedge against future conflict. But the best hedge is simply to foster the broadest possible range of trade partners.

Regional Opportunities

There have been few positive developments in the global trade space in recent years. Certainly, there has been a strong move toward increased *regionalization* in trade, and Asia, Europe, and the Americas have become ever more internally integrated as manufacturing and trade hubs.[84] Intra-regional trade has in many ways stalled, a situation exemplified best by the fact that no comprehensive round of WTO talks has succeeded since the Uruguay round in the 1990s. The failure of high-profile intra-regional trade agreements—most notably the TPP—has only added to the notion that the era of globalized trade may be ending. Recent trade negotiations have focused less on lifting trade barriers and more on labor, technology, and climate issues.

Even the burgeoning discussions about the Global South that have become popular in Washington in recent decades do not suggest that a globalized new economic approach is liable to succeed. These countries are united primarily by common developmental concerns. As Sarang Shidore of the Quincy Institute puts it, "The diversity and sprawl of the Global South implies that there will neither be a perfect definition nor perfect policy alignment among its states."[85] There are undoubtedly significant economic opportunities to be gained from interaction with these states, which contain the majority of humanity and a growing chunk of global manufacturing and critical resources. But these opportunities are most likely to be found on a region-by-region (or even country-by-country) basis. Despite this, however, significant opportunities exist for U.S. policymakers in the economic space if they are willing to embrace them.

ASIA The Trans-Pacific Partnership may be dead. But its successor agreement—the Comprehensive and Progressive Agreement for Trans-Pacific Partnership (CPTPP)—is alive and well, sustained by the other parties to the original TPP negotiations. Most of its member states would welcome an American return to the Asia trade conversation. And because the CPTPP is in most respects a clone of the U.S.-negotiated TPP, it's already well positioned to handle the most significant U.S. issues of concern when it comes to trade in Asia, including intellectual property rights and state subsidies. As one of the world's largest markets, the United States would be able to bring significant pressure to bear in reforming the CPTPP to address areas that have become problematic since 2016, such as rules on automotive imports.[86] But at heart, American membership in the CPTPP would serve the strategic aims that drove the negotiation of the original TPP. It would expand trade with important regional partners with whom the United States does not currently have free-trade agreements, such as Japan and Vietnam. Joining the CPTPP would also reduce the downside risk to the United States of being stuck on the outside of regional trade organizations while China participates, as well as offer a clear U.S. rejoinder to Chinese trade initiatives such as the Regional Comprehensive Economic Partnership.[87]

EUROPE Trade cooperation with Europe has stalled since the first Trump administration scuttled the Transatlantic Trade and Investment Partnership (TTIP) and imposed tariffs on all kinds of European exports, from cheese to aluminum. These tariffs were largely lifted under the

Biden administration, which correctly concluded that the trade war with Europe was ineffective, damaging to inter-NATO cohesion, and costly to the United States in terms of jobs.[88] But the new Trump administration appears determined to resume the tariff war. In theory, it seems difficult to imagine that the world's two most advanced industrialized economic blocs—which are formal military allies—cannot find some mutually beneficial areas of trade liberalization. Yet in practice, given that the U.S. and EU economies are roughly comparable in size, and given the highly regulated nature of both, there are substantial obstacles to a comprehensive trade agreement. Significant progress can still be made on trade in specific sectors, however, by building on the successes of the U.S.-EU Trade and Technology Council, a bilateral body that works on technology standards, data and technology governance, and investment screening, among other issues. This body has produced useful cooperation on complex issues but needs to re-engage on market access and tariff liberalization.[89] There is also potential in climate and green technology, where cooperation could well yield better benefits than protectionism.[90]

LATIN AMERICA American integration with Latin America through NAFTA was one of the great globalization stories of the 1990s, helping cement a relatively integrated transnational trade network between the United States, Canada, and Mexico. The creation of NAFTA drove a significant reorganization of supply chains and helped create an integrated energy market, among other benefits. Even its replacement with the United States–Mexico–Canada Agreement by the Trump administration did not undermine the central promise of NAFTA in integrating the three economies. But trade integration with Latin America more broadly has stalled, leaving behind a patchwork of bilateral trade agreements—something the economist Jagdesh Bhagwati has described as a "spaghetti bowl" of overlapping and conflicting standards and regulations that create significant costs for industry—rather than an integrated regional market.[91] As has been the case in other regions, the Biden administration's primary initiative toward Latin America focused more on economic inequality than on trade liberalization; the Trump administration is actively hostile to free trade.[92] There are significant costs to resisting inter-regional trade, most notably the growing number of economic migrants from Latin America who face few domestic economic opportunities and therefore seek to cross the U.S. border to work. Increased trade with Latin America and further U.S. integration with markets to the south would not only drive economic development and reduce migration pressure but would also help create a more durable American presence throughout the hemisphere, resisting Chinese incursions into space left unfilled by the United States. The possibilities for security- and development-enhancing deals are significant: Critical security-related sectors—from energy to semiconductors to cellular technology—are all potential components of an increasingly integrated regional trade infrastructure.[93]

AFRICA Opening trade with Africa presents significant and specific obstacles, as the region's underdevelopment, its reliance on raw materials and on agricultural products, and the weakness of the commercial sector all make negotiating free-trade deals challenging. At the same time, the continent presents a tremendous opportunity. Africa's demographic dividend— a population pyramid dominated by young people—and rising middle class present new markets for American companies, particularly in areas such as cellular technology, and significant opportunities for private-sector investment by American firms. The central agreement governing U.S. trade ties with the continent is the African Growth and Opportunity Act (AGOA), which is set to expire in 2025. AGOA has already been instrumental in expanding trade and economic diversification.[94] Indeed, in a region where policy has often focused almost exclusively on development aid, AGOA's focus on economic development and commercial opportunities has been highly successful. The most effective thing that any administration could do to nurture future trade with Africa would be to seek congressional renewal of AGOA and its expansion to new countries and sectors as the opportunities arise.[95]

Getting Serious

In early February 2023, an unusual news story burst into the headlines. A high-altitude balloon floating slowly across Montana had been spotted by airplane passengers. The observers initially wondered whether it was a UFO or a secret Defense Department project that had gotten out of hand.

But the government was quickly forced to announce that the balloon was of Chinese origin and most likely carried at least some surveillance capabilities. Fearing damage or injuries, the Biden administration opted not to bring the balloon down immediately, beginning a period of several days in which the balloon leisurely floated across the continental United States, trailed by fighter jets. In the meantime, politicians pontificated about the evils of China, and cable news media obsessively tracked its progress, until it was finally shot down off the coast of the Carolinas several days later, marking—rather ironically—the first confirmed air-to-air kill by an F-22 jet. The fallout didn't end there. The House Armed Services Committee held hearings about the dangers posed by the balloon; the full House of Representatives voted 419–0 to condemn the balloon. Secretary of State Anthony Blinken postponed a planned high-level trip to Beijing. The Air Force, meanwhile, scrambled fighter jets at least three more times in February, shooting down additional unknown objects, all of which were later determined to be harmless.

The balloon incident was just the most ridiculous of the anti-China hype that has come to characterize U.S. politics. States often spy on each other; an incident of this kind during the Cold War might have prompted condemnation but likely would not have created panic. Perhaps more importantly, the incident is also emblematic of the broader problem with current U.S. policy toward Asia: It is fundamentally performative and unserious. Hostile congressional committees on China—or rather, on the threat of the Chinese Communist Party, as they are typically styled—now regularly hold hearings to bang the war drums about China. U.S. politicians vie for an opportunity to travel to Taiwan and show their toughness against China, as Speaker of the House Nancy Pelosi did in August 2022, kicking off an escalation in military tensions between the island and the mainland. Even the Biden administration too often embraced meaningless gestures over productive policy. A meeting between Secretary of State Blinken, the national security adviser Jake Sullivan, and some of their Chinese counterparts in Alaska in March 2021, for example, devolved into an on-camera shouting match, as both sides attempted to lambaste the other for their policies.[96] Meanwhile, positive security achievements in the Indo-Pacific have been few and far between; the AUKUS submarine deal was riven with alliance-management and defense-industrial-base problems, and IPEF is widely perceived as an empty shell.

America cannot afford to waste its Asia policy on pontification and grandstanding by politicians. Doing so plays into China's hands: Beijing is increasingly making concrete economic and diplomatic policy gains in Asia, the Middle East, and Latin America while the United States relies on rhetoric and a flawed sense that the end of the Cold War implies that America must necessarily triumph in any new great power competition. This rhetoric—and coercive U.S. economic policies—have begun to alienate countries around the world, and as Jessica Chen Weiss has argued, there is a growing risk that America's attempts to counter China will end up undermining its own position globally. This chapter proposes a set of serious and plausible policy steps that the United States could take with respect to China. To do so will require policymakers to step back from threat inflation and instead treat seriously the question of where America fits in Asia and what it has to offer to a rapidly changing global economic system. America must lean forward, but it must do so on its own terms.

Conclusion: First Among Equals

In March 2023, Xi Jinping traveled to Moscow to meet with Vladimir Putin. Still ostracized by most leaders in the West and facing a recent arrest warrant from the International Criminal Court, the embattled Russian president was nonetheless delighted to see his Chinese counterpart. The visit reinforced the perception that Chinese trade would continue to sustain the sanctioned Russian economy. Even President Xi's attempt to tout his peace plan for Ukraine at the summit didn't blunt the celebratory mood in Moscow; the proposed plan was so heavily tilted toward Russian preferences that it would be a nonstarter in Kyiv or Western capitals. The two leaders discussed cross-border trade deals and expanding cooperation in energy and other sectors. As Xi Jinping's visit wrapped up, he made an off-the-cuff comment to his host: "Change is coming that hasn't happened in 100 years. And we're driving this change together."[1]

President Xi has expressed this sentiment before. The idea that China is emerging from a historic century of weakness and that the world is changing characterizes many of his speeches, as does the idea that this century will be China's to shape. Like many leaders of countries not entirely satisfied with U.S. hegemony, he looks to a multipolar world as a harbinger of American decline. Putin's infamous speech at the Munich Security Conference in 2007 likewise contrasted multipolarity with the perceived evils of U.S. unipolarity.[2] But although Xi or Putin may be correct on the diagnosis—the world is indeed undergoing significant structural changes—it is far from clear that the transition to a multipolar world necessitates U.S. decline or failure. There are certainly scenarios for the next few decades in which the United States overextends itself and is forced to retrench abruptly in response to crisis. But there are others in which the country wisely manages the transition into multipolarity and becomes a respected leader in a more diverse international system. Indeed, as I have argued in this book, embracing multipolarity is a winning strategy for the United States, one that allows it to nurture the rise of other capable actors in Europe and Asia, create a backstop for U.S. power, and hedge against China, Russia, and other less friendly states. The world—as Xi Jinping put it—is changing; the United States can shepherd that change in a more productive direction.

Doing so will require policymakers in Washington to embrace a more realist and prudent approach to the world. Prudence does not necessarily mean accepting the status quo; big changes in the international order—today as in past decades—will require difficult choices and shifts in U.S. strategy if the United States is to adapt effectively. But it will require policymakers to shed their unipolar mindset. America remains unique and unparalleled in many ways, but it is no longer the only power capable of shaping the international system. Policymakers must learn to engage with the emerging world on its own terms, focusing more on concrete American interests than on grand global crusades.

Realist Internationalism in Brief

They say that novelty has a quality all its own. Indeed, psychologists have found that new and exciting experiences create dopamine in the brain. Human beings are hardwired to seek novelty. Perhaps this is one reason Washington has been inundated in recent years with innovative grand strategies, such as networked strategies of "open order building," strategies of "responsible competition," and attempts to build "integrated deterrence." It is ironic that one of the few strategy documents that draws on a more classic understanding of international relations—the Trump administration's 2017 national security strategy—does not in fact define a strategy and relies instead on the more descriptive term "great power competition."[3]

Yet sometimes, old ideas persist for a reason. Realism as a formal theory may only be a century or so old, but its philosophical roots—which emphasize the importance of state sovereignty, the frailty of human nature, and the inherently tragic nature of the international system—go back millennia.[4] Throughout U.S. history, policymakers have tried to blend liberal idealism and realist prudence into strategy, but that balance has become lopsided in recent years, as policymakers took the opportunities afforded by the unipolar moment to pursue grand liberal crusades. This book argues that it is time to right the balance between liberalism and realism in U.S. foreign policy. Policymakers should not abandon their liberal ideals at home but should re-embrace core realist principles in foreign policy: focusing on interests over values, keeping threats in perspective, and seeking to manage the world rather than transform it. In doing so, they can better prepare America to flourish in an increasingly multipolar world.

At its core, this book argues that the United States must fundamentally reconceptualize its role in the world, from global hegemon to shared leadership. American strategy of the unipolar moment was one of universalism: offering security guarantees to almost any state that asked. Today, that universalism is a recipe for deterrence failure and overreach. Policymakers must learn to prioritize again and focus on commitments that are most important to core U.S. interests: protecting the U.S. homeland and the security and prosperity of Americans, as well as maintaining an acceptable global balance of power by preventing the rise of other regional hegemons. They must balance these interests against the potential for catastrophic great power war in the nuclear era. This will require changes in the mindset policymakers bring to bear on foreign policy; most importantly, they will need to define American interests significantly more narrowly in coming decades. And they will need to learn to accept that there are places, particularly in areas closest to other major competitors, where American interests are marginal and U.S. power is insufficient to compel other states to comply with our preferences. The nuclear question is particularly salient. As Robert Jervis puts it, in the nuclear era, "the pursuit of primacy" is no longer "worth the candle."[5] We have not seen a multipolar nuclear era before, but the experience of the Cold War tells us that there will be some places where U.S. interests will warrant the risk of nuclear escalation and other places where these interests are not sufficient to take such a monumental risk. Since 1991, policymakers have rarely had to draw this critical distinction in their own thinking; it is essential that they begin to do so again.

The strategy of realist internationalism outlined in this book does not prescribe a wholesale U.S. retrenchment from the world. Instead, it prescribes ruthless prioritization—most notably, a drawdown in Europe and the Middle East to focus on Asia, where the risk of a regional hegemon is the greatest. In practice, this will require a phased withdrawal from Europe as regional states pick up the burden. Although there are many barriers to coordinated continent-wide European security, there are also a variety of options available to U.S. policymakers, including fostering smaller minilateral groupings of European states focused on specific threats. In the Middle East, a U.S. drawdown should be significantly faster. American interests in the region are increasingly limited, and—except for protection of the sea lanes—there are no longer any core missions for which significant troop presence is required. Much of the American presence in the Middle East today owes to inertia rather than any specific policy choice; it is time to shed those strategic burdens.

One of the key criticisms of American retrenchment has always been that it may leave security vacuums that could be exploited by adversaries. But there are ways to resolve that problem. An unfortunate side effect—or the intention, depending on whom you ask—of America's focus on primacy since 1991 has been that it smothered the nascent military capabilities of allies in Europe and Asia under a blanket of reassurance.[6] It is time to abandon that policy and instead embrace and promote the capabilities of other friendly states. Policymakers can and should encourage other capable states to fill the gaps left by American reprioritization away from Europe and the Middle East. This will require a paradigm shift on alliances: Policymakers must start to think of them not as "sacred obligations" but as more mundane partnerships. Over time, alliances should become narrower, more flexible, and less focused on the provision of U.S. security guarantees to minor powers. At the global level, the United States should embrace the emerging multipolar order. Multipolarity is often seen as a negative for the United States because it increases the freedom of maneuver of states such as China and Russia. Yet in encouraging autonomous, but friendly, states to develop their own capabilities—turning their latent economic power into military strength—U.S. policymakers can hedge against shortfalls in our own capabilities and boost the ability of other states to resist adversaries.

In Asia, the region where the risk of a regional hegemon in the form of China is highest—and where the capabilities of regional states may not be sufficient to the task—the United States should instead engage. Forward-deployed military forces will be a part of this, though the United States will need more naval forces and fewer ground forces than it currently has in the region. But American engagement with the Indo-Pacific must be as much about economics and trade as it is about military deterrence. In this, the Obama administration was fundamentally correct ten years ago: The best counter to an assertive China is for the United States to be fully enmeshed in the politics and economics of the Indo-Pacific. And Asia is not the only place where the United States can benefit from increased economic engagement. Trade and investment can yield dividends in other areas too. In Latin America, for example, it is perhaps the best way to resolve both the current migration crisis and some of Latin America's domestic economic and security pathologies. In Africa, trade may be the key to unlocking the continent's vast demographic and economic potential. And contrary to the widespread assumptions of the past few years, trade is neither unpopular with the American people nor at the heart of public dissatisfaction with U.S. foreign policy. A realist-oriented strategy paired with economic engagement is both coherent and likely to be popular with the public.[7]

The significant U.S. strategy shifts proposed in this book may seem at odds with realism's emphasis on caution and prudence. Jonathan Kirshner, for example, has made what he describes as the "realist case for the status quo," arguing that "change is to leap into the unknown, which is generally unwelcome."[8] Stephen Brooks and William Wohlforth similarly argue against retrenchment, noting that it would be "the greatest grand strategic experiment in history" to "see how the world works with a disengaged America."[9] There are undoubtedly risks inherent in this strategy, as in any strategy. States might fail to adequately respond to threats from China or other states; the United States might be forced to come back onshore under less favorable conditions. But though possible, these outcomes do not seem likely, and the trade-offs are worth the risk. Indeed, it is a significant mistake to simply assume that the status quo is not risky; it would hardly be prudent to embrace path dependence and inertia over adaptation.

Realism does not preclude bold choices when circumstances require it; prudence suggests that America cannot continue its expansive post–Cold War foreign policy indefinitely. With growing deficits, military overextension, and increasing challenges to U.S. policies around the world, liberal primacy is likely to fail at some point. It would be significantly better to downsize U.S. force posture overseas now—while the prospects for recalibration are good—than to wait for a future crisis, when the changes will be made hastily and under duress.

Realist internationalism is undoubtedly a departure from U.S. unipolar overextension. But as an approach to the world, it is consistent with how policymakers of the past—from George Washington and Alexander Hamilton to Dwight Eisenhower or Brent Scowcroft—have thought about American foreign policy. None of these policymakers wanted America disengaged from the world. Each had different visions for engagement, from Hamilton's focus on commercial ties to Eisenhower's anti-Soviet coalition building and Scowcroft's deft diplomacy with a declining Soviet empire. But in their conduct, each embraced pragmatism and shrewdness about the state of the world and what could realistically be achieved through U.S. power. Each, in their own way, embraced Morgenthau's dictum to reject "the sentimental notion that foreign policy is a struggle between virtue and vice, with virtue bound to win."[10] Today, what is needed in U.S. foreign policy is not a grand vision of how to reshape the world in coming decades, but rather a reconceptualization of how we see the world and America's place in it. America's military power, its economic heft, and its ideological allure mean that it will always be more than just one among equals. But as power diffuses around the world, the United States is no longer capable of carrying the burden of security for the entire world. Re-embracing realism can help right the balance in foreign policy and place American foreign policy on a sounder, more sustainable footing for a multipolar world.

Temptation and the Unipolar Mindset

In the Gospel of Matthew, Satan tempts Jesus to betray God and his purpose. In the greatest of these temptations, he takes the son of God to the top of a high mountain and shows him the assembled nations of the world and their riches. "All this," he says, "I will give you if you wor-ship me."[11] Christ, of course, resists—or that story might have ended rather differently. U.S. policymakers have generally done a much poorer job of resisting temptation. America has been blessed with security and an enor-mous amount of military and economic power; from that high vantage point, it may seem obvious that the nations of the world are America's to shape. Especially in recent years, self-restraint has rarely been a feature of U.S. policy decisions. At the end of the Cold War, Jeane Kirkpatrick argued that with the Soviet threat past, the United States should attempt to be-come "a more normal nation in a normal time."[12] Washington instead took the astounding peace dividend that emerged from that struggle and went out looking for monsters to destroy in the Balkans, Iraq, and Libya. The historian Christopher Preble argues, convincingly, that it is precisely America's power that is its biggest problem: U.S. policymakers, entrusted with so much military and economic strength, simply cannot resist the temptation to use it. Even if they could commit to self-control, he argues, would other countries believe them? Would the next president concur?[13] One solution is to remove the temptation: A United States that is not present overseas and is less capable of trying to solve every problem will tempt policymakers less and allow other countries to step up. But there are limits to how much the United States can or should pull back from the world.

In any strategy that calls for continued U.S. engagement and military presence overseas, there will always be a risk that policymakers will instead choose to pursue expansive ends. Take the example of selective engage-ment, a grand strategy proposed in the early 1990s that advocated for the United States to maintain some forward presence while pursuing a limited set of international aims overseas. Though an initially compelling argument for the United States to balance between its realist and liberal impulses, selective engagement nonetheless degenerated quickly and became almost indistinguishable from more mainstream liberal internationalist approaches. By the late 1990s, Robert Art, the best-known proponent of selective engagement, was arguing that the United States not only needed to main-tain a favorable balance of power, but also had to prevent the spread of weapons of mass destruction, preserve the international economic order, foster the spread of democracy, and protect the environment.[14] These are hardly modest aims. Over time, selective engagement became such a broad paradigm that, today, it is rarely differentiated from the more overtly primacy-embracing strategy of deep engagement.[15]

The strategy in this book is potentially vulnerable to similar flaws. It can be all too easy to slide from limited ends into more expansive ones. The Obama administration is a case in point. Obama himself frequently talked like a realist. As he told the *Atlantic*'s Jeffrey Goldberg near the end of his presidency, "Almost every great world power has succumbed to overextension. . . . What I think is not smart is the idea that every time there is a problem, we send in our military to impose order. We just can't do that."[16] But in practice, his administration was as forward-leaning on foreign policy as others of the unipolar moment. Obama might have seen himself as the "don't do stupid shit" president, but he gave in to temptation in Libya, Iraq, and elsewhere.[17] He also differed from realists in his talk about the importance of alliances and international institutions. International institutions can perform important functions. They act as mechanisms for convening states on matters of shared interest such as climate change, they can provide forums for the mediation of boundary disputes, and they can smooth many of the diplomatic difficulties of international interaction through standing forums like the United Nations. Institutions permit major states to collude in taking action against smaller states to enforce rules, but they also provide voice to smaller states. In short, even from a realist perspective, institutions are hardly meaningless.[18] But there is always the risk that policymakers not only will use them instrumentally—that is, as mechanisms for conducting power politics—but might also begin to elevate their importance to the level of a core interest, making the survival or perpetuation of the international organization more important than what a state can achieve through it. This tendency to place internationalism over the national interest undermines the realist foundations of strategy.

The strategy proposed in this book can help mitigate these risks. First, the strategy described here is very explicit about the criteria for defining core U.S. interests and that it is necessary to define such interests narrowly. Unlike the extensive list of scenarios in which selective engagement might consider U.S. intervention, the list in this book is short. It does not include specific aims like preventing the spread of weapons of mass destruction or protecting civilians. Indeed, in some ways the mistake made by proponents of selective engagement in the 1990s was to take such a "kitchen sink" approach to U.S. interests. Preventing nuclear proliferation, for example, is not a core U.S. interest. It could *become* a concern for U.S. policymakers under the strategy proposed in this book, but only if it reached the point of significantly imperiling U.S. security or economic prosperity—something that is highly unlikely. On its own, for example, realist internationalism would not consider the risk of proliferation sufficient to warrant U.S. military action. Tying policy choices explicitly to foundational interests makes it much easier to be selective in those decisions.

Second, policymakers must be crystal clear about the true function played by the international institutions and alliances more commonly associated with liberal theories of international relations. Alliances and institutions can be useful for convening states on topics of mutual importance—for example, climate change or arms control—for coordination, and for smoothing the process of engagement with other states in trade negotiations and diplomacy. But they are not in and of themselves functional ways to enforce any kind of international law; they will not become so over time. And indeed, though there will be many places where the strategy in this book overlaps in practice with the prescriptions of liberal or progressive thinkers, here I wish to be clear: Anarchy cannot be easily overcome in the international system, and we are not in the process of building a better world. Instead, this book presents a strategy for managing the world as it exists in ways that protect and benefit the American people. This requires keeping the role of institutions or ideas in international relations in perspective and accepting that they matter mostly on the margins.

Finally, the only area in which this strategy calls for a significant U.S. forward-deployed military presence is in the Indo-Pacific. One of the central flaws with selective- or deep-engagement strategies is that forward-deployed military forces sometimes become self-sustaining. We see this today in Iraq, where U.S. troops are present to "deter militias," whose central purpose is to attack U.S. troops; it is perpetual presence as a self-fulfilling prophecy. In other places, U.S. bases can become a barrier to policy choice, whether that is the failure to criticize autocratic host governments for their human rights records or alliance entanglement dynamics. In Europe and the Middle East, this book calls for U.S. retrenchment, which would constrain policymakers' temptations and reduce the likelihood that the United States will be drawn back into relatively unimportant conflicts—at least in those regions.

But ultimately, we must remember that policymakers are human and are subject to human emotions, hubris, and frailties. It is unsurprising that when tempted with massive power and the prospect of reshaping the world, many choose to throw caution to the wind. These tendencies can be mitigated, however, by providing clear guidelines about U.S. interests and adopting restrictive guidance for the use of U.S. military force. This could take the form of the Weinberger or Powell Doctrines, each of which presents specific criteria that must be met before force can be used and focuses on whether vital interests are threatened, whether the objective is militarily achievable, and whether the U.S. public will support it. Though little can prevent a determined policymaker from engaging in foreign policy crusades, these steps can at least reduce the risks, provide a rubric by which Americans can judge policymakers on foreign policy, and help keep policymakers honest.

The Domestic Politics of Getting to Restraint

One problem with the literature on U.S. grand strategy—this book included—is that it tends to treat the implementation of policy and the domestic politics of foreign policy as simple, clean, and almost irrelevant to the formulation of strategy, ignoring the messy compromises and bureaucratic politics that often bog down such discussions in practice. This is why books on grand strategy sound so different from bloated U.S. national security strategies, in which bureaucratic constituencies inside the U.S. government jockey to highlight their own priorities. Some argue that this renders grand strategy a largely useless, navel-gazing exercise. Peter Dombrowski and Simon Reich stress this point, noting that "the very idea of a single, one-size-fits-all grand strategy has little utility in the twenty-first century," when the U.S. military finds it increasingly difficult to implement "policies based on singular grand strategic visions drawn up on metaphorical chessboards by academics or Washington policymakers."[19]

Others argue that the world has become too chaotic, unpredictable, or impossible to understand for any unifying vision for U.S. foreign policy that matches means to ends to be viable; the best we can do, they imply, is muddle through.[20] This is a fundamentally false idea. There have been multipolar eras before, and leaders and states have formulated strategies— even if only implicitly—for how to navigate them. New technology may change the way that states communicate with or spy on one another, but they're fundamentally engaged in the same processes of cooperation and competition. Throwing out the *idea* of strategy simply because policymakers have done a poor job articulating and sticking to a strategy in recent years is no better than jettisoning the baby with the bathwater. Instead, we should acknowledge both the positives of grand strategic visions—that they allow policymakers to more clearly define what the United States is trying to achieve in the world and how to prioritize scarce resources across those ends—and their limitations. Strategies are at best a guide to the world, a rubric that policymakers can use when making difficult decisions.[21]

They are also subject to domestic political limitations, and in this context, it is worth briefly exploring what the constraints on a more realist grand strategy would be—and whether the domestic environment is favorable or unfavorable. Perhaps the most obvious question surrounds public opinion. Polling is often cited by those who support a more restrained strategy to support their case. Different polls are cited by those who support today's strategy of liberal primacy, and still other polls by those who favor a more aggressive strategy. Looking at the numbers, you can find strong support among the American public for continued global engagement, strong support for NATO, and belief that the United States was right to support Ukraine in its current war. You can also find polling that suggests Americans prefer economic engagement to military intervention, want allies to pay more toward their own defense, and believe that U.S. policymakers should press for peace in Ukraine. None of this should come as a surprise to those who remember that one of the most popular primers for students on basic probability is the aptly titled *How to Lie with Statistics*.[22] Indeed, what public-opinion polling on foreign policy mostly shows is that politicians and pundits are very good at cherry-picking specific numbers to support their own positions. But even though individual numbers or specific moments in time may be suspect, there are some broad trends worth noting. Americans remain broadly supportive of global engagement, but the form of engagement they prefer is shifting. Polling by Gallup in 2023, for example, asked Americans their preferences about America's role in the world; a plurality (about 45 percent) wanted America to play a major role in the world, but only 20 percent wanted America to play the leading role.[23] These numbers are shifting over time, with growth primarily in the "minor role" or "no role" category. Generational differences contribute too: Americans under the age of forty are less likely to favor military action and more likely to list transnational concerns like climate change as their primary foreign policy concerns.[24]

More complicated is the ongoing debate about whether public opinion really matters for foreign policy. The Duke of Wellington once infamously said that the Battle of Waterloo was won on the playing fields of Eton, implying that elite education and consensus was one reason for Britain's victories in the Napoleonic Wars. Many of today's biggest foreign policy debates likewise originated in the classrooms of America's top universities; foreign policy is fundamentally an elite preoccupation. The public certainly has opinions on foreign policy, but it tends to be of low salience: Voters do not typically prioritize it, and it is usually latent unless activated in some way by media coverage or a specific interest group.[25] In short, voters mostly care about foreign policy when led by politicians. Worse, policymakers themselves sometimes base their foreign policy choices on their perceptions of what will be popular, which creates a tangled, circular mess of connections between public opinion, elite cues, and foreign policy. But research suggests that the biggest impact on public opinion is typically seen when credible foreign policy elites diverge from the existing consensus on foreign policy.[26] This is roughly the process that we saw in the campaign to end the "forever wars," when a combination of credible elite dissent and highly motivated interest groups in the form of peace organizations and veterans' groups helped build a groundswell of support for withdrawal from Afghanistan in the run-up to the election of 2020. This suggests that it will be challenging to build domestic political support for a more realist or restrained grand strategy: Public opinion may be trending in the right direction, but it will almost certainly take some level of elite contestation and a critical mass of elite defections from the liberal or primacist consensus to yield change; popular dissatisfaction with foreign policy alone is unlikely to yield results.

Public opinion also suggests another danger point for implementing a more realist grand strategy: Periods of change can yield unpleasant surprises that themselves make it more difficult to implement policy reforms. After the fall of the Soviet Union, for example, Eastern European economies underwent a profound period of transition that roughly mirrored a J-shaped curve; almost everywhere, economic conditions got worse before they got better. The transition these states underwent was a necessary one—there was no other way to get from a command economy to a more open, market-based system—yet during that downward economic swing, many people suffered. In several post-communist states, early elections were held at the low point of the curve, allowing the short-term winners to lock in their position before reforms truly had time to take hold. It is no surprise that, in these cases, reforms stalled.[27]

A similar dynamic is often at play in attempts to reform U.S. foreign policy, where attempts to retrench can produce messy results in the short term. The Obama administration, for example, was successful in reducing troop levels in Iraq and Afghanistan, but the fear that accompanied the rise of ISIS in Iraq prompted the administration to send troops back into that theater almost immediately. The Biden administration appears to have suffered a similar psychological blow after the withdrawal from Afghanistan; the negative media coverage of the catastrophic collapse of Kabul soured the administration on new or innovative foreign policy thinking by high-lighting the public relations risks.[28] This suggests that if any administration is to be successful in transitioning to a more realist grand strategy, policy-makers must begin early and be willing to tolerate some setbacks without changing course. It is also notable how much easier Richard Nixon—re-elected with a significant majority—found it to shift U.S. foreign policy than more narrowly elected first-time presidents such as Jimmy Carter or Joe Biden.

Growing partisanship in U.S. foreign policy poses another risk. Tradi-tionally, there has been broader agreement between both major parties on foreign policy than on domestic policy. Indeed, as we've explored in pre-vious chapters, many of the cleavages in foreign policy debates run not between Republicans and Democrats but rather within parties or between the executive and Congress.[29] But partisanship has been increasing in foreign policy. Some research suggests that partisanship is making it harder for Congress to exert oversight in foreign policy, and other research sug-gests that Republican and Democratic preferences on foreign policy seem to be diverging. Issues on the margins of foreign policy—notably trade and immigration—have become more divisive, and differences are increasingly emerging on such topics as international institutions, Israel, Russia, China, and Ukraine. These more rapid shifts on specific issues are largely elite driven and may not be as durable as the broad trends discussed earlier. But they can nonetheless shape foreign policy.[30]

Bipartisanship is not necessarily an unalloyed good in foreign policy, where it often tends toward reflexive hawkishness or criticism of administrations that are "not tough enough" on adversaries. Indeed, simply because a foreign policy consensus is bipartisan does not mean that it should go unchallenged. But partisanship on specific foreign policy issues can carry its own risks. In recent years, relations with both Israel and Saudi Arabia have become increasingly politicized as both countries have effectively aligned themselves with Republican leaders. Democrats, meanwhile, have swung in a more hawkish direction on Russia, in large part thanks to the controversies surrounding the 2016 election and Trump's first impeachment. The case of the Iran nuclear deal is particularly salient here. Talks began during the presidency of George W. Bush and continued under the Obama administration. But by 2016, opposition to the deal had become a Republican litmus test; President Trump's choice to pull the United States out of the deal was a profound reversal in U.S. policy and left European states and Iran in the difficult position of choosing to uphold either the deal or the U.S. sanctions.[31] The extreme swings between administrations were damaging for Iran policy and for America's ability to negotiate credible nonproliferation deals more broadly. Extreme partisanship on specific issues can thus undermine coherent foreign policy. If a realist internationalist strategy is to be implemented, it will likely need to draw support from some subset of both political parties—not merely from one.

A final area of consideration is bureaucratic contestation over the resources that flow from any significant shift in U.S. strategy. Perhaps the most notable of these is defense spending. Though it's beyond the scope of this book to assess in concrete terms what a realist internationalist strategy would mean for the defense budget, we know from prior assessments that any shift to a more restrained or realist strategy could shrink the defense budget by up to one-third if done wisely.[32] Most likely, even an improved strategy would not yield this level of savings unless the implementing administration were also able to tackle Pentagon administrative and procurement bloat. Even modest cuts to the defense budget, however, would likely face political pushback from within the bureaucracy. The strategy outlined in this book would almost certainly require a redistribution of resources across the military services—fewer resources for the army and more for the navy, for example—in ways that might prompt similar pushback.

To fully realize the benefits of a more realist strategy would also require increased core budgets and personnel for the Departments of State and Commerce, as well as the intelligence services (with a focus on collection, not on operations). This money would likely have to come from the Pentagon, where the many things that do not improve U.S. war-fighting capabilities could be trimmed; that includes bloated service staffs, excess base capacity, and unnecessary functions that could be performed by civilian agencies.[33] Recapitalizing and reorganizing the State Department is a particular priority; in recent years, budget cuts and morale issues have hollowed out the agency, leaving fewer and fewer genuine diplomats, many of whom focus almost entirely on alliance management. Although money will form some of the solution here, there is also a political-will problem.[34] The department needs less focus on functional bureaus with responsibility for abstract principles such as human rights and religious freedom, and more dedicated staff with deep regional or functional experience. Even though this is less pressing, resources should be prioritized away from the Treasury Department's Office of Financial Assets Control—the bastion of sanctions enforcement—and toward the Office of the U.S. Trade Representative or the Department of Commerce, both of which are better positioned to work on trade and investment issues. Each of these steps would be intensely challenging to achieve. At a minimum, however, we can say that a more realist strategy could easily be implemented within current budgetary constraints, even if the reprioritization of those resources may prove politically difficult.

Fools, Drunks, and the United States of America

The German statesman Otto von Bismarck, a realist's realist, reputedly remarked that "God has a special Providence for fools, drunks, and the United States of America." Although the quote is probably apocryphal, the meaning behind it is clear. Even in Bismarck's time—mere decades after the U.S. Civil War, during all the upheavals of reconstruction and industrialization—it was increasingly apparent that the rising nation had been unusually blessed with geography, resources, and even human capital. While European states squabbled at power politics and scrapped over territory, America was expanding into the West, gobbling up more land and power. And even at the turn of the twentieth century, when the United States finally got drawn into idealistic worldbuilding crusades and European and Asian wars, those blessings continued to provide a robust economy, burgeoning industry, and a vibrant and diverse society. George Washington was wrong when he argued in his farewell address that America's "detached and distant situation invites and enables us to pursue a different course" than international power politics, but he was not wrong that America does so from a tremendously privileged position.[35] This is not the sense one gets today in Washington, where the city's foreign policy elites appear increasingly besieged. The country has recently engaged in yet another contentious election. International crises appear omnipresent. And the challenges to the U.S. position in the international system are growing. Foreign visitors land in Washington and head to the think tank of their choice to ask, in worried tones, what will happen to American leadership going forward.

But although there have undoubtedly been some setbacks for the United States in recent years, there's also an element of psychological trickery going on here. When you have been top dog for three decades, almost entirely unchallenged, with the whole world as your sphere of influence, *any* kind of challenge can seem like a reversal in fortune. Humans are, fundamentally, loss averse, and the idea of retrenchment, or even just of changing course, can seem daunting and even defeatist—surrendering influence and power to an uncaring world. But Bismarck's dictum is still fundamentally correct: America occupies an exceedingly privileged place in the international system and, more important, an exceedingly secure one. To put it another way: The era of nation-building may be over, and the world may be moving toward multipolarity, but that does not mean the United States has become less secure. Indeed, the very fact that it has the option to step back, reconsider its commitments, and prioritize its approach to the world highlights just how much breathing space the United States has in which to engage in course correction.

It would be a far bigger risk to let fear of the unknown lock us into a strategy that is a poor fit for the rapidly changing world. The political scientists Paul McDonald and Joseph Parent point out that retrenchment "is not the devil great powers don't know, but the devil they know best. . . . Nostalgia is no solution to decline."[36] The same could be said more broadly about strategic course correction. Although it is not always politically easy to engage in a significant about-face on foreign policy, it is no less necessary. As Lord Salisbury once put it, "The commonest error in politics is sticking to the carcasses of dead policies."[37] The vibrant debate on the future of U.S. policy that has characterized Washington discussions over the past five years is the result of a growing realization that the unipolar moment is ending. Growing Chinese and Russian revisionism, the relative decline of U.S. economic power, the shifting military balance in certain areas, and even growing domestic political backlash on foreign policy strategy all suggest that a change is in order. But that debate will be for naught if policymakers simply fiddle around the edges of existing policies and avoid making the difficult changes that are needed if the United States is to thrive in the coming multipolar era. Washington must learn once again how to engage with the world most effectively.

If policymakers ignore everything else in this book, let them at least take this principle: The world is changing; do not let the past be a straitjacket.

Notes

Introduction: A Normal Nation

Epigraph: Robert L. Bartley et al., "America's Purpose Now," *National Interest,* no. 21 (1990): 26–61.

1. MacKenzie Sigalos, " 'The Davos Underground': A Final Take on the Secretive Parties of the World's Rich and Powerful," *CNBC,* January 31, 2024, www.cnbc.com/2024/01/31/the-davos-underground-inside-the-secret-parties-of-the-elite-world.html.

2. *Global Risks Report 2023* (World Economic Forum, January 11, 2023), www.weforum.org/publications/global-risks-report-2023/digest.

3. Richard N. Haass, "The Age of Nonpolarity: What Will Follow U.S. Dominance," *Foreign Affairs* 87, no. 3 (2008): 44–56; Christopher Layne, "This Time It's Real: The End of Unipolarity and the *Pax Americana,*" *International Studies Quarterly* 56, no. 1 (2012): 203–13, https://doi.org/10.1111/j.1468-2478.2011.00704.x; Fareed Zakaria, "The Self-Destruction of American Power," *Foreign Affairs* 98, no. 4 (2019): 10–16; Stephen G. Brooks and William C. Wohlforth, "The Myth of Multipolarity," *Foreign Affairs* 102, no. 3 (2023), www.foreignaffairs.com/united-states/china-multipolarity-myth; Michael Beckley, *Unrivaled: Why America Will Remain the World's Sole Superpower* (Cornell University Press, 2018).

4. Brooks and Wohlforth, "The Myth of Multipolarity."

5. "Did the Unipolar Moment Ever End?," Ask the Experts, *Foreign Affairs,* May 23, 2023, www.foreignaffairs.com/ask-the-experts/did-unipolar-moment-ever-end.

6. Mark Leonard, "China Is Ready for a World of Disorder," *Foreign Affairs* 102, no. 4 (2023), www.foreignaffairs.com/united-states/china-ready-world-disorder.

7. "Macron Criticised for Saying Europe Should Take Independent Stance on Taiwan," *Reuters,* April 10, 2023, www.reuters.com/world/macron-criticised-saying-europe-should-take-independent-stance-taiwan-2023-04-10.

8. Bryan Harris and Joe Leahy, "Lula Vows Partnership with China to 'Balance World Geopolitics,'" *Financial Times,* April 15, 2023, www.ft.com/content/766ed3aa-3f51-4035-8573-43254c9756d5.

9. Barry Posen, *Restraint: A New Foundation for U.S. Grand Strategy* (Cornell University Press, 2015), 4.

10. Jennifer Lind and William C. Wohlforth, "The Future of the Liberal Order Is Conservative," *Foreign Affairs* 98, no. 2 (2019), www.foreignaffairs.com/articles/united-states/2019-02-12/future-liberal-order-conservative.

11. Randall L. Schweller, "Three Cheers for Trump's Foreign Policy: What the Establishment Misses," *Foreign Affairs* 97, no. 5 (2018), www.foreignaffairs.com/articles/world/2018-08-13/three-cheers-trumps-foreign-policy.

12. Scott Pelley, "President Joe Biden: The 2023 60 Minutes Interview Transcript," CBS, October 15, 2023, www.cbsnews.com/news/president-joe-biden-2023-60-minutes-transcript; Jeffrey Jones, "Fewer Americans Want U.S. Taking Major Role in World Affairs," Gallup, March 3, 2023, https://news.gallup.com/poll/471350/fewer-americans-taking-major-role-world-affairs.aspx.

13. Alexander Ward, *The Internationalists: The Fight to Restore American Foreign Policy After Trump* (Portfolio/Penguin, 2024).

14. David Samuels, "The Aspiring Novelist Who Became Obama's Foreign-Policy Guru," *New York Times Magazine,* May 5, 2016, www.nytimes.com/2016/05/08/magazine/the-aspiring-novelist-who-became-obamas-foreign-policy-guru.html.

15. Nadia Schadlow, "The End of American Illusion," *Foreign Affairs* 99, no. 5 (2020), www.foreignaffairs.com/articles/americas/2020-08-11/end-american-illusion; H. R. McMaster, *Battlegrounds: The Fight to Defend the Free World* (HarperCollins, 2020); Leon Panetta, foreword to *Defending Forward: Securing America by Projecting Military Power Abroad,* ed. Bradley Bowman (Foundation for Defense of Democracies, December 2020), www.fdd.org/wp-content/uploads/2020/12/fdd-monograph-defending-forward.pdf; Matt Pottinger, testimony before the House Select Committee on the Strategic Competition Between the United States and the Chinese Communist Party (Washington, D.C., February 28, 2023), www.congress.gov/118/meeting/house/115402/witnesses/HHRG-118-ZS00-Wstate-PottingerM-20230228.pdf; Elbridge Colby, *The Strategy of Denial: American Defense in an Age of Great Power Conflict* (Yale University Press, 2021).

16. Robert Kagan, "A Superpower, Like It or Not," *Foreign Affairs* 100, no. 2 (2021), www.foreignaffairs.com/articles/united-states/2021-02-16/superpower-it-or-not.

17. Jim Garamone, "NATO Stands Together as Biden Reaffirms U.S. Commitment to Alliance," U.S. Department of Defense News, June 15, 2021, www.defense.gov/News/News-Stories/Article/Article/2658794/nato-stands-together-as-biden-reaffirms-us-commitment-to-alliance; Mira Rapp-Hooper, *Shields of the Republic: The Triumph and Peril of America's Alliances* (Harvard University Press, 2020); Michael O'Hanlon, *The Art of War in an Age of Peace: U.S. Grand Strategy and Resolute Restraint* (Yale University Press, 2021); Thomas J. Wright, *All Measures Short of War:*

The Contest for the Twenty-First Century and the Future of American Power (Yale University Press, 2017).

18. Heather Hurlburt, "Back to Basics: The Core Goals a 'Progressive' Foreign Policy Must Address," Policy Roundtable: The Future of Progressive Foreign Policy, *Texas National Security Review,* December 4, 2018, https://tnsr.org/roundtable/policy-roundtable-the-future-of-progressive-foreign-policy; Van Jackson, "Left of Liberal Internationalism: Grand Strategies Within Progressive Foreign Policy Thought," *Security Studies* 31, no. 4 (2022): 553–92, https://doi.org/10.1080/09636412.2022.2132874.

19. *Foreign Policy Is Possible: A Series of Lefty Policy Briefs* (Fellow Travelers, June 2021), https://fellowtravelersdotblog.files.wordpress.com/2021/06/foreign-policy-is-possible-june2021.pdf.

20. David Samuels, "The Aspiring Novelist Who Became Obama's Foreign-Policy Guru," *New York Times Magazine,* May 5, 2016, www.nytimes.com/2016/05/08/magazine/the-aspiring-novelist-who-became-obamas-foreign-policy-guru.html.

21. Kenneth N. Waltz, *Theory of International Politics* (Addison-Wesley, 1979); Jonathan Kirshner, *An Unwritten Future: Realism and Uncertainty in World Politics* (Princeton University Press, 2022).

22. Jonathan Rauch, "Learning From Ike," *Atlantic,* April 17, 2007, www.theatlantic.com/magazine/archive/2007/04/learning-from-ike/305875.

23. Joshua R. Itzkowitz Shifrinson, *Rising Titans, Falling Giants: How Great Powers Exploit Power Shifts* (Cornell University Press, 2018); M. E. Sarotte, *1989: The Struggle to Create Post–Cold War Europe,* new and rev. ed. (Princeton University Press, 2014); Bartholomew H. Sparrow, *The Strategist: Brent Scowcroft and the Call of National Security* (PublicAffairs, 2015).

24. William C. Wohlforth, "Realism," in *The Oxford Handbook of International Relations,* ed. Christian Reus-Smit and Duncan Snidal (Oxford University Press, 2009), 131–49, https://doi.org/10.1093/oxfordhb/9780199219322.003.0007.

25. Rauch, "Learning from Ike."

26. Colin Dueck, "The Strategy of Retrenchment and Its Consequences," E-Notes (Foreign Policy Research Institute, April 13, 2015), www.fpri.org/article/2015/04/the-strategy-of-retrenchment-and-its-consequences.

27. Paul K. MacDonald and Joseph M. Parent, "Graceful Decline? The Surprising Success of Great Power Retrenchment," *International Security* 35, no. 4 (2011): 7–44, https://doi.org/10.1162/ISEC_a_00034.

28. Hans J. Morgenthau, "The Primacy of the National Interest," *American Scholar* 18, no. 2 (1949): 207–12; Joseph S. Nye, "Redefining the National Interest," *Foreign Affairs* 78, no. 4 (1999): 22–35, https://doi.org/10.2307/20049361.

29. Keir Giles, "Russian Nuclear Intimidation: How Russia Uses Nuclear Threats to Shape Western Responses to Aggression," Research Paper (Chatham House (Royal Institute of International Affairs), March 29, 2023), https://doi.org/10.55317/9781784135645.

30. Richard K. Betts, *Nuclear Blackmail and Nuclear Balance* (Brookings Institution Press, 1987).

31. Kirshner, *An Unwritten Future.*

32. Rebecca Friedman Lissner, "What Is Grand Strategy? Sweeping a Conceptual Minefield," *Texas National Security Review* 2, no. 1 (2018), https://doi.org/10.26153/TSW/868; Hal Brands, *What Good Is Grand Strategy? Power and Purpose in American Statecraft from Harry S. Truman to George W. Bush,* paperback print (Cornell University Press, 2015), 1.

33. David A. Baldwin, *Economic Statecraft* (Princeton University Press, 1985); Robert Gilpin, *War and Change in World Politics* (Cambridge University Press, 2002).

34. Michael Howard, "The Forgotten Dimensions of Strategy," *Foreign Affairs* 57, no. 5 (1979), www.foreignaffairs.com/articles/1979-06-01/forgotten-dimensions-strategy; Elizabeth Borgwardt, Christopher McKnight Nichols, and Andrew Preston, eds., *Rethinking American Grand Strategy* (Oxford University Press, 2021); Thierry Balzacq, Peter Dombrowski, and Simon Reich, "Is Grand Strategy a Research Program? A Review Essay," *Security Studies* 28, no. 1 (2019): 58–86, https://doi.org/10.1080/09636412.2018.1508631; Nina Silove, "Beyond the Buzzword: The Three Meanings of 'Grand Strategy,'" *Security Studies* 27, no. 1 (2018): 27–57, https://doi.org/10.1080/09636412.2017.1360073; Lawrence Freedman, *Strategy: A History* (Oxford University Press, 2013); Ionut C. Popescu, "Grand Strategy vs. Emergent Strategy in the Conduct of Foreign Policy," *Journal of Strategic Studies* 41, no. 3 (2018): 438–60, https://doi.org/10.1080/01402390.2017.1288109.

35. Simon Reich and Peter J. Dombrowski, *The End of Grand Strategy: US Maritime Operations in the Twenty-First Century* (Cornell University Press, 2017); Daniel W. Drezner, Ronald R. Krebs, and Randall Schweller, "The End of Grand Strategy," *Foreign Affairs* 99, no. 3 (2020), www.foreignaffairs.com/articles/world/2020-04-13/end-grand-strategy.

36. Brands, *What Good Is Grand Strategy?,* 2.

37. John Lewis Gaddis, *On Grand Strategy* (Penguin, 2018), 21.

Chapter 1. The Decline and Fall of the Unipolar Moment

1. George H. W. Bush, "Address Before a Joint Session of the Congress on the Persian Gulf Crisis and the Federal Budget Deficit" (speech, Washington D.C., September 11, 1990), https://bush41library.tamu.edu/archives/public-papers/2217.

2. James D. Bryan and Jordan Tama, "The Prevalence of Bipartisanship in U.S. Foreign Policy: An Analysis of Important Congressional Votes," *International Politics* 59, no. 5 (2022): 874–97, https://doi.org/10.1057/s41311-021-00348-7.

3. John Lewis Gaddis, *Strategies of Containment: A Critical Appraisal of American National Security Policy During the Cold War,* rev. and expanded ed. (Oxford University Press, 2005).

4. Bruce D. Berkowitz, "After the Crusade: American Foreign Policy for Post-Superpower Age," *ORBIS* 42, no. 3 (1998): 465; John Dumbrell, "America in the 1990s: Searching for Purpose," in *U.S. Foreign Policy* (Oxford University Press, 2012), https://doi.org/10.1093/hepl/9780199585816.003.0005.

5. Stacie E. Goddard and Ronald R. Krebs, "Legitimating Primacy After the Cold War: How Liberal Talk Matters to U.S. Foreign Policy," in *Before and After the Fall: World Politics and the End of the Cold War,* ed. Fritz Bartel and Nuno P. Monteiro (Cambridge University Press, 2021), 132–50, https://doi.org/10.1017/97811089 10194.009.

6. Posen, *Restraint,* 7; Michael Mastanduno, "Preserving the Unipolar Moment: Realist Theories and U.S. Grand Strategy After the Cold War," *International Security* 21, no. 4 (1997): 49–88, https://doi.org/10.1162/isec.21.4.49; Hal Brands, *Making the Unipolar Moment: U.S. Foreign Policy and the Rise of the Post–Cold War Order* (Cornell University Press, 2016); Patrick Porter, "Why America's Grand Strategy Has Not Changed: Power, Habit, and the U.S. Foreign Policy Establishment," *International Security* 42, no. 04 (2018): 9–46, https://doi.org/10.1162/isec_a_00311; Michael Mandelbaum, *Mission Failure: America and the World in the Post–Cold War Era* (Oxford University Press, 2016).

7. John J. Mearsheimer, "Bound to Fail: The Rise and Fall of the Liberal International Order," *International Security* 43, no. 4 (2019): 23, https://doi.org/10.1162/ isec_a_00342.

8. Colin Dueck, "Ideas and Alternatives in American Grand Strategy, 2000–2004," *Review of International Studies* 30, no. 4 (2004): 511–35.

9. *The National Security Strategy of the United States of America* (The White House, September 2002), https://georgewbush-whitehouse.archives.gov/nsc/nss/2002.

10. Brands, *Making the Unipolar Moment,* 356.

11. Michael Mandelbaum, "The Inadequacy of American Power," *Foreign Affairs* 81, no. 5 (2002), www.foreignaffairs.com/articles/united-states/2002-09-01/inadequacy-american-power.

12. *Defense Strategy for the 1990s: The Regional Defense Strategy* (Office of the Secretary of Defense, January 1993); Jim Mann, *Rise of the Vulcans: The History of Bush's War Cabinet* (Penguin Books, 2004).

13. G. John Ikenberry, *After Victory: Institutions, Strategic Restraint, and the Rebuilding of Order after Major Wars,* new ed. (Princeton University Press, 2019), 273.

14. Mearsheimer, "Bound to Fail: The Rise and Fall of the Liberal International Order," 8.

15. Brands, *Making the Unipolar Moment.*

16. "Spiegel Interview: 'America Had No Verdun,'" *New York Times,* March 24, 2003, www.nytimes.com/2003/03/24/international/europe/spiegel-interview-quotamerica-had-no-verdunquot.html.

17. Robert A. Pape, "Soft Balancing Against the United States," *International Security* 30, no. 1 (2005): 10.

18. Patrick Porter, *The False Promise of Liberal Order: Nostalgia, Delusion and the Rise of Trump* (Polity, 2020).

19. Nuno Monteiro and Fritz Bartel, eds., *Before and After the Fall: World Politics and the End of the Cold War* (Cambridge University Press, 2021), 354.

20. Jake Sullivan, "The World After Trump: How the System Can Endure," *Foreign Affairs* 97, no. 2 (2018), https://www.foreignaffairs.com/articles/2018-03-05/world-after-trump.

21. Joshua R. Itzkowitz Shifrinson, "Deal or No Deal? The End of the Cold War and the U.S. Offer to Limit NATO Expansion," *International Security* 40, no. 4 (2016): 7–44, https://doi.org/10.1162/ISEC_a_00236; M. E. Sarotte, *Not One Inch: America, Russia, and the Making of Post–Cold War Stalemate* (Yale University Press, 2021); Fritz Bartel, *The Triumph of Broken Promises: The End of the Cold War and the Rise of Neoliberalism* (Harvard University Press, 2022).

22. Strobe Talbott, *The Russia Hand: A Memoir of Presidential Diplomacy*, paperback ed. (Random House, 2003); James M. Goldgeier and Michael McFaul, *Power and Purpose: U.S. Policy Toward Russia After the Cold War* (Brookings Institution Press, 2003).

23. Svetlana Savranskaya and Tom Blanton, "NATO Expansion: What Yeltsin Heard," Briefing Book No. 621, National Security Archive, March 16, 2018, https://nsarchive.gwu.edu/briefing-book/russia-programs/2018-03-16/nato-expansion-what-yeltsin-heard.

24. James M. Goldgeier, *Not Whether but When: The U.S. Decision to Enlarge NATO* (Brookings Institution Press, 1999); Stuart Croft et al., "NATO's Triple Challenge," *International Affairs* 76, no. 3 (2000): 495–518; M. E. Sarotte, "Containment Beyond the Cold War," *Foreign Affairs* 100, no. 6 (2021), www.foreignaffairs.com/articles/russia-fsu/2021-10-19/containment-beyond-cold-war.

25. Arms Control Association, "Open Letter: Opposition to NATO Expansion," June 26, 1997, www.armscontrol.org/act/1997-06/arms-control-today/opposition-nato-expansion; Elaine Sciolino, "NATO's Salesman Finds the U.S. Tough Territory," *New York Times,* November 9, 1997, www.nytimes.com/1997/11/09/world/natos-salesman-finds-the-us-tough-territory.html.

26. John Kornblum, "NATO's Second Half Century—Tasks for an Alliance," NATO on Track for the 21st Century, Conference Report (Netherlands Atlantic Commission, 1994).

27. John S. Duffield, "NATO's Functions After the Cold War," *Political Science Quarterly* 109, no. 5 (1994): 785–86, https://doi.org/10.2307/2152531.

28. *Study on NATO Enlargement* (North Atlantic Treaty Organization, September 3, 1995), http://www.nato.int/cps/en/natohq/official_texts_24733.htm.

29. Mark Baker, "U.S.: Rumsfeld's 'Old' And 'New' Europe Touches on Uneasy Divide," *Radio Free Europe/Radio Liberty,* January 24, 2003, www.rferl.org/a/1102012.html; Andrew A. Michta, "NATO Enlargement Post-1989: Successful Adaptation or Decline?," *Contemporary European History* 18, no. 3 (2009): 363.

30. Vladimir V. Putin, "Putin's Prepared Remarks at 43rd Munich Conference on Security Policy" (speech, Munich Security Conference, Munich, February 12, 2007), http://www.washingtonpost.com/wp-dyn/content/article/2007/02/12/AR2007021200555.html.

31. James Goldgeier and Joshua R. Itzkowitz Shifrinson, eds., *Evaluating NATO Enlargement: From Cold War Victory to the Russia-Ukraine War* (Springer International, 2023), https://doi.org/10.1007/978-3-031-23364-7.

32. David A. Shlapak and Michael Johnson, *Reinforcing Deterrence on NATO's Eastern Flank: Wargaming the Defense of the Baltics* (RAND Corporation, January 29, 2016), www.rand.org/pubs/research_reports/RR1253.html.

33. Max Bergmann, James Lamond, and Siena Cicarelli, "The Case for EU Defense," Center for American Progress, June 1, 2021, www.americanprogress.org/article/case-eu-defense; Mark Cancian, "The European Reassurance Initiative," Critical Questions, Center for Strategic and International Studies, February 9, 2016, www.csis.org/analysis/european-reassurance-initiative.

34. Gustav Gressel, "After Crimea: Does NATO Have the Means to Defend Europe?," *ECFR* (blog), April 2, 2019, https://ecfr.eu/article/commentary_after_crimea_does_nato_have_the_means_to_defend_europe.

35. John J. Mearsheimer, "Why the Ukraine Crisis Is the West's Fault," *Foreign Affairs* 93, no. 5 (2014), www.foreignaffairs.com/articles/russia-fsu/2014-08-18/why-ukraine-crisis-west-s-fault; Michael McFaul, Stephen Sestanovich, and John J. Mearsheimer, "Faulty Powers: Who Started the Ukraine Crisis?," *Foreign Affairs* 93, no. 6 (2014): 167–78; Alexander J. Motyl, "The Surrealism of Realism: Misreading the War in Ukraine," *World Affairs* 177, no. 5 (2015): 75–84; "Was NATO Enlargement a Mistake?," Ask the Experts, *Foreign Affairs,* April 19, 2022, www.foreignaffairs.com/ask-the-experts/2022-04-19/was-nato-enlargement-mistake.

36. Sarotte, "Containment Beyond the Cold War."

37. Samantha Power, *"A Problem from Hell": America and the Age of Genocide* (Basic Books, 2013).

38. *Report of the Secretary-General Pursuant to General Assembly Resolution 53/35: The Fall of Srebrenica* (United Nations, November 15, 1999), 107, https://digitallibrary.un.org/record/372298.

39. Francis Mading Deng, ed., *Sovereignty as Responsibility: Conflict Management in Africa* (Brookings Institution, 1996).

40. Nicholas J. Wheeler, "Reflections on the Legality and Legitimacy of NATO's Intervention in Kosovo," *International Journal of Human Rights* 4, nos. 3–4 (2000): 144–63, https://doi.org/10.1080/13642980008406897.

41. "Two Concepts of Sovereignty," *Economist,* September 16, 1999, www.economist.com/international/1999/09/16/two-concepts-of-sovereignty.

42. Gareth Evans, "R2P: The Dream and the Reality" (speech, European Centre for the Responsibility to Protect Annual Lecture, Leeds University, November 26, 2020), www.globalr2p.org/publications/r2p-the-dream-and-the-reality.

43. CNN Wire Staff, "Rebel Leader Calls for 'Immediate Action' on No-Fly Zone," *CNN,* March 10, 2011, http://www.cnn.com/2011/WORLD/africa/03/09/libya.civil.war/index.html.

44. Micah Zenko, "The Big Lie About the Libyan War," *Foreign Policy,* March 22, 2016, https://foreignpolicy.com/2016/03/22/libya-and-the-myth-of-humanitarian-intervention.

45. Alan J. Kuperman, "A Model Humanitarian Intervention? Reassessing NATO's Libya Campaign," *International Security* 38, no. 1 (2013): 105–36.

46. Marc Lynch, "What's Really at Stake in the Syria Debate," *War on the Rocks,* October 10, 2016, https://warontherocks.com/2016/10/whats-really-at-stake-in-the-syria-debate.

47. Leon Wieseltier, "Lessons from the Rubble of Palmyra," *Atlantic,* September 4, 2015, www.theatlantic.com/international/archive/2015/09/rubble-palmyra-syria-isis/403921.

48. Jeffrey Goldberg, "The Obama Doctrine," *Atlantic,* March 10, 2016, www.theatlantic.com/magazine/archive/2016/04/the-obama-doctrine/471525.

49. *National Security Strategy of the United States of America* (The White House, October 2022), 22 (hereafter cited as 2022 *National Security Strategy*), www.whitehouse.gov/wp-content/uploads/2022/10/Biden-Harris-Administrations-National-Security-Strategy-10.2022.pdf.

50. Courtney Alter, "CNN: Full Transcript of the Fifth Republican Debate," *Time,* December 16, 2015, https://time.com/4150816/republican-debate-las-vegas-transcript.

51. Reem Nadeem, "A Look Back at How Fear and False Beliefs Bolstered U.S. Public Support for War in Iraq," *Pew Research Center* (blog), March 14, 2023, www.pewresearch.org/politics/2023/03/14/a-look-back-at-how-fear-and-false-beliefs-bolstered-u-s-public-support-for-war-in-iraq.

52. Andrew Prokop, "Donald Trump Issued a Remarkably Blunt Denunciation of the Iraq War During the Debate," *Vox,* December 16, 2015, www.vox.com/2015/12/16/10296032/donald-trump-gop-debate-iraq-war.

53. Nadeem, "A Look Back at How Fear and False Beliefs Bolstered U.S. Public Support for War in Iraq."

54. Stephen Cook, "Twenty Years After the War to Oust Saddam, Iraq Is a Shaky Democracy," *Council on Foreign Relations* (blog), March 17, 2023, www.cfr.org/article/twenty-years-after-war-oust-saddam-iraq-shaky-democracy.

55. Stewart M. Patrick, "How Do Warren and Sanders' Progressive Foreign Policy Visions Stack Up?," *World Politics Review,* October 28, 2019, www.worldpoliticsreview.com/how-do-warren-and-sanders-progressive-foreign-policy-visions-stack-up.

56. Barack Obama, "Obama's Remarks on Iraq and Afghanistan" (speech, Woodrow Wilson International Center for Scholars, Washington D.C., July 15, 2008), www.nytimes.com/2008/07/15/us/politics/15text-obama.html.

57. Jessica Stern, "Obama and Terrorism," *Foreign Affairs* 94, no. 5 (2015), www.foreignaffairs.com/articles/obama-and-terrorism.

58. "Petraeus: Afghan War Has Turned a Corner," *BBC News,* July 22, 2011, www.bbc.com/news/world-us-canada-14257679; Craig Whitlock, "Confidential Documents Reveal U.S. Officials Failed to Tell the Truth About the War in Afghanistan," *Washington Post,* December 9, 2019, www.washingtonpost.com/graphics/2019/investigations/afghanistan-papers/afghanistan-war-confidential-documents.

59. Nadeem, "A Look Back at How Fear and False Beliefs Bolstered U.S. Public Support for War in Iraq."

60. Harry Enten, "Americans Sour on Obama's Foreign Policy," *FiveThirtyEight,* June 6, 2014, https://fivethirtyeight.com/features/americans-sour-on-obamas-foreign-policy.

61. "The Partisan Divide on Political Values Grows Even Wider," Pew Research Center, October 5, 2017, www.pewresearch.org/politics/2017/10/05/3-foreign-policy.

62. Craig Whitlock, *The Afghanistan Papers: A Secret History of the War* (Simon & Schuster, 2021).

63. Bartel, *The Triumph of Broken Promises,* 19.

64. William J. Clinton, "President Clinton's Remarks on the Passage of the China Trade Bill" (speech, Washington D.C., May 25, 2000), www.nytimes.com/library/world/asia/052500clinton-trade-text.html.

65. Thomas L. Friedman, "Foreign Affairs Big Mac I," Opinion, *New York Times,* December 8, 1996, www.nytimes.com/1996/12/08/opinion/foreign-affairs-big-mac-i.html.

66. Henry S. Farber and Joanne Gowa, "Polities and Peace," *International Security* 20, no. 2 (1995): 123–46, https://doi.org/10.1162/isec.20.2.123; John R. Oneal and Bruce M. Russet, "The Classical Liberals Were Right: Democracy, Interdependence, and Conflict, 1950–1985," *International Studies Quarterly* 41, no. 2 (1997): 267–94, https://doi.org/10.1111/1468-2478.00042; Erik Gartzke, "The Capitalist Peace," *American Journal of Political Science* 51, no. 1 (2007): 166–91, https://doi.org/10.1111/j.1540-5907.2007.00244.x; Christopher F. Gelpi and Joseph M. Grieco, "Democracy, Interdependence, and the Sources of the Liberal Peace," *Journal of Peace Research* 45, no. 1 (2008): 17–36, https://doi.org/10.1177/00223433 07084921.

67. "Albright Interview on NBC-TV 'The Today Show,'" U.S. Department of State Archive, February 19, 1998, https://1997-2001.state.gov/statements/1998/980219a.html.

68. Robert Zoellick, "Whither China? From Membership to Responsibility" (speech, National Committee on U.S.-China Relations, New York City, September 21, 2005), www.ncuscr.org/wp-content/uploads/2020/04/migration_Zoellick_remarks_notes06_winter_spring.pdf.

69. *A National Security Strategy of Engagement and Enlargement* (The White House, July 1994), https://history.defense.gov/Portals/70/Documents/nss/nss1994.pdf.

70. Ann Harrison, "Globalization and Poverty," NBER Working Paper No. 12347 (National Bureau of Economic Research, March 3, 2007), www.nber.org/papers/w12347.

71. J. Adam Tooze, *Crashed: How a Decade of Financial Crises Changed the World* (Penguin Books, 2019), 458–59.

72. Alex Ward, "Read: Bernie Sanders's Big Foreign Policy Speech," *Vox,* September 21, 2017, www.vox.com/world/2017/9/21/16345600/bernie-sanders-full-text-transcript-foreign-policy-speech-westminster.

73. Ian Bremmer, *Us vs. Them: The Failure of Globalism* (Portfolio/Penguin, 2018).

74. Tom Wyler et al., *Making U.S. Foreign Policy Work Better for the Middle Class* (Carnegie Endowment for International Peace, September 23, 2020), 5, https://carnegieendowment.org/2020/09/23/making-u.s.-foreign-policy-work-better-for-middle-class-pub-82728.

75. Jason W. Davidson, "The Enduring Importance of Revisionism and Status-Quo Seeking," in *The Origins of Revisionist and Status-Quo States*, ed. Jason W. Davidson (Palgrave Macmillan US, 2006), 1–18, https://doi.org/10.1007/978-1-137-09201-4_1.

76. *National Security Strategy of the United States of America* (The White House, December 2017) (hereafter cited as 2017 *National Security Strategy*), www.whitehouse.gov/wp-content/uploads/2017/12/NSS-Final-12-18-2017-0905-2.pdf.

77. Bruce M. Russett, Thomas Risse-Kappen, and John J. Mearsheimer, "Back to the Future, Part III: Realism and the Realities of European Security," *International Security* 15, no. 3 (1990): 216–22, https://doi.org/10.2307/2538912.

78. Steven Ward, *Status and the Challenge of Rising Powers* (Cambridge University Press, 2017); J. Davidson, *The Origins of Revisionist and Status-Quo States* (Springer, 2016).

79. Korinna Horta, *The Asian Infrastructure Investment Bank: A Multilateral Bank Where China Sets the Rules* (Heinrich Boll Stiftung, April 2019), www.boell.de/en/2019/03/26/asian-infrastructure-investment-bank-aiib-multilateral-bank-where-china-sets-rules.

80. Bruce Jones and Andrew Yeo, "China and the Challenge to Global Order," Policy Brief (Brookings Institution, November 2022), www.brookings.edu/articles/china-and-the-challenge-to-global-order.

81. Michael Mandelbaum, "America in a New World," *The American Interest,* May 23, 2016, www.the-american-interest.com/2016/05/23/america-in-a-new-world; Colin Dueck, *Age of Iron: On Conservative Nationalism* (Oxford University Press, 2019).

82. 2017 *National Security Strategy.*

83. Kurt Campbell et al., *Extending American Power: Strategies to Expand U.S. Engagement in a Competitive World Order* (Center for a New American Security, May 2016), www.cnas.org/publications/reports/extending-american-power-strategies-to-expand-u-s-engagement-in-a-competitive-world-order.

84. "Open Letter on Trump from GOP National Security Leaders," *War on the Rocks,* March 3, 2016, https://warontherocks.com/2016/03/open-letter-on-donald-trump-from-gop-national-security-leaders.

85. Maureen Dowd, "Donald the Dove, Hillary the Hawk," Opinion, *New York Times,* April 30, 2016, www.nytimes.com/2016/05/01/opinion/sunday/donald-the-dove-hillary-the-hawk.html.

86. Maggie Haberman and David E. Sanger, "Transcript: Donald Trump Expounds on His Foreign Policy Views," *New York Times,* March 26, 2016, www.nytimes.com/2016/03/27/us/politics/donald-trump-transcript.html.

87. Stephen M. Walt, *The Hell of Good Intentions: America's Foreign Policy Elite and the Decline of U.S. Primacy* (Farrar, Straus and Giroux, 2018), 91.

88. John Hudson, "Inside Hillary Clinton's Massive Foreign-Policy Brain Trust," *Foreign Policy*, February 10, 2016, https://foreignpolicy.com/2016/02/10/inside-hillary-clintons-massive-foreign-policy-brain-trust.

89. Mira Rapp-Hooper (@MiraRappHooper), "Thinking of U.S. Marines at Battle of Chosin River: Retreat, hell! We're attacking in a different direction. Thanks @ Carter_PE, wise words," Nov 10, 2016, https://x.com/MiraRappHooper/status/796688860642181120?s=20; Ulrike Franke (@RikeFranke), "9 November 1938: Night of Broken Glass, 9 November 1989 Fall of the Berlin Wall, 9 November 2016: End of the Liberal Order #shickalstag," November 9, 2016, https://x.com/RikeFranke/status/796274064285454336?s=20.

90. Mira Rapp-Hooper, "Deciphering Trump's Asia Policy," *Foreign Affairs*, November 22, 2016, www.foreignaffairs.com/articles/asia/2016-11-22/deciphering-trumps-asia-policy; Aharon Klieman and Yoel Guzansky, "Reading Trump's Middle East Policy," *Foreign Affairs*, November 17, 2016, www.foreignaffairs.com/articles/united-states/2016-11-17/reading-trumps-middle-east-policy.

91. Wyler et al., *Making U.S. Foreign Policy Work Better for the Middle Class;* Julianne Smith, " 'Across the Pond, In the Field': Bringing U.S. Foreign Policy Out of the Washington Bubble," *Pittsburgh Post-Gazette*, October 18, 2017, *https://www.post-gazette.com/opinion/Op-Ed/2017/10/18/Across-the-Pond-In-the-Field-U-S-foreign-policy-Washington-bubble-Center-New-American-Security-Julianne-Smith/stories/201710190029*; "Debating America's Role in the World," Brookings Institution, accessed March 7, 2023, www.brookings.edu/tags/debating-americas-role-in-the-world.

92. Lara Seligman, "The Afghanistan Deal That Never Happened," *Politico*, August 11, 2022, www.politico.com/news/magazine/2022/08/11/the-afghanistan-deal-00050916.

Chapter 2. New World, New Debates

1. Joseph R. Biden, "Remarks by President Biden Ahead of the One-Year Anniversary of Russia's Brutal and Unprovoked Invasion of Ukraine" (speech, Warsaw, Poland, February 21, 2023), www.whitehouse.gov/briefing-room/speeches-remarks/2023/02/21/remarks-by-president-biden-ahead-of-the-one-year-anniversary-of-russias-brutal-and-unprovoked-invasion-of-ukraine.

2. Melvyn P. Leffler, *For the Soul of Mankind: The United States, the Soviet Union, and the Cold War* (Hill and Wang, 2008).

3. Mark Leonard and Ivan Krastev, "Peace versus Justice: The Coming European Split over the War in Ukraine," European Council on Foreign Relations, June 15, 2022, https://ecfr.eu/publication/peace-versus-justice-the-coming-european-split-over-the-war-in-ukraine.

4. Jennifer Agiesta, "CNN Poll: Majority of Americans Oppose More U.S. Aid for Ukraine in War with Russia," *CNN*, August 4, 2023, www.cnn.com/2023/08/04/politics/cnn-poll-ukraine/index.html.

5. Robert Jervis, "American Grand Strategy: Untangling the Debates," in *The Oxford Handbook of Grand Strategy*, ed. Thierry Balzacq and Ronald R. Krebs (Oxford University Press, 2021), 442.

6. Robert Jervis, "International Primacy: Is the Game Worth the Candle?," *International Security* 17, no. 4 (1993): 58, https://doi.org/10.2307/2539021.

7. If, indeed, there ever was. Walter Russell Mead argues that the "isolationist vs. internationalist" dichotomy is the central dividing cleavage of U.S. foreign policy. But as Stephen Wertheim argues, the term "isolationist" has always been more of a pejorative—used to win domestic political battles over the future of U.S. foreign policy—than it has been an accurate description of foreign policy views. See Stephen Wertheim, *Tomorrow, the World: The Birth of U.S. Global Supremacy* (Belknap Press of Harvard University Press, 2020); Walter Russell Mead, *Special Providence: American Foreign Policy and How It Changed the World* (Routledge, 2009).

8. 2017 *National Security Strategy.*

9. "The Rise and Fall of the Responsibility to Protect," *World101* (blog), Council on Foreign Relations, April 20, 2023, https://world101.cfr.org/understanding-international-system/building-blocks/rise-and-fall-responsibility-protect.

10. Hal Brands, "U.S. Grand Strategy in an Age of Nationalism: Fortress America and Its Alternatives," *Washington Quarterly* 40, no. 1 (2017): 73–94, https://doi.org/10.1080/0163660X.2017.1302740.

11. Wyler et al., "Making U.S. Foreign Policy Work Better for the Middle Class."

12. Janet Yellen, "Remarks by Secretary of the Treasury Janet L. Yellen on the U.S.-China Economic Relationship" (speech, Johns Hopkins School of Advanced International Studies, August 28, 2023), https://home.treasury.gov/news/press-releases/jy1425; Jake Sullivan, "Remarks by National Security Advisor Jake Sullivan on Renewing American Economic Leadership" (speech, Brookings Institution, April 27, 2023), www.whitehouse.gov/briefing-room/speeches-remarks/2023/04/27/remarks-by-national-security-advisor-jake-sullivan-on-renewing-american-economic-leadership-at-the-brookings-institution.

13. Graham Allison, "The Myth of the Liberal Order," *Foreign Affairs* 97, no. 4 (2018), www.foreignaffairs.com/united-states/myth-liberal-order; Porter, *The False Promise of Liberal Order;* Michael Barnett, "The End of a Liberal International Order That Never Existed," *The Global* (blog), April 16, 2019, https://theglobal.blog/2019/04/16/the-end-of-a-liberal-international-order-that-never-existed; Kyle M. Lascurettes, *Orders of Exclusion: Great Powers and the Strategic Sources of Foundational Rules in International Relations* (Oxford University Press, 2020).

14. Porter, *The False Promise of Liberal Order,* 14.

15. Ikenberry, *After Victory;* Daniel Deudney and G. John Ikenberry, "Realism, Liberalism and the Iraq War," *Survival* 59, no. 4 (2017): 7–26.

16. Robert Kagan, *The Jungle Grows Back: America and Our Imperiled World* (Alfred A. Knopf, 2018), 4.

17. Joseph R. Biden, "Remarks by President Biden at the White House Correspondents' Association Dinner" (speech, Washington Hilton, May 1, 2022), www.whitehouse.gov/briefing-room/speeches-remarks/2022/05/01/remarks-by-president-biden-at-the-white-house-correspondents-association-dinner; 2022 *National Security Strategy.*

18. Wright, *All Measures Short of War,* 188.

19. Rebecca Lissner and Mira Rapp-Hooper, *An Open World: How America Can Win the Contest for Twenty-First-Century Order* (Yale University Press, 2020); O'Hanlon, *The Art of War in an Age of Peace.*

20. Garamone, "NATO Stands Together as Biden Reaffirms U.S. Commitment to Alliance."

21. O'Hanlon, *The Art of War in an Age of Peace,* 1–2.

22. Mead, *Special Providence,* 4.

23. Max Boot, "Trump Is Turning U.S. Foreign Policy into a Protection Racket," Opinion, *Washington Post,* March 11, 2019, www.washingtonpost.com/opinions/2019/03/11/trump-is-turning-us-foreign-policy-into-protection-racket.

24. Ted Cruz, "Sen. Cruz on the Senate Floor: I Will Use All Options To Stop Biden-Putin Nord Stream 2 Pipeline," press release, August 11, 2021, www.cruz.senate.gov/newsroom/press-releases/sen-cruz-on-the-senate-floor-i-will-use-all-options-to-stop-biden-putin-nord-stream-2-pipeline; Rebecca Heinrichs, Peter Rough, and Bartosz Bieliszczuk, "The Future of the Russian Nord Stream 2 Pipeline" (panel discussion, Hudson Institute, August 30, 2023), www.hudson.org/foreign-policy/transcript-the-future-of-the-russian-nord-stream-2-pipeline.

25. Schadlow, "The End of American Illusion."

26. McMaster, *Battlegrounds.*

27. Dueck, *Age of Iron.*

28. Colby, *The Strategy of Denial.*

29. Pottinger, testimony before the House Select Committee on the Strategic Competition Between the United States and the Chinese Communist Party.

30. John Laloggia, "As New Tariffs Take Hold, More See Negative Than Positive Impact for the U.S.," *Pew Research Center* (blog), July 19, 2018, www.pewresearch.org/short-reads/2018/07/19/as-new-tariffs-take-hold-more-see-negative-than-positive-impact-for-the-u-s.

31. Jeet Heer, "What's Behind the New Calls to Invade Mexico," *Nation,* April 4, 2023, www.thenation.com/article/politics/invade-mexico-amlo-cartels.

32. Jeffrey Goldberg, "A Senior White House Official Defines the Trump Doctrine: 'We're America, Bitch,'" *Atlantic,* June 11, 2018, www.theatlantic.com/politics/archive/2018/06/a-senior-white-house-official-defines-the-trump-doctrine-were-america-bitch/562511.

33. Barry R. Posen, "The Rise of Illiberal Hegemony," *Foreign Affairs* 97, no. 2 (2018), www.foreignaffairs.com/united-states/rise-illiberal-hegemony; Michael Beckley, "Why This Could Be an Illiberal American Century," *Foreign Affairs* 99, no. 6 (2020), www.foreignaffairs.com/articles/united-states/2020-10-06/illiberal-american-century-rogue-superpower.

34. Daniel McDowell, *Bucking the Buck: U.S. Financial Sanctions and the International Backlash Against the Dollar* (Oxford University Press, 2023).

35. Loren DeJonge Schulman, "Progressives Should Embrace the Politics of Defense," Policy Roundtable: The Future of Progressive Foreign Policy, *Texas National*

Security Review, December 4, 2018, https://tnsr.org/roundtable/policy-roundtable-the-future-of-progressive-foreign-policy.

36. Robert Farley, "The LCS, Apple Pie, and What Not," *Lawyers, Guns, and Money* (blog), January 4, 2011, https://lawyersgunsmon.wpengine.com/2011/01/the-lcs-apple-pie-and-what-not.

37. Jackson, "Left of Liberal Internationalism: Grand Strategies Within Progressive Foreign Policy Thought."

38. Hurlburt, "Back to Basics: The Core Goals a 'Progressive' Foreign Policy Must Address."

39. *Foreign Policy Is Possible: A Series of Lefty Policy Briefs.*

40. Anatol Lieven and John Hulsman, *Ethical Realism: A Vision for America's Role in the World* (Vintage Books, 2006); Daniel Bessner, "Realism in U.S. Foreign Policy," *Foreign Exchanges* (Substack), October 13, 2020, https://fx.substack.com/p/realism-in-us-foreign-policy; Robert Wright, " 'Progressive Realism': In Search of a Foreign Policy," Opinion, *New York Times,* July 18, 2006, www.nytimes.com/2006/07/18/opinion/18iht-edwright.2231959.html; Katrina vanden Heuvel, "Needed: A Clear Foreign Policy of Progressive Realism," Opinion, *Washington Post,* January 22, 2019, www.washingtonpost.com/opinions/needed-a-clear-foreign-policy-of-progressive-realism/2019/01/22/9743994c-1dbe-11e9-9145-3f74070bbdb9_story.html.

41. Dwight Eisenhower, "The Chance for Peace" (speech, American Society of Newspaper Editors, Washington D.C., April 16, 1953), www.presidency.ucsb.edu/documents/address-the-chance-for-peace-delivered-before-the-american-society-newspaper-editors.

42. Daniel Benaim, "A Progressive Course Correction for U.S.-Saudi Relations," The Century Foundation, June 25, 2020, https://tcf.org/content/report/progressive-course-correction-u-s-saudi-relations.

43. Michael Walzer, *A Foreign Policy for the Left* (New Haven: Yale University Press, 2018).

44. Robert Wright, "American Foreign Policy Has an Empathy Problem," *Nation,* December 21, 2016, www.thenation.com/article/archive/american-foreign-policy-has-an-empathy-problem.

45. Kate Kizer, "A U.S. Grand Strategy for a Values-Driven Foreign Policy," in *New Voices in Grand Strategy* (Center for a New American Security, 2018), www.cnas.org/publications/reports/new-voices-in-grand-strategy.

46. Jackson, "Left of Liberal Internationalism: Grand Strategies Within Progressive Foreign Policy Thought."

47. Daniel H. Nexon, "Toward a Neo-Progressive Foreign Policy," *Foreign Affairs,* September 4, 2018, www.foreignaffairs.com/articles/united-states/2018-09-04/toward-neo-progressive-foreign-policy.

48. Jackson, "Left of Liberal Internationalism: Grand Strategies Within Progressive Foreign Policy Thought," 576.

49. Suzanne Maloney, "Deception and the Iran Deal: Did the Obama Administration Mislead America, or Did the Rhodes Profile?," Brookings Institution, May 11,

2016, www.brookings.edu/articles/deception-and-the-iran-deal-did-the-obama-ad-ministration-mislead-america-or-did-the-rhodes-profile.

50. Ganesh Sitaraman, "The Emergence of Progressive Foreign Policy," *War on the Rocks,* April 15, 2019, https://warontherocks.com/2019/04/the-emergence-of-progressive-foreign-policy; Jennifer Harris, "Making Trade Address Inequality," *Democracy: A Journal of Ideas,* no. 48 (Spring 2018), https://democracyjournal.org/magazine/48/making-trade-address-inequality.

51. Tarak Barkawi, "Wishful Strategies," *Security Studies* 32, no. 2 (2023): 371–77, https://doi.org/10.1080/09636412.2023.2200969.

52. Emma Ashford, "Strategies of Restraint," *Foreign Affairs* 100, no. 5 (2021), www.foreignaffairs.com/articles/united-states/2021-08-24/strategies-restraint.

53. Eugene Gholz, Daryl G. Press, and Harvey M. Sapolsky, "Come Home, America: The Strategy of Restraint in the Face of Temptation," *International Security* 21, no. 4 (1997): 5–48, https://doi.org/10.1162/isec.21.4.5.

54. Posen, *Restraint;* Miranda Priebe et al., *Implementing Restraint: Changes in U.S. Regional Security Policies to Operationalize a Realist Grand Strategy of Restraint* (RAND Corporation, 2021), www.rand.org/pubs/research_reports/RRA739-1.html; Andrew J. Bacevich, *The Age of Illusions: How America Squandered Its Cold War Victory* (Metropolitan Books, Henry Holt, 2020); John J. Mearsheimer, *The Great Delusion: Liberal Dreams and International Realities* (Yale University Press, 2018).

55. Christopher Layne, *The Peace of Illusions: American Grand Strategy from 1940 to the Present* (Cornell University Press, 2007), 204.

56. Stephen Walt, "How American Foreign Policy Inspires Resistance, Insurgency, and Terrorism," *Big Think,* 2016, https://bigthink.com/the-present/stephen-walt-how-american-foreign-policy-inspires-resistance-insurgency-and-terrorism.

57. Bessner, "Realism in U.S. Foreign Policy,"; Van Jackson, "Do Realists and Leftists Want the Same Thing?," *Inkstick,* March 30, 2022, https://inkstickmedia.com/do-realists-and-leftists-want-the-same-thing.

58. Posen, *Restraint;* Gholz, Press, and Sapolsky, "Come Home, America."

59. John J. Mearsheimer and Stephen M. Walt, "The Case for Offshore Balancing," *Foreign Affairs* 95, no. 4 (2016): 70–83; Walt, *The Hell of Good Intentions;* Christopher Layne, "America's Middle East Grand Strategy After Iraq: The Moment for Offshore Balancing Has Arrived," *Review of International Studies* 35, no. 1 (2009): 5–25; Layne, *The Peace of Illusions.*

60. William Ruger and Christopher Preble, "No More of the Same: The Problem with Primacy," *War on the Rocks,* August 31, 2016, https://warontherocks.com/2016/08/no-more-of-the-same-the-problem-with-primacy.

61. Daniel Deudney and G. John Ikenberry, "Misplaced Restraint: The Quincy Coalition Versus Liberal Internationalism," *Survival* 63, no. 4 (2021): 7–32, https://doi.org/10.1080/00396338.2021.1956187.

62. Wright, *All Measures Short of War;* Deudney and John Ikenberry, "Misplaced Restraint"; Hal Brands, *American Grand Strategy in the Age of Trump* (Brookings Institution Press, 2018).

63. Henry Kissinger and Cyrus Vance, "Bipartisan Objectives for American Foreign Policy," *Foreign Affairs* 66, no. 5 (1988): 899, https://doi.org/10.2307/20043570.

64. Bryan and Tama, "The Prevalence of Bipartisanship in U.S. Foreign Policy"; James M. McCormick and Eugene R. Wittkopf, "Bipartisanship, Partisanship, and Ideology in Congressional-Executive Foreign Policy Relations, 1947–1988," *Journal of Politics* 52, no. 4 (1990): 1077–1100, https://doi.org/10.2307/2131683.

65. Christopher Tuttle, "Foreign Policy Bipartisanship's Mixed Blessings," *Renewing America* (blog), Council on Foreign Relations, May 31, 2022, www.cfr.org/blog/foreign-policy-bipartisanships-mixed-blessings.

66. Schulman, "Progressives Should Embrace the Politics of Defense."

Chapter 3. Naval Gazing

1. Thomas Callendar, "The Nation Needs a 400-Ship Navy," Special Report No. 205 (Heritage Foundation, October 26, 2018), www.heritage.org/sites/default/files/2018-10/SR205.pdf.

2. Sam Lagrone and Mallory Shelborne, "CNO Gilday: 'We Need a Naval Force of Over 500 Ships,'" *USNI News,* February 19, 2022, https://news.usni.org/2022/02/18/cno-gilday-we-need-a-naval-force-of-over-500-ships.

3. Brad Lendon, "China Has Built the World's Largest Navy: Now What's Beijing Going to Do with It?," *CNN,* March 6, 2021, www.cnn.com/2021/03/05/china/china-world-biggest-navy-intl-hnk-ml-dst/index.html; David Lague and Benjamin Kang Lim, "China's Vast Fleet Is Tipping the Balance in the Pacific," *Reuters,* April 30, 2019, www.reuters.com/investigates/special-report/china-army-navy/.

4. Andrew Flowers, Sebastian Dettmers, and Chris Forman, "The Great People Shortage Hits China," *Business Insider,* February 1, 2023, www.businessinsider.com/china-shrinking-population-worker-labor-shortage-grim-omen-global-economy-2023-2.; Albee Zhang and Farah Master, "China's First Population Drop in Six Decades Sounds Alarm on Demographic Crisis," *Reuters,* January 18, 2023, www.reuters.com/world/china/chinas-population-shrinks-first-time-since-1961-2023-01-17.

5. Bret Stephens, "China's Decline Became Undeniable This Week: Now What?," Opinion, *New York Times,* January 18, 2023, www.nytimes.com/2023/01/17/opinion/china-population-decline.html.

6. The most notable is Beckley, *Unrivaled.* See also Matthew Kroenig, *The Return of Great Power Rivalry: Democracy versus Autocracy from the Ancient World to the U.S. and China* (Oxford University Press, 2020); Evan Braden Montgomery, "Primacy and Punishment: U.S. Grand Strategy, Maritime Power, and Military Options to Manage Decline," *Security Studies* 29, no. 4 (2020): 769–96; Stephen G. Brooks, "Power Transitions, Then and Now: Five New Structural Barriers That Will Constrain China's Rise," *China International Strategy Review* 1, no. 1 (2019): 65–83; Brian D. Blankenship and Benjamin Denison, "Is America Prepared for Great-Power Competition?," *Survival* 61, no. 5 (2019): 43–64; Nicholas Kitchen and Michael Cox, "Power, Structural Power, and American Decline," *Cambridge Review of International Affairs* 32, no. 6 (2019): 734–52; Graham T. Allison, *Destined for War: Can America and China Escape Thucydides's Trap?* (Houghton Mifflin Harcourt, 2017).

7. Joseph S. Nye Jr., "The Changing Nature of World Power," *Political Science Quarterly* 105, no. 2 (1990), 177, https://doi.org/10.2307/2151022.

8. Michael J. Mazarr, *The Societal Foundations of National Competitiveness* (RAND Corporation, 2022), https://doi.org/10.7249/RRA499-1.

9. Nuno P. Monteiro, *Theory of Unipolar Politics* (Cambridge University Press, 2014), 42.

10. The alternative is measuring power by outcomes, which is deeply problematic both from the point of view of social-scientific deduction and from the point of view of assessing current trends with policy relevance. If you can only measure power in retrospect, it is not a particularly useful metric.

11. Charles Glaser, in contrast, argues that we should explicitly exclude military capabilities from measures of power, as those are themselves derivative of other latent power measures. Nuno Monteiro and others disagree on this point. For more on this debate, see Charles L Glaser, "Why Unipolarity Doesn't Matter (Much)," *Cambridge Review of International Affairs* 24, no. 2 (2011): 135, https://doi.org/10.1080/09557571.2011.570740; Monteiro, *Theory of Unipolar Politics,* 38–39.

12. W. Gardner Selby, "U.S. Army Was Smaller Than the Army for Portugal Before World War II," Politifact, June 13, 2014, www.politifact.com/factchecks/2014/jun/13/ken-paxton/us-army-was-smaller-army-portugal-world-war-ii.

13. Michael Beckley, "The Power of Nations: Measuring What Matters," *International Security* 43, no. 2 (2018): 7–44, https://doi.org/10.1162/isec_a_00328.

14. "Wealth Accounting," World Bank, last updated October 2024, https://datacatalog.worldbank.org/search/dataset/0042066.

15. Randall L. Schweller, "Grand Strategy Under Nonpolarity," in *The Oxford Handbook of Grand Strategy,* ed. Balzacq and Krebs, 690–705, https://doi.org/10.1093/oxfordhb/9780198840299.001.0001.

16. Mauro Gilli, "H-Diplo/ISSF Roundtable 11-11 on *Unrivaled: Why America Will Remain the World's Sole Superpower,*" H-Diplo (blog), February 22, 2020, https://networks.h-net.org/node/28443/discussions/5868657/h-diploissf-roundtable-11-11-unrivaled-why-america-will-remain#_Toc32489616.

17. Mazarr, *The Societal Foundations of National Competitiveness.*

18. All economic data is from the World Bank. The Atlas method (which shows China rapidly closing the gap) seeks to smooth out exchange rate volatility, whereas the purchasing power parity (PPP) method (which shows China having surpassed the United States) focuses on controlling for differences in relative prices across countries.

19. Susannah Patton, Jack Sato, and Herve Lemahieu, "Lowy Institute Asia Power Index," https://power.lowyinstitute.org/downloads/lowy-institute-asia-power-index-2019-methodology.pdf.

20. "U.S. Defense Spending Compared to Other Countries," Peterson Foundation, May 11, 2022, www.pgpf.org/chart-archive/0053_defense-comparison.

21. Jo Inge Bekkevold, "Why China Is Not a Superpower," *Foreign Policy,* March 2, 2023, https://foreignpolicy.com/2023/03/02/china-superpower-us-new-cold-war-rivalry-geopolitics.

22. Sydney Freedberg, "US Defense Budget Not That Much Bigger Than China, Russia: Gen. Milley," *Breaking Defense,* May 22, 2018, https://breakingdefense.sites.breakingmedia.com/2018/05/us-defense-budget-not-that-much-bigger-than-china-russia-gen-milley; Toby Harshaw, "China Outspends the U.S. on Defense? Here's the Math," *Bloomberg,* May 25, 2018, www.bloomberg.com/opinion/articles/2018-05-25/china-outspends-the-u-s-on-the-military-here-s-the-math.

23. "Lowy Institute Asia Power Index."

24. *Military and Security Developments Involving the People's Republic of China 2020: Annual Report to Congress* (Office of the Secretary of Defense, 2020), 6, https://media.defense.gov/2020/Sep/01/2002488689/-1/-1/1/2020-dod-china-military-power-report-final.pdf.

25. Ali Wyne, *America's Great-Power Opportunity: Revitalizing U.S. Foreign Policy to Meet the Challenges of Strategic Competition* (Polity, 2022), 38.

26. Economic data is from the World Bank. The CINC score is from the Correlates of War Project. See J. David Singer, "Reconstructing the Correlates of War Dataset on Material Capabilities of States, 1816–1985," *International Interactions* 14, no. 2 (1988): 115–32.

27. Monteiro, *Theory of Unipolar Politics,* 46; "Lowy Institute Asia Power Index."

28. Randall L. Schweller, *Deadly Imbalances: Tripolarity and Hitler's Strategy of World Conquest* (Columbia University Press, 1998), 22.

29. Mearsheimer contends that unbalanced multipolarity is a system in which three or more great powers dominate and a significant difference in power between these states makes at least one of them a potential hegemon. See John J. Mearsheimer, *The Tragedy of Great Power Politics,* updated ed. (W. W. Norton, 2003).

30. Kerstin Cuhls, Annelieke Van Der Giessen, and Hannes Toivanen, *Models of Horizon Scanning—How to Integrate Horizon Scanning into European Research and Innovation Policies* (European Commission Directorate General for Research and Innovation, 2015), https://doi.org/10.2777/338823.

31. "World Population Prospects 2022," United Nations Population Division, accessed August 1, 2022, https://population.un.org/wpp/Graphs/Probabilistic/Ratios/OADR/65plus/15-64/156.

32. Michael Beckley and Hal Brands, *Danger Zone: The Coming Conflict with China* (W. W. Norton, 2022).

33. David Dollar, Yiping Huang, and Yang Yao, "Global Clout, Domestic Fragility," *Finance & Development,* June 2021, www.imf.org/en/Publications/fandd/issues/2021/06/the-future-of-china-dollar-huang-yao.

34. Bert Hofman, "China's Demography Is Not Destiny," *Bert's Newsletter* (blog), January 18, 2023, https://berthofman.substack.com/p/chinas-demography-is-not-destiny.

35. Luke Rogers, "COVID-19, Declining Birth Rates and International Migration Resulted in Historically Small Population Gains," U.S. Census Bureau, December 21, 2021, www.census.gov/library/stories/2021/12/us-population-grew-in-2021-slowest-rate-since-founding-of-the-nation.html.

36. Jeff Wise, "America's Population Could Use a Boom," *Intelligencer (New York Magazine)*, January 3, 2023, https://nymag.com/intelligencer/2023/01/americas-population-could-use-a-boom.html.

37. Adam Taylor, "Long Closed to Most Immigration, Japan Looks to Open Up amid Labor Shortage," *Washington Post*, November 18, 2021, www.washingtonpost.com/world/2021/11/18/japan-labor-shortage-immigration.

38. John Reed and Chloe Cornish, "Can India Build a Military Strong Enough to Deter China?," *Financial Times*, December 12, 2022, www.ft.com/content/333aa07e-93ff-4e97-95c4-548bdccb5661.

39. *Jacobellis v. Ohio*, 378 U.S. 184, 197 (1964) (Stewart, J., concurring).

40. Brooks and Wohlforth, "The Myth of Multipolarity"; Joshua Shifrinson et al., "The Long Unipolar Moment?," *Foreign Affairs* 102, no. 6 (2023), www.foreignaffairs.com/responses/long-unipolar-moment-american-dominance#polarity-is-what-states-make-of-it.

41. Bruce Bueno de Mesquita and David Lalman, "Empirical Support for Systemic and Dyadic Explanations of International Conflict," *World Politics* 41, no. 1 (1988): 1–20, https://doi.org/10.2307/2010477.

42. Kenneth N. Waltz, *Theory of International Politics* (Addison-Wesley, 1979).

43. Robert Jervis and Seweryn Bialer, eds., *Soviet-American Relations After the Cold War* (Duke University Press, 1991), 9–10.

44. Karl W. Deutsch and J. David Singer, "Multipolar Power Systems and International Stability," *World Politics* 16, no. 3 (1964): 390–406, https://doi.org/10.2307/2009578; Marco Nilsson, "The Magnitude of Warfare Revisited—System Polarity and War Duration," *Journal of Strategic Security* 14, no. 2 (2021): 25–46, https://doi.org/10.5038/1944-0472.14.2.1885; Dale C. Copeland, "Neorealism and the Myth of Bipolar Stability: Toward a New Dynamic Realist Theory of Major War," *Security Studies* 5, no. 3 (1996): 29–89, https://doi.org/10.1080/09636419608429276.

45. John J. Mearsheimer, "Back to the Future: Instability in Europe After the Cold War," *International Security* 15, no. 1 (1990): 5–56, https://doi.org/10.2307/2538981.

46. Bob Woodward, *Rage* (Simon & Schuster UK, 2020), 194.

47. Bret Stephens, *America in Retreat: The New Isolationism and the Coming Global Disorder*, paperback ed. (Sentinel, 2015).

48. Nils Petter Gleditsch et al., "Armed Conflict, 1946–2001: A New Dataset," *Journal of Peace Research* 39, no. 5 (2002): 615–37, https://doi.org/10.1177/0022343302039005007; Monteiro, *Theory of Unipolar Politics*.

49. Joseph Grieco, "Structural Realism and the Problem of Polarity and War," in *Power in World Politics*, ed. Felix Berenskoetter and Michael J. Williams (Routledge, 2007), 64.

50. Glenn Snyder, *Alliance Politics* (Cornell University Press, 1997).

51. Shifrinson, *Rising Titans, Falling Giants*.

52. Stephen Van Evera, "Primed for Peace: Europe After the Cold War," *International Security* 15, no. 3 (1990): 7, https://doi.org/10.2307/2538906.

53. Paul C. Avey, "Just Like Yesterday? New Critiques of the Nuclear Revolution," *Texas National Security Review* 6, no. 2 (2023): 9–31, https://tnsr.org/2023/04/just-like-yesterday-new-critiques-of-the-nuclear-revolution.

54. Kenneth N. Waltz, "The Emerging Structure of International Politics," *International Security* 18, no. 2 (1993): 74, https://doi.org/10.2307/2539097.

55. 2022 *National Security Strategy.*

56. Jessica Chen Weiss, "The China Trap," *Foreign Affairs* 101, no. 5 (2022), www.foreignaffairs.com/china/china-trap-us-foreign-policy-zero-sum-competition.

57. 2022 *National Security Strategy.*

58. Paul Stares, "Averting Major Power War," Discussion Paper Series on Managing Global Disorder (Council on Foreign Relations, February 2023), www.cfr.org/report/averting-major-power-war.

59. Economic data is from the World Bank. The GINC score is calculated from the Correlates of War Project. See Singer, "Reconstructing the Correlates of War Dataset on Material Capabilities of States, 1816–1985."

60. Iliya Kusa, "The Ukraine-Russia Grain Deal," *Wilson Center Focus Ukraine* (blog), January 9, 2023, www.wilsoncenter.org/blog-post/ukraine-russia-grain-deal-success-or-failure.

61. Cornell Overfield, "Turkey Must Close the Turkish Straits Only to Russian and Ukrainian Warships," *Lawfare* (blog), March 5, 2022, www.lawfareblog.com/turkey-must-close-turkish-straits-only-russian-and-ukrainian-warships.

62. Lauren Frayer, "A Year into the Ukraine War, the World's Biggest Democracy Still Won't Condemn Russia," *NPR*, February 20, 2023, www.npr.org/2023/02/20/1156478956/russia-india-relations-oil-modi-putin.

Chapter 4. Realist Internationalism

1. *Air Force One* (Sony Pictures Releasing, 1997), www.imdb.com/title/tt0118571.

2. Dina Smeltz et al., "2022 Survey of Public Opinion on U.S. Foreign Policy," Chicago Council on Global Affairs, October 20, 2022, https://globalaffairs.org/research/public-opinion-survey/2022-chicago-council-survey.

3. Laura Silver, "Americans Are Divided over U.S. Role Globally and Whether International Engagement Can Solve Problems," *Pew Research Center* (blog), June 10, 2022, www.pewresearch.org/short-reads/2022/06/10/americans-are-divided-over-u-s-role-globally-and-whether-international-engagement-can-solve-problems; Aidan Connaughton, Laura Clancy, and Sneha Gubbala, "Far More Americans See U.S. Influence on the World Stage Getting Weaker Than Stronger," *Pew Research Center* (blog), December 22, 2022, www.pewresearch.org/short-reads/2022/12/22/far-more-americans-see-u-s-influence-on-the-world-stage-getting-weaker-than-stronger.

4. John Bew, "We Are Realists Now . . . or Are We?," *War on the Rocks*, July 23, 2014, https://warontherocks.com/2014/07/we-are-realists-now-or-are-we.

5. Kirshner, *An Unwritten Future.*

6. Patrick Stewart, "What Would 'Restraint' Really Mean for U.S. Foreign Policy?," *World Politics Review*, November 4, 2019, www.worldpoliticsreview.com/articles/28317/what-would-restraint-really-mean-for-u-s-foreign-policy.

7. Kirshner, *An Unwritten Future*, 139.

8. Samuel Charap and Timothy J. Colton, *Everyone Loses: The Ukraine Crisis and the Ruinous Contest for Post-Soviet Eurasia* (Routledge, 2017); Stephen Wertheim, "The Ukraine Temptation," *Foreign Affairs*, April 12, 2022, www.foreignaffairs.com/articles/united-states/2022-04-12/ukraine-temptation; Mike Sweeney, "A Plan for U.S. Withdrawal from the Middle East," Defense Priorities, December 21, 2020, www.defensepriorities.org/explainers/a-plan-for-us-withdrawal-from-the-middle-east; Michael Mazarr and Patrick Porter, "Countering China's Adventurism over Taiwan: A Third Way," Lowy Institute, May 14, 2021, www.lowyinstitute.org/publications/countering-china-s-adventurism-over-taiwan-third-way-0.

9. Michael C. Desch, "Henry Kissinger: An Occasional Realist," *The American Conservative*, September 15, 2020, www.theamericanconservative.com/henry-kissinger-an-occasional-realist.

10. Hans J. Morgenthau and Kenneth W. Thompson, *Politics Among Nations: The Struggle for Power and Peace* (McGraw-Hill, 1993).

11. Colin Elman, "Horses for Courses: Why *Not* Neorealist Theories of Foreign Policy?," *Security Studies* 6, no. 1 (1996): 26, https://doi.org/10.1080/09636419608429297.

12. Gideon Rose, "Neoclassical Realism and Theories of Foreign Policy," *World Politics* 51, no. 1 (1998): 144–72, https://doi.org/10.1017/S0043887100007814; Steven E. Lobell, Norrin M. Ripsman, and Jeffrey W. Taliaferro, eds., *Neoclassical Realism, the State, and Foreign Policy* (Cambridge University Press, 2009); Norrin M. Ripsman, Jeffrey W. Taliaferro, and Steven E. Lobell, *Neoclassical Realist Theory of International Politics* (Oxford University Press, 2016); Randall L. Schweller, "The Progressiveness of Neoclassical Realism," in *Progress in International Relations Theory*, ed. Elman Colin and Miriam Fendius Elman (MIT Press, 2003), https://doi.org/10.7551/mitpress/5627.003.0012.

13. Robert Jervis, *Perception and Misperception in International Politics*, new ed. (Princeton University Press, 2017), 90.

14. Elbridge A. Colby and A. Wess Mitchell, "The Age of Great-Power Competition," *Foreign Affairs* 99, no. 1 (2020), www.foreignaffairs.com/articles/2019-12-10/age-great-power-competition.

15. Christopher Gelpi, Jason Reifler, and Peter Feaver, "Iraq the Vote: Retrospective and Prospective Foreign Policy Judgments on Candidate Choice and Casualty Tolerance," *Political Behavior* 29, no. 2 (2007): 151–74, https://doi.org/10.1007/s11109-007-9029-6.

16. Erica Borghard, "Reality Check #3: The Uses and Abuses of Deterrence," Atlantic Council, March 1, 2021, www.atlanticcouncil.org/content-series/reality-check/reality-check-3-the-uses-and-abuses-of-deterrence.

17. Dani Rodrik and Stephen M. Walt, "How to Build a Better Order," *Foreign Affairs* 101, no. 5 (2022), www.foreignaffairs.com/world/build-better-order-great-power-rivalry-dani-rodrik-stephen-walt.

18. Robert J. Art, *A Grand Strategy for America* (Cornell University Press, 2003); Barry R. Posen and Andrew L. Ross, "Competing Visions for U.S. Grand Strategy,"

International Security 21, no. 3 (1996): 5, https://doi.org/10.2307/2539272; Robert Litwak, *Deterring Nuclear Terrorism* (Wilson Center, 2016).

19. Toby Dalton and Eric Brewer, "South Korea's Nuclear Flirtations Highlight the Growing Risks of Allied Proliferation," Carnegie Endowment for International Peace, February 13, 2023, https://carnegieendowment.org/posts/2023/02/south-koreas-nuclear-flirtations-highlight-the-growing-risks-of-allied-proliferation; Jennifer Lind and Daryl G. Press, "Should South Korea Build Its Own Nuclear Bomb?," Opinion, *Washington Post*, October 7, 2021, www.washingtonpost.com/outlook/should-south-korea-go-nuclear/2021/10/07/a40bb400-2628-11ec-8d53-67cf-b452aa60_story.html; Laura Sukin and Toby Dalton, "Why South Korea Shouldn't Build Its Own Nuclear Bombs," *War on the Rocks,* October 26, 2021, https://warontherocks.com/2021/10/why-south-korea-shouldnt-build-its-own-nuclear-bombs.

20. Francis J. Gavin, "Same as It Ever Was: Nuclear Alarmism, Proliferation, and the Cold War," *International Security* 34, no. 3 (2010): 7–37, https://doi.org/10.1162/isec.2010.34.3.7.

21. Scott D. Sagan and Kenneth N. Waltz, *The Spread of Nuclear Weapons: A Debate Renewed* (Norton, 2003).

22. Todd S. Sechser and Matthew Fuhrmann, *Nuclear Weapons and Coercive Diplomacy* (Cambridge University Press, 2016), https://doi.org/10.1017/9781316227305.

23. Ash Tellis, Christine Fair, and Jamison Medby, *Limited Conflicts Under the Nuclear Umbrella: Indian and Pakistani Lessons from the Kargil Crisis* (RAND Corporation, 2001), https://doi.org/10.7249/MR1450; Michael Krepon, "The Stability-Instability Paradox," *Arms Control Wonk* (blog), November 2, 2010, www.armscontrolwonk.com/archive/402911/the-stability-instability-paradox.

24. Ikenberry, *After Victory,* 23–26.

25. Joseph S. Nye, *Understanding International Conflicts: An Introduction to Theory and History,* 7th ed. (Pearson Longman, 2009), 276–77.

26. Mearsheimer, *The Tragedy of Great Power Politics,* 40–41.

27. Jeff Colgan, *Partial Hegemony: Oil Politics and International Order* (Oxford University Press, 2021).

28. Robert Gilpin, *War and Change in World Politics* (Cambridge University Press, 1981), 28.

29. Henry Farrell and Abraham L. Newman, "Weaponized Interdependence: How Global Economic Networks Shape State Coercion," *International Security* 44, no. 1 (2019): 42–79, https://doi.org/10.1162/isec_a_00351; Tooze, *Crashed.*

30. See, for example, Colby, *The Strategy of Denial.*

31. "Secretary Rice Addresses U.S.-Russia Relations at the German Marshall Fund" (speech, Washington, D.C., September 18, 2008), https://2001-2009.state.gov/secretary/rm/2008/09/109954.htm.

32. Evan N. Resnick, "What's Missing in the Debate over Spheres of Influence," *Americas' Global Role* (Chatham House), March 17, 2020, https://americas.chathamhouse.org/article/whats-missing-in-the-debate-over-spheres-of-influence.

33. Graham Allison, "The New Spheres of Influence," *Foreign Affairs* 99, no. 2 (2020), https://www.foreignaffairs.com/articles/united-states/2020-02-10/new-spheres-influence.

34. Rapp-Hooper, *Shields of the Republic,* 5.

35. 2022 *National Security Strategy.*

36. Snyder, *Alliance Politics,* 192.

37. "Defense Planning Guidance, FY 1994–1999 (Draft)," U.S. Department of Defense, April 16, 1992, www.archives.gov/files/declassification/iscap/pdf/2008-003-docs1-12.pdf.

38. Alex Emmons, "Saudi Arabia Planned to Invade Qatar Last Summer: Rex Tillerson's Efforts to Stop It May Have Cost Him His Job," *Intercept,* August 1, 2018, https://theintercept.com/2018/08/01/rex-tillerson-qatar-saudi-uae.

39. Alexander Lanoszka, *Atomic Assurance: The Alliance Politics of Nuclear Proliferation* (Cornell University Press, 2018), 22, https://doi.org/10.7591/cornell/9781501729188.001.0001.

40. Vesna Danilovic, "The Sources of Threat Credibility in Extended Deterrence," *Journal of Conflict Resolution* 45, no. 3 (2001): 341–69, https://doi.org/10.1177/0022002701045003005; David S. Yost, "Assurance and U.S. Extended Deterrence in NATO," *International Affairs* 85, no. 4 (2009): 755–80, https://doi.org/10.1111/j.1468-2346.2009.00826.x; Susan Colbourn, *Euromissiles: The Nuclear Weapons That Nearly Destroyed NATO* (Cornell University Press, 2022).

41. "Defense Planning Guidance, FY 1994–1999 (Draft)."

42. Jennifer Lind, "Article Review 52 on 'The Myth of Entangling Alliances,' *International Security* 39:4," H-Diplo/ISSF, April 13, 2016, https://issforum.org/articlereviews/52-entangling-alliances; Beckley, *Unrivaled.*

43. Colby Lutz and Darrell Driver, "Burden-Sharing Dilemmas and NATO's Tumultuous Summer," *War Room* (blog), September 27, 2018, https://warroom.armywarcollege.edu/articles/natos-tumultuous-summer.

44. "Funding NATO," North Atlantic Treaty Organization, accessed October 28, 2024, https://www.nato.int/cps/en/natohq/topics_67655.htm; *OECD Economic Outlook, Interim Report: Confronting Inflation and Low Growth* (OECD, September 2023), https://doi.org/10.1787/1f628002-en; *OECD Labour Force Statistics 2022* (OECD, April 2023), https://doi.org/10.1787/dcoc92f0-en.

45. Raluka Csernatoni, "The EU's Defense Ambitions: Understanding the Emergence of a European Defense Technological and Industrial Complex," Working Paper (Carnegie Endowment for International Peace, December 2021), https://carnegieendowment.org/files/Csernatoni_EU_Defense_v2.pdf.

46. Lind and Wohlforth, "The Future of the Liberal Order Is Conservative."

47. "Text of Speech by Robert Gates on the Future of NATO," *Atlantic Council* (blog), June 10, 2011, www.atlanticcouncil.org/blogs/natosource/text-of-speech-by-robert-gates-on-the-future-of-nato.

48. David Welna, "Under Trump, NATO Nations Get More U.S. Troops and Military Spending," *NPR,* December 3, 2019, www.npr.org/2019/12/03/784444270/under-trump-nato-nations-get-more-u-s-troops-and-military-spending.

49. Glenn H. Snyder, "The Security Dilemma in Alliance Politics," *World Politics* 36, no. 4 (1984): 475, https://doi.org/10.2307/2010183.

50. Jeremy Suri, "The Promise and Failure of American Grand Strategy After the Cold War," Foreign Policy Research Institute, March 13, 2010, www.fpri.org/article/2010/03/the-promise-and-failure-of-american-grand-strategy-after-the-cold-war; Christopher M. Hemmer, *American Pendulum: Recurring Debates in U.S. Grand Strategy* (Cornell University Press, 2015); Thomas J. Hirschfeld, *U.S. Grand Strategy for the 1990s and Beyond* (RAND Corporation, 1990), www.rand.org/pubs/notes/N3180.html; Posen and Ross, "Competing Visions for U.S. Grand Strategy," 5.

51. Bruce D. Berkowitz, "Handicapping the George Kennan Sweepstakes," *Orbis* 42, no. 3 (1998): 465–73, https://doi.org/10.1016/S0030-4387(98)90036-9.

52. Heather Hurlburt, "More Diplomacy, Less Intervention, but for What? Making Sense of the Grand Strategy Debate," *Lawfare* (blog), June 7, 2019, www.lawfaremedia.org/article/more-diplomacy-less-intervention-what-making-sense-grand-strategy-debate.

53. Posen and Ross, "Competing Visions for U.S. Grand Strategy," 6.

54. Jervis, "American Grand Strategy: Untangling the Debates," 442.

55. Christopher Layne, *The Peace of Illusions: American Grand Strategy from 1940 to the Present* (Cornell University Press, 2007); Posen, *Restraint;* Mearsheimer and Walt, "The Case for Offshore Balancing."

56. Art, *A Grand Strategy for America;* Stephen G. Brooks and William C. Wohlforth, *World Out of Balance: International Relations and the Challenge of American Primacy* (Princeton University Press, 2008); Stephen G. Brooks and William C. Wohlforth, *America Abroad: The United States' Global Role in the 21st Century* (Oxford University Press, 2016); Ikenberry, *After Victory;* Anne-Marie Slaughter, *The Chessboard and the Web: Strategies of Connection in a Networked World* (Yale University Press, 2018); Wright, *All Measures Short of War.*

57. Francis Fukuyama, *America at the Crossroads: Democracy, Power, and the Neoconservative Legacy,* paperback ed. (Yale University Press, 2007); William Kristol and Robert Kagan, "Toward a Neo-Reaganite Foreign Policy," *Foreign Affairs* 75, no. 4 (1996), www.foreignaffairs.com/articles/1996-07-01/toward-neo-reaganite-foreign-policy; Hal Brands, "Choosing Primacy: U.S. Strategy and Global Order at the Dawn of the Post–Cold War Era," *Texas National Security Review* 1, no. 2 (2018): 8–33, https://doi.org/10.15781/T2VH5D166; "Defense Planning Guidance, FY 1994–1999 (Draft)."

58. Mastanduno, "Preserving the Unipolar Moment: Realist Theories and U.S. Grand Strategy After the Cold War"; Posen and Ross, "Competing Visions for U.S. Grand Strategy"; Brooks and Wohlforth, *America Abroad;* Posen, *Restraint.*

59. Posen and Ross, "Competing Visions for U.S. Grand Strategy," 20.

60. Edward Luce, "What the CIA Thinks: William Burns on the New World Disorder," *Financial Times,* May 13, 2022, www.ft.com/content/03860857-e160-4920-9e81-28527dda5560.

61. Tom Nichols (@radiofreetom), "Speaking of why realism is nonsense, a great passage in this new @anneapplebaum piece," Twitter, March 1, 2022, https://x.com/radiofreetom/status/1498850713207726080.

62. Desch, "Henry Kissinger."

63. Robert G. Gilpin, "No One Loves a Political Realist," *Security Studies* 5, no. 3 (1996): 3–26, https://doi.org/10.1080/09636419608429275.

Chapter 5. Pull Back

1. Olaf Scholz, "Policy Statement by Olaf Scholz, Chancellor of the Federal Republic of Germany and Member of the German Bundestag" (speech, German Bundestag, Berlin, February 27, 2022), www.bundesregierung.de/breg-en/news/policy-statement-by-olaf-scholz-chancellor-of-the-federal-republic-of-germany-and-member-of-the-german-bundestag-27-february-2022-in-berlin-2008378.

2. Jeremy Shapiro and Jana Puglierin, "The Art of Vassalization: How Russia's War on Ukraine Has Transformed Transatlantic Relations," *War on the Rocks,* June 29, 2023, https://warontherocks.com/2023/06/the-art-of-vassalization-how-russias-war-on-ukraine-has-transformed-transatlantic-relations.

3. Klaus Dodds, *Geopolitics: A Very Short Introduction* (Oxford University Press, 2007).

4. Lili Bayer, "Meet von Der Leyen's 'Geopolitical Commission,'" *Politico,* December 4, 2019, www.politico.eu/article/meet-ursula-von-der-leyen-geopolitical-commission.

5. Jaehan Park, "Rethinking Geopolitics: Geography as an Aid to Statecraft," *Texas National Security Review* 6, no. 4 (2023): 79–100, https://doi.org/10.26153/TSW/48843.

6. Joshua Shifrinson, "Time to Consolidate NATO?," *Washington Quarterly* 40, no. 1 (2017): 109–23, https://doi.org/10.1080/0163660X.2017.1302742.

7. Patrick Porter, *The Global Village Myth: Distance, War, and the Limits of Power* (Hurst, 2015).

8. Daniel Immerwahr, *How to Hide an Empire: A History of the Greater United States* (Farrar, Straus and Giroux, 2019).

9. Henry Farrell and Abraham Newman, *Underground Empire: How America Weaponized the World Economy* (Henry Holt, 2023).

10. Stephen M. Walt, *The Origins of Alliances* (Cornell University Press, 1990).

11. Gabriela Iveliz Rosa Hernández, "Allies Ponder the Future of the CFE Treaty," *Arms Control Today,* September 2023, www.armscontrol.org/act/2023-09/news/allies-ponder-future-cfe-treaty; Jim Garamone, "Milley Proposes Rotational Forces in Permanent Bases Across Eastern Europe," *DOD News,* April 5, 2022, www.defense.gov/News/News-Stories/Article/Article/2990320/milley-proposes-rotational-forces-in-permanent-bases-across-eastern-europe.

12. Chris Brown, "While the UK and Europe Can Be Proud of Their Role in Libya, There Was a Dependence on U.S. Support and This Cannot Be Relied Upon in Future Conflicts," *London School of Economics Blog* (blog), September 2, 2011, https://blogs.lse.ac.uk/politicsandpolicy/libya-eu-uk-role.

13. Ulrich Kühn, Tristan Volpe, and Bert Thompson, "Tracking the German Nuclear Debate," Carnegie Endowment for International Peace, updated March 5, 2020, https://carnegieendowment.org/posts/2018/08/tracking-the-german-nuclear-debate?lang=en; François Diaz-Maurin, "Germany Debates Nuclear Weapons, Again: But Now It's Different," *Bulletin of the Atomic Scientists* (blog), March 15, 2024, https://thebulletin.org/2024/03/germany-debates-nuclear-weapons-again-but-now-its-different; François Diaz-Maurin, "France Wants to Extend Its Nuclear Umbrella to Europe: But Is Macron Ready to Trade Paris for Helsinki?," *Bulletin of the Atomic Scientists* (blog), May 10, 2024, https://thebulletin.org/2024/05/france-wants-to-extend-its-nuclear-umbrella-to-europe-but-is-macron-ready-to-trade-paris-for-helsinki.

14. Michael J. Mazarr, "Why America Still Needs Europe," *Foreign Affairs,* April 17, 2023, www.foreignaffairs.com/united-states/why-america-still-needs-europe; Max Bergmann and Sophia Besch, "Why European Defense Still Depends on America," *Foreign Affairs,* March 7, 2023, www.foreignaffairs.com/ukraine/why-european-defense-still-depends-america; Max Bergmann and Benjamin Haddad, "Europe Needs to Step Up on Defense," *Foreign Affairs,* November 18, 2021, www.foreignaffairs.com/articles/europe/2021-11-18/europe-needs-step-defense; Nathalie Tocci, "The Paradox of Europe's Defense Moment," *Texas National Security Review* 6, no. 1 (2022/2023): 99–108, https://doi.org/10.26153/TSW/44441.

15. Nathalie Tocci, "European Strategic Autonomy: What It Is, Why We Need It, How to Achieve It" (paper, Istituto Affari Internazionali, February 24, 2021), www.iai.it/en/pubblicazioni/european-strategic-autonomy-what-it-why-we-need-it-how-achieve-it.

16. Max Bergmann, "Europe on Its Own," *Foreign Affairs,* August 22, 2022, www.foreignaffairs.com/europe/europe-its-own.

17. Shapiro and Puglierin, "The Art of Vassalization."

18. "Polish PM Blasts 'Short-Sighted' European Opening to China After Macron Visit," *Agence France Presse,* April 13, 2023, www.france24.com/en/live-news/20230413-polish-pm-blasts-short-sighted-european-opening-to-china-after-macron-visit.

19. José Ignacio Torreblanca, "Onwards and Outwards: Why the EU Needs to Move from Strategic Autonomy to Strategic Interdependence," European Council on Foreign Relations, August 24, 2023, https://ecfr.eu/article/onwards-and-outwards-why-the-eu-needs-to-move-from-strategic-autonomy-to-strategic-interdependence.

20. Shapiro and Puglierin, "The Art of Vassalization."

21. Mathieu Droin, "NATO and the European Union: The Burden of Sharing," Center for Strategic and International Studies, January 17, 2023, www.csis.org/analysis/nato-and-european-union-burden-sharing.

22. Madeleine Albright, press conference (NATO Headquarters Press Conference, Brussels, December 8, 1998), www.nato.int/docu/speech/1998/s981208x.htm.

23. Mark Hannah, Lucas Robinson, and Zuri Linetsky, *Order and Disorder: Views of U.S. Foreign Policy in a Fragmented World* (Eurasia Group Foundation, October 2023), https://instituteforglobalaffairs.org/wp-content/uploads/2023/10/2023-Order-Disorder.pdf.

24. Eva Michaels, "European Strategic Autonomy 2.0: What Europe Needs to Get Right," *Carnegie Europe* (blog), June 29, 2023, https://carnegieeurope.eu/strategiceurope/90077.

25. Council of the European Union, "A Strategic Compass for Security and Defence," No. 7371/22, March 21, 2022, https://data.consilium.europa.eu/doc/document/ST-7371-2022-INIT/en/pdf; Nick Witney, "The EU's Strategic Compass: Brand New, Already Obsolete," *ECFR* (blog), European Council on Foreign Relations, March 31, 2022, https://ecfr.eu/article/the-eus-strategic-compass-brand-new-already-obsolete.

26. Hannah Aries, Bastian Giegerich, and Tim Lawrenson, "The Guns of Europe: Defence-Industrial Challenges in a Time of War," *Survival* 65, no. 3 (2023): 7–24, https://doi.org/10.1080/00396338.2023.2218716.

27. Max Bergmann and Otto Svendsen, *Transforming European Defense: A New Focus on Integration* (Center for Strategic and International Studies, June 15, 2023), www.csis.org/analysis/transforming-european-defense-new-focus-integration.

28. Ben Barry et al., "Defending Europe: Scenario-Based Capability Requirements for NATO's European Members," IISS Research Paper (International Institute for Strategic Studies, May 10, 2019), www.iiss.org/research-paper/2019/05/defending-europe; Barry R. Posen, "Europe Can Defend Itself," *Survival* 62, no. 6 (2020): 7–34, https://doi.org/10.1080/00396338.2020.1851080; Stephen G. Brooks and Hugo Meijer, "Europe Cannot Defend Itself: The Challenge of Pooling Military Power," *Survival* 63, no. 1 (2021): 33–40, https://doi.org/10.1080/00396338.2021.1881251; Barry R. Posen, "In Reply: To Repeat, Europe Can Defend Itself," *Survival* 63, no. 1 (2021): 41–49, https://doi.org/10.1080/00396338.2021.1881252.

29. Hillary Clinton, "America's Pacific Century," *Foreign Policy,* October 11, 2011, https://foreignpolicy.com/2011/10/11/americas-pacific-century; Barack Obama, "Remarks By President Obama to the Australian Parliament" (speech, Canberra, Australia, November 17, 2011), https://obamawhitehouse.archives.gov/the-press-office/2011/11/17/remarks-president-obama-australian-parliament.

30. Barry et al., "Defending Europe: Scenario-Based Capability Requirements."

31. Matthew Karnitschnig, "Disbelief and Betrayal: Europe Reacts to Biden's Afghanistan 'Miscalculation,'" *Politico,* August 16, 2021, www.politico.eu/article/europe-reacts-bidens-afghanistan-withdrawal.

32. Barry et al., "Defending Europe: Scenario-Based Capability Requirements."

33. Bergmann and Svendsen, "Transforming European Defense."

34. A barometer poll in 2023 found that 77 percent of European respondents favored a more integrated common defense and security policy. "Eurobarometer Survey," Eurobarometer (European Commission), accessed January 5, 2024, https://europa.eu/eurobarometer/surveys/detail/3052.

35. Andrew J. Bacevich, *America's War for the Greater Middle East: A Military History,* paperback ed. (Random House, 2017).

36. Clinton, "America's Pacific Century."

37. Unlike Europe, the region has no major cross-national military alliances. Instead, a "hub-and-spokes" model dominates; the United States maintains strong semi-formal and informal security commitments to regional states including Israel, Jordan, Saudi Arabia, and Kuwait.

38. Rashaan Ayesh, "Where U.S. Troops and Military Assets Are Deployed in the Middle East," *Axios*, January 8, 2020, www.axios.com/2019/09/21/where-us-troops-deployed-middle-east.

39. U.S. Department of State, *Foreign Relations of the United States, 1977–1980*, ed. Adam M. Howard, vol. 18, *Middle East Region; Arabian Peninsula*, ed. Kelly M. McFarland (Government Publishing Office, 2015), doc. no. 45 (editorial note), https://history.state.gov/historicaldocuments/frus1977-80v18/d45.

40. Some (such as Eugene Gholz and Daryl Press) would argue that the energy-security situation was never profound enough to require U.S. military presence in the Gulf, noting that energy markets are typically robust in their response to even moderate disruptions. But this ignores the question of wartime necessity, which scholars such as Rose Kelanic have highlighted as a fear that drove U.S. policy through much of the late Cold War. Eugene Gholz and Daryl G. Press, "Enduring Resilience: How Oil Markets Handle Disruptions," *Security Studies* 22, no. 1 (2013): 139–47, https://doi.org/10.1080/09636412.2013.757167; Rosemary A. Kelanic, "The Petroleum Paradox: Oil, Coercive Vulnerability, and Great Power Behavior," *Security Studies* 25, no. 2 (2016): 181–213, https://doi.org/10.1080/09636412.2016.1171966.

41. Alexander B. Downes, *Catastrophic Success: Why Foreign-Imposed Regime Change Goes Wrong* (Cornell University Press, 2021); Alexander B. Downes and Jonathan Monten, "Forced to Be Free?: Why Foreign-Imposed Regime Change Rarely Leads to Democratization," *International Security* 37, no. 4 (2013): 90–131, https://doi.org/10.1162/ISEC_a_00117; William G. Nomikos, Alexander B. Downes, and Jonathan Monten, "Reevaluating Foreign-Imposed Regime Change," *International Security* 38, no. 3 (2013): 184–95; Alexander B. Downes and Lindsey A. O'Rourke, "You Can't Always Get What You Want: Why Foreign-Imposed Regime Change Seldom Improves Interstate Relations," *International Security* 41, no. 2 (2016): 43–89, https://doi.org/10.1162/ISEC_a_00256.

42. Thomas Schelling, "An Astonishing 60 Years: The Legacy of Hiroshima," *Proceedings of the National Academy of Sciences of the United States of America* 103, no. 6 (2006): 6089–93.

43. Charles L. Glaser and Rosemary A. Kelanic, "Getting Out of the Gulf," *Foreign Affairs* 96, no. 1 (2017), www.foreignaffairs.com/articles/persian-gulf/2016-12-12/getting-out-gulf; Charles L. Glaser and Rosemary A. Kelanic, eds., *Crude Strategy: Rethinking the U.S. Military Commitment to Defend Persian Gulf Oil* (Georgetown University Press, 2016); John Glaser, "Status, Prestige, Activism and the Illusion of American Decline," *Washington Quarterly* 41, no. 1 (2018): 173–97, https://doi.org/10.1080/01636 60X.2018.1445903; Gholz and Press, "Enduring Resilience"; Eugene Gholz and Daryl G. Press, "Protecting 'The Prize': Oil and the U.S. National Interest," *Security Studies* 19, no. 3 (2010): 453–85, https://doi.org/10.1080/09636412.2010.505865.

44. Anthony H. Cordesman, "The Gulf Military Balance and U.S. Commitments to the Gulf," Center for Strategic and International Studies, December 9, 2019, www.csis.org/analysis/gulf-military-balance-and-us-commitments-gulf.

45. Eugene Gholz, "Nothing Much to Do: Why America Can Bring All Troops Home from the Middle East," Quincy Paper No. 7 (Quincy Institute for Responsible Statecraft, June 24, 2021), https://quincyinst.org/report/nothing-much-to-do-why-america-can-bring-all-troops-home-from-the-middle-east.

46. Faris Al-Sulayman and Jon B. Alterman, "China's Essential Role in the Gulf States' Energy Transitions," Center for Strategic and International Studies, December 11, 2023, www.csis.org/analysis/chinas-essential-role-gulf-states-energy-transitions; Tim Niblock, "Problems and Opportunities for China in Developing Its Role in the Gulf Region," *Asian Journal of Middle Eastern and Islamic Studies* 11, no. 3 (2017): 1–11, https://doi.org/10.1080/25765949.2017.12023305; Imad Mansour, "Treading with Caution: China's Multidimensional Interventions in the Gulf Region," *China Quarterly* 239 (2019): 656–78, https://doi.org/10.1017/S0305741018001777; Jonathan Fulton, "China Between Iran and the Gulf Monarchies," *Middle East Policy* 28, no. 3–4 (2021): 203–16, https://doi.org/10.1111/mepo.12589.

47. 2022 *National Defense Strategy* (U.S. Department of Defense, 2018), https://media.defense.gov/2022/Oct/27/2003103845/-1/-1/1/2022-national-defense-strategy-npr-mdr.pdf.

48. Robert O. Work, "A Slavish Devotion to Forward Presence Has Nearly Broken the U.S. Navy," *USNI Proceedings,* December 1, 2021; Becca Wasser, *Campaign of Denial* (Center for a New American Security, August 22, 2023), www.cnas.org/publications/reports/campaign-of-denial.

49. It should be noted that similar problems—as well as concerns about backlash—apply to the growing network of counterterrorism bases in Africa, and a similar logic of withdrawal should be applied to them.

50. Ilan Goldenberg et al., *When Less Is More: Rethinking U.S. Military Strategy and Posture in the Middle East* (Center for a New American Security, November 4, 2021), www.cnas.org/publications/reports/when-less-is-more.

51. Caitlin Talmadge, "Closing Time: Assessing the Iranian Threat to the Strait of Hormuz," *International Security* 33, no. 1 (2008): 82–117, https://doi.org/10.1162/isec.2008.33.1.82.

52. Gholz, "Nothing Much to Do."

53. Renanah Miles Joyce and Brian Blankenship, "The Market for Foreign Bases," *Security Studies* 33, no. 2 (2024): 194–223, https://doi.org/10.1080/09636412.2023.2271387.

54. Joyce and Blankenship, "The Market for Foreign Bases."

55. Sweeney, "A Plan for U.S. Withdrawal from the Middle East."

56. "Missiles of Iran," Missile Threat, CSIS Missile Defense Project, last updated August 10, 2021, https://missilethreat.csis.org/country/iran.

57. Courtney Kube, "This U.S. Base in Syria Is Key to Combating ISIS and Countering Iran," *NBC News,* October 23, 2018, www.nbcnews.com/news/military/inside-remote-u-s-base-syria-central-combating-isis-countering-n922991.

58. Daniel Magruder, "Al Tanf Garrison: America's Strategic Baggage in the Middle East," Brookings Institution, November 20, 2020, www.brookings.edu/articles/al-tanf-garrison-americas-strategic-baggage-in-the-middle-east.

59. Alex Horton, Dan Lamothe, and Abigail Hauslohner, "A Split Emerges as Biden Struggles to Deter Attacks on U.S. Troops," *Washington Post*, November 19, 2023, www.washingtonpost.com/national-security/2023/11/19/iranian-proxy-attacks-us-troops; Grant Rumley and David Schenker, "The Future of Al-Tanf Garrison in Syria," PolicyWatch 3553, Washington Institute for Near East Policy, December 6, 2021, www.washingtoninstitute.org/policy-analysis/future-al-tanf-garrison-syria; "Al-Tanf, Syria," Global Flashpoints, International Crisis Group, accessed December 14, 2017, www.crisisgroup.org/trigger-list/iran-usisrael-trigger-list/flashpoints/al-tanf-syria.

60. "Why Iran Is Hard to Intimidate," *Economist*, February 6, 2024, www.economist.com/middle-east-and-africa/2024/02/06/why-iran-is-hard-to-intimidate.

Chapter 6. Lean Forward

1. 2017 *National Security Strategy;* Jim Garamone, "White House Report Recommends Multi-Pronged Approach to Counter China," *DOD News,* June 5, 2020. www.defense.gov/News/News-Stories/Article/Article/2210283/white-house-report-recommends-multi-pronged-approach-to-counter-china.

2. Campbell et al., "Extending American Power: Strategies to Expand U.S. Engagement in a Competitive World Order"; Robert Zoellick, "Whither China: From Membership to Responsibility?" (speech, National Committee on U.S.-China Relations, New York, September 21, 2005), https://2001-2009.state.gov/s/d/former/zoellick/rem/53682.htm.

3. Uri Friedman, "The New Concept Everyone in Washington Is Talking About," *Atlantic,* August 6, 2019, www.theatlantic.com/politics/archive/2019/08/what-genesis-great-power-competition/595405.

4. Øystein Tunsjø, *The Return of Bipolarity in World Politics: China, the United States, and Geostructural Realism* (Columbia University Press, 2018).

5. Ryan Hass, *Stronger: Adapting America's China Strategy in an Age of Competitive Interdependence* (Yale University Press, 2021), 16.

6. Mearsheimer, *The Tragedy of Great Power Politics,* 142.

7. David C. Kang, "China, Hegemony, and Leadership in East Asia," in *Responding to China's Rise: US and EU Strategies,* ed. Vinod K. Aggarwal and Sara A. Newland (Springer International, 2015), 27–49, https://doi.org/10.1007/978-3-319-10034-0_2; Colby, *The Strategy of Denial.*

8. Paula Dobriansky, "Should U.S. Foreign Policy Focus on Great-Power Competition?," Ask the Experts, *Foreign Affairs,* October 13, 2020, www.foreignaffairs.com/ask-the-experts/2020-10-13/should-us-foreign-policy-focus-great-power-competition; Hal Brands, "The Chinese Century?," *National Interest,* February 19, 2018, https://nationalinterest.org/feature/the-chinese-century-24557.

9. Lissner and Rapp-Hooper, *An Open World,* 25; From the academic to the conspiratorial: Rush Doshi, *The Long Game: China's Grand Strategy to Displace American*

Order (Oxford University Press, 2023); Michael P. Pillsbury, *The Hundred-Year Marathon: China's Secret Strategy to Replace America as the Global Superpower* (Henry Holt, 2015); Robert Spalding, *War Without Rules: China's Playbook for Global Domination* (Sentinel, 2022).

10. Aaron L. Friedberg, "An Answer to Aggression," *Foreign Affairs* 99, no. 5 (2020), www.foreignaffairs.com/articles/china/2020-08-11/ccp-answer-aggression.

11. Michael Mazarr and Hal Brands, "Navigating Great Power Rivalry in the 21st Century," *War on the Rocks,* April 5, 2017, https://warontherocks.com/2017/04/navigating-great-power-rivalry-in-the-21st-century.

12. Alastair Iain Johnston, "Is China a Status Quo Power?," *International Security* 27, no. 4 (2003): 5–56.

13. Jervis, *Perception and Misperception in International Politics,* 68.

14. Weiss, "The China Trap."

15. Van Jackson, *Pacific Power Paradox: American Statecraft and the Fate of the Asian Peace* (Yale University Press, 2023); Hass, *Stronger.*

16. Sanjay Pulipaka and Mohit Musaddi, "In Defence of the 'Indo-Pacific' Concept," Issue Brief No. 493 (Observer Research Foundation, September 2021), www.orfonline.org/public/uploads/posts/pdf/20230423113824.pdf.

17. Evan A. Feigenbaum, "An Indo-Pacific Economic Framework" (testimony before the House Foreign Affairs Committee, Washington D.C., March 1, 2022), https://carnegieendowment.org/2022/03/01/indo-pacific-economic-framework-pub-86564.

18. Ryan Hass and Jude Blanchette, "The Right Way to Deter China from Attacking Taiwan," *Foreign Affairs,* November 8, 2023, www.foreignaffairs.com/china/right-way-deter-china-attacking-taiwan.

19. Mark F. Cancian, Matthew Cancian, and Eric Heginbotham, *The First Battle of the Next War: Wargaming a Chinese Invasion of Taiwan* (Center for Strategic and International Studies, January 9, 2023), www.csis.org/analysis/first-battle-next-war-wargaming-chinese-invasion-taiwan.

20. Colby, *The Strategy of Denial;* Christina Lai, "Bound to Lead: US-Taiwan Relations, Security Networks, and The Future of AUKUS," *International Journal: Canada's Journal of Global Policy Analysis* 78, no. 3 (2023): 417–34, https://doi.org/10.1177/00207020231197761.

21. Brendan Rittenhouse Green and Caitlin Talmadge, "Then What? Assessing the Military Implications of Chinese Control of Taiwan," *International Security* 47, no. 1 (2022): 7–45, https://doi.org/10.1162/isec_a_00437.

22. Daryl G. Press, *Calculating Credibility: How Leaders Assess Military Threats* (Cornell University Press, 2005).

23. Kelly A. Grieco and Jennifer Kavanagh, "America Can't Surpass China's Power in Asia," *Foreign Affairs,* January 16, 2024, www.foreignaffairs.com/united-states/america-cant-surpass-chinas-power-asia.

24. Mazarr and Porter, "Countering China's Adventurism over Taiwan: A Third Way."

25. Miranda Priebe et al., *The Limits of Restraint: The Military Implications of a Restrained U.S. Grand Strategy in the Asia-Pacific* (RAND Corporation, 2022), 33, https://doi.org/10.7249/RRA739-4.

26. Green and Talmadge, "Then What?," 9.

27. Priebe et al., *The Limits of Restraint*, 24.

28. Mazarr and Porter, "Countering China's Adventurism over Taiwan: A Third Way."

29. Michael Swaine, Jessica Lee, and Rachel Odell, "Toward an Inclusive and Balanced Regional Order: A New U.S. Strategy in East Asia," Quincy Paper No. 5 (Quincy Institute for Responsible Statecraft, January 2021), https://quincyinst.org/wp-content/uploads/2021/02/A-New-U.S.-Strategy-in-East-Asia.pdf.

30. James Timbie and James O. Ellis Jr., "A Large Number of Small Things: A Porcupine Strategy for Taiwan," *Texas National Security Review* 5, no. 1 (2021/2022): 83–93, https://doi.org/10.15781/GKAW-3709.

31. "China Island Tracker," Asia Maritime Transparency Initiative, accessed February 27, 2024, https://amti.csis.org/island-tracker/china.

32. Priebe et al., *The Limits of Restraint*, 57.

33. Jennifer Kavanagh, "Japan's New Defense Budget Is Still Not Enough," *Carnegie Endowment for International Peace* (blog), February 8, 2023, https://carnegieendowment.org/2023/02/08/japan-s-new-defense-budget-is-still-not-enough-pub-88981.

34. Benjamin Schreer, "Arming Without Aiming? Challenges for Japan's Amphibious Capability," *War on the Rocks*, October 2, 2020, https://warontherocks.com/2020/10/arming-without-aiming-challenges-for-japans-amphibious-capability.

35. Priebe et al., *The Limits of Restraint*, 21.

36. Clint Work, "Seoul Isn't Kabul," *Foreign Policy*, February 28, 2024, https://foreignpolicy.com/2021/08/18/south-korea-usa-troops-withdraw-kim-jong-un-moon-seoul-kabul; Alex Velez-Green, "The Case for Urgency Against China," *The Heritage Foundation* (blog), September 13, 2023, www.heritage.org/asia/commentary/the-case-urgency-against-china.

37. Grieco and Kavanagh, "America Can't Surpass China's Power in Asia"; Posen, *Restraint*, 161.

38. Luke Nicastro, *U.S. Defense Infrastructure in the Indo-Pacific: Background and Issues for Congress*, CRS Report R47589 (Congressional Research Service, June 6, 2023), https://crsreports.congress.gov/product/pdf/R/R47589.

39. Renanah Miles Joyce and Brian Blankenship, "Access Denied? The Future of U.S. Basing in a Contested World," *War on the Rocks*, February 1, 2021, http://warontherocks.com/2021/02/access-denied-the-future-of-u-s-basing-in-a-contested-world.

40. Sameer Lalwani and Heather Byrne, "The Elephant in the Room: Auditing the Past and Future of the U.S.-India Partnership," *War on the Rocks*, June 26, 2019, https://warontherocks.com/2019/06/the-elephant-in-the-room-auditing-the-past-and-future-of-the-u-s-india-partnership.

41. John Hawksworth, Hannah Audino, and Rob Clarry, *The Long View: How Will the Global Economic Order Change by 2050?* (PwC, February 2017), www.pwc.com/gx/en/world-2050/assets/pwc-the-world-in-2050-full-report-feb-2017.pdf.

42. John Hemmings, "Should the Quad Become a Formal Alliance?," *Journal of Indo-Pacific Affairs* 5, no. 2 (2022): 65–77; Daniel Depetris, "What the Quad Is, Is Not, and Should Not Be," *Defense Priorities Explainers* (blog), September 22, 2021, www.defensepriorities.org/explainers/what-the-quad-is-is-not-and-should-not-be.

43. Jennifer Kavanagh, "Networks and Competitive Advantage in a Contested World" (working paper, Carnegie Endowment for International Peace, November 28, 2022), https://carnegieendowment.org/2022/11/28/networks-and-competitive-advantage-in-contested-world-pub-88461; Zack Cooper, "The Era of Coalitions: The Shifting Nature of Alignments in Asia," *FULCRUM* (blog), February 23, 2023, https://fulcrum.sg/the-era-of-coalitions-the-shifting-nature-of-alignments-in-asia.

44. O'Hanlon, *The Art of War in an Age of Peace.*

45. Zdzisław Lachowski, *Confidence- and Security-Building Measures in the New Europe,* SIPRI Research Report No. 18 (Oxford University Press, 2004).

46. Kurt M. Campbell and Jake Sullivan, "Competition Without Catastrophe," *Foreign Affairs* 98, no. 5 (2019), www.foreignaffairs.com/china/competition-with-china-catastrophe-sullivan-campbell.

47. Ulrich Kühn and Heather Williams, "Behavioral Arms Control and East Asia," *Journal for Peace and Nuclear Disarmament* 7, no. 1 (2024): 143–56, https://doi.org/10.1080/25751654.2024.2337965.

48. Grieco and Kavanagh, "America Can't Surpass China's Power in Asia."

49. Ward, "Read: Bernie Sanders's Big Foreign Policy Speech."

50. Jeremy Diamond, "Trump Slams Globalization, Promises to Upend Economic Status Quo," *CNN,* June 28, 2016, www.cnn.com/2016/06/28/politics/donald-trump-speech-pennsylvania-economy/index.html.

51. Jake Sullivan and Jennifer Harris, "America Needs a New Economic Philosophy: Foreign Policy Experts Can Help," *Foreign Policy,* February 7, 2020, https://foreignpolicy.com/2020/02/07/america-needs-a-new-economic-philosophy-foreign-policy-experts-can-help.

52. Gavin Bade, "Joe Biden Wants a 'New Economic World Order': It's Never Looked More Disordered," *Politico,* May 25, 2023, www.politico.com/news/2023/05/25/joe-bidens-economy-trade-china-00096781.

53. Ana Swanson, "Biden's Pacific Trade Pact Suffers Setback After Criticism from Congress," *New York Times,* November 13, 2023, www.nytimes.com/2023/11/13/business/economy/indo-pacific-trade-delay.html.

54. Elaine Dezenski and John C. Austin, "Rebuilding America's Economy and Foreign Policy with 'Ally-Shoring,'" Brookings Institution, June 8, 2021, www.brookings.edu/articles/rebuilding-americas-economy-and-foreign-policy-with-ally-shoring; Peter Coy, "'Onshoring' Is So Last Year: The New Lingo Is 'Friend-Shoring,'" *Bloomberg,* June 24, 2021, www.bloomberg.com/news/articles/2021-06-24/-onshoring-is-so-last-year-the-new-lingo-is-friend-shoring.

55. World Trade Organization, *World Trade Report 2023: Re-Globalization for a Secure, Inclusive and Sustainable Future* (World Trade Organization, 2023), www.wto.org/english/res_e/booksp_e/wtr23_e/wtr23_e.pdf.

56. Farrell and Newman, *Underground Empire.*

57. Daniel W. Drezner, Henry Farrell, and Abraham Newman, eds., *The Uses and Abuses of Weaponized Interdependence* (Brookings Institution Press, 2021).

58. Yellen, "Remarks by Secretary of the Treasury Janet L. Yellen on the U.S.-China Economic Relationship"; Sullivan, "Remarks by National Security Advisor Jake Sullivan on Renewing American Economic Leadership."

59. Farrell and Newman, *Underground Empire*, 3.

60. McDowell, *Bucking the Buck;* Drezner, Farrell, and Newman, *The Uses and Abuses of Weaponized Interdependence;* Agathe Demarais, *Backfire: How Sanctions Reshape the World Against U.S. Interests* (Columbia University Press, 2022).

61. Erica York, "Tracking the Economic Impact of Tariffs," Tax Foundation, July 7, 2023, https://taxfoundation.org/research/all/federal/tariffs-trump-trade-war.

62. Farrell and Newman, *Underground Empire.*

63. Sullivan, "Remarks by National Security Advisor Jake Sullivan on Renewing American Economic Leadership."

64. Mercy Kuo, "The State of China's Semiconductor Industry," *Diplomat,* October 2, 2023, https://thediplomat.com/2023/10/the-state-of-chinas-semiconductor-industry; Qianer Liu, "How Huawei Surprised the U.S. with a Cutting-Edge Chip Made in China," *Financial Times,* November 30, 2023, www.ft.com/content/327414d2-fe13-438e-9767-333cdb94c7e1.

65. Andrew David et al., *Russia Shifting Import Sources Amid U.S. and Allied Export Restrictions: China Feeding Russia's Technology Demands* (Silverado Policy Accelerator, January 1, 2023), https://cdn.sanity.io/files/0wfzc71x/production/6745ea42c21d65d6709231e0e7767bd5de57469b.pdf.

66. Jake Sullivan, "Remarks by National Security Advisor Jake Sullivan on the Biden-Harris Administration's National Security Strategy" (speech, Georgetown University, October 12, 2022), www.whitehouse.gov/briefing-room/speeches-remarks/2022/10/13/remarks-by-national-security-advisor-jake-sullivan-on-the-biden-harris-administrations-national-security-strategy.

67. Demarais, *Backfire,* 254–55.

68. Farrell and Newman, *Underground Empire*, 7.

69. Daniel W. Drezner, "The Biden Administration's Zombie Foreign Economic Policy," Perspective, *Washington Post,* April 12, 2022, www.washingtonpost.com/outlook/2022/04/12/biden-administrations-zombie-foreign-economic-policy.

70. Van Jackson, "America's Asia Strategy Has Reached a Dead End," *Foreign Policy,* September 1, 2022, https://foreignpolicy.com/2022/01/09/us-southeast-asia-china-biden-economic-strategy-geopolitics.

71. Ash Jain, Matthew Kroenig, and Marianne Schneider-Petsinger, *A Democratic Trade Partnership: Ally Shoring to Counter Coercion and Secure Supply Chains* (Atlantic Council, June 1, 2022), www.atlanticcouncil.org/in-depth-research-reports/report/strategic-decoupling-building-a-democratic-trade-and-economic-partnership-d-tep.

72. Emily Benson and Ethan B. Kapstein, "The Limits of 'Friend-Shoring,'" Center for Strategic and International Studies, February 1, 2023, www.csis.org/analysis/limits-friend-shoring.

73. Robert B. Zoellick, *America in the World: A History of U.S. Diplomacy and Foreign Policy* (Twelve, 2020); Dale C. Copeland, *A World Safe for Commerce: American Foreign Policy from the Revolution to the Rise of China* (Princeton University Press, 2024); Kelly Grieco, Kei Koga, and Zack Cooper, "In Forum: 2024—U.S. Strategy and the Indo-Pacific," 9Dashline, January 31, 2024, www.9dashline.com/article/in-forum-2024-us-strategy-and-the-indo-pacific.

74. "America's Crumbling Trade Initiative in Asia," *Economist*, November 23, 2023, www.economist.com/asia/2023/11/23/americas-crumbling-trade-initiative-in-asia.

75. Karl Friedhoff and Lama El Baz, "Most Americans See Value in International Trade," Chicago Council on Global Affairs, October 8, 2023, https://globalaffairs.org/research/public-opinion-survey/most-americans-see-value-international-trade.

76. Scott Lincicome, "US Trade Data for 2023 Debunk Common Globalization Myths," *Cato Institute* (blog), February 9, 2024, www.cato.org/blog/us-trade-data-2023-debunk-common-globalization-myths.

77. Pablo D. Fajgelbaum and Amit K. Khandelwal, "Measuring the Unequal Gains from Trade," *Quarterly Journal of Economics* 131, no. 3 (2016): 1113–80, https://doi.org/10.1093/qje/qjw013.

78. Brooks and Wohlforth, *America Abroad*.

79. Eugene Gholz and Daryl G. Press, "The Effects of Wars on Neutral Countries: Why It Doesn't Pay to Preserve the Peace," *Security Studies* 10, no. 4 (2001): 1–57, https://doi.org/10.1080/09636410108429444.

80. Bryan Rooney et al., *Does the U.S. Economy Benefit from U.S. Alliances and Forward Military Presence?* (RAND Corporation, 2022), https://doi.org/10.7249/RRA739-5.

81. Gholz and Press, "Enduring Resilience."

82. Rosemary A. Kelanic, *Black Gold and Blackmail: Oil and Great Power Politics* (Cornell University Press, 2020).

83. World Trade Organization, *Re-Globalization for a Secure, Inclusive and Sustainable Future*.

84. Shannon K. O'Neil, *The Globalization Myth: Why Regions Matter* (Yale University Press, 2022).

85. Sarang Shidore, "Winning the Majority: A New U.S. Bargain with the Global South," Quincy Brief No. 33 (Quincy Institute for Responsible Statecraft, November 2022), https://quincyinst.org/research/winning-the-majority-a-new-u-s-bargain-with-the-global-south.

86. Clete Willems, "12 Ways to Get the U.S. Back into TPP," Hinrich Foundation, February 7, 2023, www.hinrichfoundation.com/research/article/us-china/how-to-get-the-us-back-into-the-tpp.

87. Congressional Research Service, *CPTPP: Overview and Issues for Congress*" IF12078, version 6 (Congressional Research Service, June 16, 2023), https://crsreports.congress.gov/product/pdf/IF/IF12078.

88. Sanjay Patnaik and James Kunhardt, "Biden Could Reduce Inflation, Mitigate a Recession, and Strengthen Democracy with a New EU-US Trade Agreement," Brookings Institution, August 30, 2022, www.brookings.edu/articles/biden-could-reduce-inflation-mitigate-a-recession-and-strengthen-democracy-with-a-new-eu-us-trade-agreement.

89. Emily Benson, "The Fifth Ministerial of the U.S.-EU Trade and Technology Council," Center for Strategic and International Studies, February 7, 2024, www.csis.org/analysis/fifth-ministerial-us-eu-trade-and-technology-council.

90. Trevor Sutton and Mike Williams, "A New Horizon in U.S. Trade Policy," Center for American Progress, March 14, 2023, www.americanprogress.org/article/a-new-horizon-in-u-s-trade-policy.

91. Daniel Raisbeck, "U.S. Policy Toward Latin America," in *Cato Handbook for Policymakers*, 9th ed. (Cato Institute, 2022), www.cato.org/cato-handbook-policy-makers/cato-handbook-policymakers-9th-edition-2022/us-policy-toward-latin-america.

92. Michael Stott, "US Reluctance on Trade Deals Sends Latin America towards China," *Financial Times*, May 24, 2023, www.ft.com/content/19ff62c3-5c75-4ba7-8f73-75a7a902aa90.

93. Inu Manak and Gabriel Cabanas, "The United States Needs a Bold Vision for Trade in the Americas," *Council on Foreign Relations Renewing America* (blog), November 28, 2023, www.cfr.org/blog/united-states-needs-bold-vision-trade-americas.

94. Daniel F. Runde and Sundar R. Ramanujam, "Beyond 2025: The Future of the African Growth and Opportunity Act," Center for Strategic and International Studies, March 4, 2022, www.csis.org/analysis/beyond-2025-future-african-growth-and-opportunity-act.

95. Frannie Leautier, *AGOA and the Future of US-Africa Trade* (Atlantic Council, October 26, 2023), www.atlanticcouncil.org/in-depth-research-reports/report/agoa-and-the-future-of-us-africa-trade.

96. Barbara Plett-Usher, "US and China Trade Angry Words at High-Level Alaska Talks," *BBC News*, March 19, 2021, www.bbc.com/news/world-us-canada-56452471.

Conclusion: First Among Equals

1. James Kynge, "China Is Tightening Its Embrace with Russia as It Builds Bulwarks," *Financial Times*, September 18, 2023, www.ft.com/content/bbaa4006-318e-4dbe-b7d4-3c21aa5e8887.

2. Putin, "Putin's Prepared Remarks at 43rd Munich Conference on Security Policy."

3. Anne-Marie Slaughter, *The Chessboard and the Web: Strategies of Connection in a Networked World* (Yale University Press, 2018); Wright, *All Measures Short of War*; 2017 *National Security Strategy*.

4. Matthew Specter, *Atlantic Realists: Empire and International Political Thought Between Germany and the United States* (Stanford University Press, 2022), http://www.sup.org/books/title/?id=28906; Emma Ashford, "In Praise of Lesser Evils," *Foreign Affairs* 101, no. 5 (2022), www.foreignaffairs.com/reviews/praise-lesser-evils-realism-foreign-policy-emma-ashford.

5. Robert Jervis, "International Primacy: Is the Game Worth the Candle?," *International Security* 17, no. 4 (1993): 52, https://doi.org/10.2307/2539021.

6. Stephen Wertheim, "Iraq and the Pathologies of Primacy," *Foreign Affairs* 102, no. 3 (2023), www.foreignaffairs.com/united-states/iraq-and-pathologies-primacy.

7. Friedhoff and El Baz, "Most Americans See Value in International Trade."

8. Kirshner, *An Unwritten Future,* 234.

9. Brooks and Wohlforth, *America Abroad,* 199.

10. Hans J. Morgenthau, *In Defense of the National Interest: A Critical Examination of American Foreign Policy* (University Press of America, 1982).

11. Matt. 4:9.

12. Bartley et al., "America's Purpose Now."

13. Christopher A. Preble, *The Power Problem: How American Military Dominance Makes Us Less Safe, Less Prosperous, and Less Free* (Cornell University Press, 2009).

14. Art, *A Grand Strategy for America.*

15. Posen, *Restraint;* Paul C. Avey, Jonathan N. Markowitz, and Robert Reardon, "Disentangling Grand Strategy: International Relations Theory and U.S. Grand Strategy," *Texas National Security Review* 2, no. 1 (2018): 28–51, https://tnsr.org/2018/11/disentangling-grand-strategy-international-relations-theory-and-u-s-grand-strategy.

16. Goldberg, "The Obama Doctrine."

17. John Glaser and Trevor Thrall, "Were We Watching the Same Presidency? Obama Was Not a Restrainer," *War on the Rocks,* March 14, 2017, https://warontherocks.com/2017/03/were-we-watching-the-same-presidency-obama-was-not-a-restrainer.

18. Randall L. Schweller and David Priess, "A Tale of Two Realisms: Expanding the Institutions Debate," *Mershon International Studies Review* 41, no. 1 (1997): 1, https://doi.org/10.2307/222801.

19. Simon Reich and Peter J. Dombrowski, *The End of Grand Strategy: U.S. Maritime Operations in the Twenty-First Century* (Cornell University Press, 2017), 3.

20. Drezner, Krebs, and Schweller, "The End of Grand Strategy."

21. Rebecca Friedman Lissner, "What Is Grand Strategy? Sweeping a Conceptual Minefield," *Texas National Security Review* 2, no. 1 (2018): 52–73, https://doi.org/10.26153/TSW/868.

22. Darrell Huff and Irving Geis, *How to Lie with Statistics,* paperback reissue (Norton, 1993).

23. Jones, "Fewer Americans Want U.S. Taking Major Role in World Affairs"; Dina Smeltz and Craig Kafura, "Americans Grow Less Enthusiastic About Active U.S. Engagement Abroad," Chicago Council on Global Affairs, October 12, 2023, https://globalaffairs.org/research/public-opinion-survey/americans-grow-less-enthusiastic-about-active-us-engagement-abroad.

24. Hannah, Robinson, and Linetsky, "Order and Disorder: Views of U.S. Foreign Policy in a Fragmented World"; Dina Smeltz and Emily Sullivan, "Young Americans Question U.S. Global Engagement," Chicago Council on Global Affairs, March 22, 2023, https://globalaffairs.org/research/public-opinion-survey/young-americans-question-us-global-engagement.

25. Elizabeth N. Saunders, "Will Foreign Policy Be a Major Issue in the 2016 Election? Here's What We Know," *Washington Post*, December 7, 2021, www.washingtonpost.com/news/monkey-cage/wp/2016/01/26/will-foreign-policy-be-a-major-issue-in-the-2016-election-heres-what-we-know; Joshua Busby, "Foreign Policy Salience and the 2016 Election: Evidence from the ANES Survey," *Duck of Minerva*, May 23, 2016, www.duckofminerva.com/2016/05/foreign-policy-salience-and-the-2016-election-evidence-from-the-anes-survey.html.

26. Philip J. Powlick and Andrew Z. Katz, "Defining the American Public Opinion/ Foreign Policy Nexus," *Mershon International Studies Review* 42, no. 1 (1998): 29, https://doi.org/10.2307/254443.

27. Adam Przeworski, *Democracy and the Market: Political and Economic Reforms in Eastern Europe and Latin America* (Cambridge University Press, 1991); Joel S. Hellman, "Winners Take All: The Politics of Partial Reform in Postcommunist Transitions," *World Politics* 50, no. 2 (1998): 203–34, https://doi.org/10.1017/S0043887100008091.

28. Ward, *The Internationalists*.

29. Gordon M. Friedrichs and Jordan Tama, "Polarization and U.S. Foreign Policy: Key Debates and New Findings," *International Politics* 59, no. 5 (2022): 767–85, https://doi.org/10.1057/s41311-022-00381-0.

30. James Goldgeier and Elizabeth N. Saunders, "The Unconstrained Presidency," *Foreign Affairs* 97, no. 5 (2018), www.foreignaffairs.com/united-states/unconstrained-presidency; Dina Smeltz, "Are We Drowning at the Water's Edge? Foreign Policy Polarization Among the U.S. Public," *International Politics* 59, no. 5 (2022): 786–801, https://doi.org/10.1057/s41311-022-00376-x; Helen V. Milner and Dustin Tingley, *Sailing the Water's Edge: The Domestic Politics of American Foreign Policy* (Princeton University Press, 2016), https://doi.org/10.1515/9781400873821.

31. Riccardo Alcaro, "All Is Not Quiet on the Western Front," IAI Papers 18/07 (Istituto Affari Internazionali, 2018), www.iai.it/en/pubblicazioni/all-not-quiet-western-front.

32. Jacob Cohn and Ryan Boone, eds., *How Much Is Enough? Alternative Defense Strategies* (Center for Strategic and Budgetary Studies, November 28, 2016), https://csbaonline.org/research/publications/how-much-is-enough-alternative-defense-strategies/publication/1.

33. Mark Cancian, "Focus DoD on Its Warfighting Mission," *National Interest*, July 27, 2020, https://nationalinterest.org/blog/skeptics/focus-dod-its-warfighting-mission-165544.

34. William J. Burns, "The Damage at the State Department Is Worse Than You Can Imagine," *Atlantic*, March 12, 2020, www.theatlantic.com/ideas/archive/2020/03/how-rebuild-state-department/607837.

35. "Washington's Farewell Address," The Avalon Project, https://avalon.law.yale.edu/18th_century/washing.asp.

36. Paul K. MacDonald and Joseph M. Parent, *Twilight of the Titans: Great Power Decline and Retrenchment*, 196.

37. Steven E. Meyer, "Carcass of Dead Policies: The Irrelevance of NATO," *Parameters* 33, no. 4 (2003), https://doi.org/10.55540/0031-1723.2176.

Index